DHAMMA ABOARD EVOLUTION

AF132686

Dhamma
Aboard Evolution

A Study of the Aggañña Sutta in Relation to Westernscience

(Second Edition)

Venerable Bhikkhu Mihita, Ph.D.

US Fulbright Scholar;
Canadian Buddhist Scholar;
Lifetime Buddhist Practitioner

MOTILAL BANARSIDASS
INTERNATIONAL
DELHI

Second Edition : Delhi, 2025
First Edition : 2014

© AUTHOR
All Rights Reserved

ISBN : 978-93-48911-15-5

Also available at
MOTILAL BANARSIDASS INTERNATIONAL
H.O. : 41 U.A. Bungalow Road, (Back Lane)Jawahar Nagar, Delhi - 110 007
4261 (basement) Lane #3,Ansari Road, Darya Ganj, New Delhi - 110 002
203 Royapettah High Road, Mylapore, Chennai - 600 004
12/1A, 2nd Floor, Bankim Chatterjee Street, Kolkata - 700 073
Stockist : Motilal Books, Ashok Rajpath, Near Kali Mandir, Patna - 800 004

No part of this book may be reproduced in any form or by any electronic or mechanical means including information storage and retrieval systems without permission in writing from the publishers, excepts by a reviewer who may quote brief passages in a review.

Printed in India
MOTILAL BANARSIDASS INTERNATIONAL

DEDICATION

To the Pioneers in Buddhadhianscience and Westernscience

Dr. W. F. F Jayasuriya

Author of *The Psychology and Philosophy of Buddhism*, 1963, Colombo, Sri Lanka: YMBA Press.

Prof. Buddhadasa P. Kirtisinghe

Editor, *Buddhism and Science*, Motilal Banarsidass, 1984, and Interdisciplnary Biologist and Evolutionary Scientist.

Prof. K. N. Jayatilleke

Author of *Early Buddhist Theory of Knowledge*, London: George Allen & Unwin, 1963

To my 'beautiful friends' (*kalyāṇa mitta*), for help in my Sanskrit Studies:

Prof. Sumana Lal Kekulawala

Vice Chancellor, Vidyalankara University, Sri Lanka, and my Sanskrit teacher at Ananda College, Colombo.

K D Somaratna (B A Hons.)

Colleague, and Sanskrit
Teacher at Ananda College,
Colombo .

ACKNOWLEDGEMENT

relating to the use of the original Pali Text Society text of chapters 10-16 of the Aggañña Sutta, in this Second Edition

Digha-Nikaya of the Sutta-Pitaka,
Vol. III; Patikavagga, Suttantas 24-34.
Based on the edition by T.W. Rhys Davids and J.E. Carpenter, London : Pali Text Society 1911.

Input by the Dhammakaya Foundation, Thailand, 1989-1996
[GRETIL-Version vom 2.10.2014]

NOTICE
This file is (C) Copyright the Pali Text Society and the Dhammakaya Foundation, 2015.

This work is licensed under a Creative Commons Attribution-ShareAlike 4.1 International License.

These files are provided by courtesy of the Pali Text Society for scholarly purposes only.

In principle they represent a digital edition (without revision or correction) of the printed editions of the complete set of Pali canonical texts published by the PTS. While they have been subject to a process of checking, it should not be assumed that there is no divergence from the printed editions and it is strongly recommended that they are checked against the printed editions before quoting.

Thank you (First Edition)

I thank Prof. Victor Bruce Matthews (of Acadia University, Nova Scotia), Ven. Ajahn Punnadhammo Mahathero (Abbot, Arrow River Forest Meditation Centre, Thunder Bay) and Ven. Mahathera Madawela Punnaji (former Abbot , Toronto Mahavihara), for their kind consent to write a Foreword. They provide the reader a taste of what to expect. While Prof. Matthews seeks to place the research in the context of western scholarship, Mahathero Punnadhammo places it squarely against the issues raised by the Agganna Sutta, showing the inadequacy of both materialistic and theistic positions on the issue of the origins of the universe. Pointing out how many a scholar have erroneously thought that the Buddha was ignorant about the origin of the world, or at least avoided the subject, Punnaji Mahathero notes how this study shows that the Buddha was not only discussing the important subject of genesis, but also how he was ahead of modern science. So we respectfully invite the reader to go through their Forewords by way of preparing oneself for the long haul.

My thanks also go to Prof. Lily de Silva (of the University of Peradeniya, Sri Lanka) and Dr. Rupert Sheldrake (British biologist), for their kind comments (see back cover) on Part I of this work, originally published in the *Canadian Journal of Buddhist Studies* (No. 9, 2013). And to those others who have commented as well, supportively or otherwise. They have all served as an encouragement in my humble efforts.

I thank my wife Swarna for the many hours lost in companionship, and also for her help with the Index. It is to Johnny Osorio of JTPrinting that my thanks go to for setting the text into book as well as translating my concepts into a cover design. I thank Tai and Jonathan, both of JT Printing, for an expeditious job in printing the book, and for their continuing support for my work in the area of Dhamma.

Hope you will enjoy my study as much as I have getting it into your hands.

Wishing you the best in health and happiness!
Suwanda H J Sugunasiri

Toronto, Canada
August 2014

Thank You (Second Edition)

This is an edited version of *Dhamma Aboard Evolution: a Canonical Study of the Aggañña Sutta in Relation to Science*, 2014, written under my lay name, Sugunasiri, Suwanda H. J. This edition comes with two changes in the subtitle, now reading: *a Buddhianscientific Study of the Aggañña Sutta in Relation to Westernscience*.

The changes made in the text in this Edition primarily relate to deleting the final chapters of the earlier edition (16-17), and the Appendix, with no direct relevance to the study. This study is based in paragraphs 10-16 of the *Aggañña Sutta*. In the original publication, the chapters were introduced only in its translation. So a critical addition in this version are the paragraphs 10-16 in Pali, as in the original PTS Edition.

I thank the Pali Text Society for kindly authorizing its use for this scholarly purpose, and the Dhammakaya Foundation, Thailand, 1989-1996, for facilitating it. (See 'Acknowledgement' above for details). I thank my colleague Dr. Bryan Levman for kindly facilitating its availability.

It is with deep gratitude I thank Prof. Peter Harvey of the University of Sunderland, UK, for putting in the time to do a close reading of the earlier version, and offering detailed comments on my interpretations. Though nothing but natural as such comments would be, in such a complex Discourse that has challenged scholars, at my age 89, I have no choice but to leave such discussion to future scholars. But the typos identified and other editorial comments made are now incorporated.

Finally, I thank Mr. Abhisheik Jain of Motilal Banarsidass International, India, for publishing this Second Edition, and his staff Mrs. Poonam for getting the job well done.

Hope you will enjoy my study as much as I have getting it into your hands.

Wishing you the best in health and happiness!

Ven. Bhikkhu Mihita
Toronto, Canada
June 2025

CONTENTS

PREFACE xv

FOREWORD I: Prof. Victor Bruce Mathews. xxvii

FOREWORD II: Ven. Ajahn Punnadhammo Mahathero xxix

FOREWORD III: Ven. Mahathera Madawela Punnaji' xxxvi

PART I 1

PART II 129

BIBLIOGRAPHY 201

ABBREVIATIONS 206

INDEX 207

DETAILED CONTENTS

PART I

1. Introduction 1
2. Outline of Aggañña Sutta 5
3. Original Pali Text and Translation
of Aggañña Sutta # 10-16 11
3.1 Original Pali Text 11
3.2 Translation.. 17
4. Notes to the Translation 21
5. Aggañña Sutta # 10-21 as Cosmic Narrative 43
6. Two Seeming Chronological Paradoxes 75
6.1 Fingers, Food, Humans and Earth 75
6.2 *Lingua* Precedes *Linga*.................................... 81
7. Going Traditional: Ābhassara Beings
Finding a Footing on Earth 95
8. A Seeming Spiritual Paradox?
Kāma-taṇhā-jettisoned Ābhassara Beings
Engage in Sex! 101
8.1 Ābhassara Beings: A Heretical View 102
8.2 Two Types of Ābhassara Beings 105
8.3 Beings Reckoned Just as Beings' as
New Strand of Sentience 107
8.4 Why Introduce Ābhassara Beings? 109
8.5 Ride on a Straw Horse 110
9. Finding a Footing on Earth Revisited
in Relation to Westernscience 111
10. A Concluding Overview 121

PART II

11. Cutting through the Vedic Myth 129
12. Intended Audience 147
13. Unfolding the Primeval as Buddha's Intent 169
14. 'Dhamma is Best' as Buddha's Real Intent 179
15 Closure 191
15.1 Aggañña Sutta a Clumsy Patchwork? 191
15.2 A Clumsy Patchwork of Research? 193
15.3 Beauty Lies in the Eye of the Beholder 195
15.4 Going Interdisciplinary at One's Own Peril! 197
15.5 Concluding Remarks 198

FIGURES

Fig. 1 Four Phases in the Devolutionary/Evolutionary Cycle of the Universe (speculatively developed based in the Aggañña Sutta) 44

Fig. 2 Benchmarks identified by the Buddha as against the Benchmarks of Evolution in Westernscience 66

Fig. 3 Stages of Linguistic Growth in Beings and Food Type as Indicative of the Evolutionary Phases 70

Fig. 4 A Comparative Evolutionary Perspective as between the Buddha and Westernscience 123

Fig. 5 Some Common Elements in the Vedic Creation Hymn and the *Aggañña* Sutta 132

Fig. 6 Some Contrastive Elements in the Vedic Creation Hymn and the *Aggañña* Sutta.......................134

Fig. 7 Parallels Between Lines in # 3 and # 9 using *tumhe* 148

Fig. 8 Graduated Sequence of Information Release by the Buddha of his Knowledge of the Primeval 157

Fig. 9 Indicative Reciprocal Micro-conditioning Process as between Loss of Luminosity in Sentient Beings and Appearance of the Sun 184

Namo tassa bhagavato arahato sammāsambuddhassa!

'Homage to the Fortunate One, the Worthy One, the Fully Enlightened One.'

PREFACE

The Discourse under study, number 27 of the *Dīgha Nikāya*, is titled *aggañña sutta*, analyzeable as *agga-* + *-(ñ)ña, - ña* meaning 'knowledge' or 'knowing'. But *agga-* is rich in meaning; it means 'ancient', 'primeval' and 'end' on the one hand, and 'beginning' 'first, 'foremost', 'best', etc., on the other. So *agga-* in relation to the process of Evolution can be said to refer to the 'beginning' process, and 'best' in relation to the Dhamma. We see this latter meaning at the end of the Sutta, "Of these four classes [meaning Khattiya, Brāhmaṇa, Vessa, Sudda, listing them in the order the Buddha does], Vāseṭṭha, one who becomes a monk, becoming worthy [i.e., Arahant] with defilements jettisoned, … in whom the fetters of becoming are destroyed … indeed is properly called the best [or 'deserve the highest praise'] among them" (# 30).

As will be seen in our analysis, in # 10-16 of the Discourse, the Buddha is laying out the parameters of the unfolding of the universe. What this intricate and succinct segment of a mere seven paragraph does is to give a comprehensive understanding of the reality of the universe, in its physical, human and vegetation dimensions, interactively. Yet, in introducing the lines quoted above, at the very end of the Sutta, the Buddha seems to be telling us, 'It's great that you now know the beginnings of the universe (in this Evolutionary phase). But you know what, what's best is knowing the Dhamma'. This, then, is the wordplay that the Buddha engages in, providing a treasure trove for the language as art afficianados.

It was quite accidentally that I got into this study. Writing a popular piece, "Life there was before Earth" (see Bibliography), in a comparative thrust in relation to Westernscience, it was sent to a respected scholar, when I was kindly directed to an article by Prof. Collins (see Bibliography). This was an extensive research on the *aggañña sutta,* opening up a whole new world to me. Interesting it was alright, but I just could not quite stomach his view that segment # 10-16 of the Sutta was nothing but 'satire'. (See 16.1 for a little longer treatment.)

The article introduced me to another treatment of the Sutta, by Prof. Gombrich (see Bibliography). He took the segment to be a 'parody' of the Vedic 'aetiological myth' of Creation. This, too, I found not sitting well with me. I could not just believe it – that the Buddha would spend his time on satire or parody just for its own sake. This is not to say that there is no satire and wit in the Buddha's Teachings, but to the extent that I can fathom, it has always been as a communication strategy, a means to an end, and not as an end in itself.

This is when I took a serious look at the *aggañña sutta*. In the opening segment, the Buddha tells us of an Ābhassara Being existing in the Devolutionary phase. So my first question to myself was who these Beings were. By definition, a Being has a consciousness; and so, in the text, they are 'mind-based'. But a consciousness cannot exist without a material body, given the characterization of sentience as 'mindbody' (*nāmarūpa*). So how could we understand this material form? The traditional meaning of Ābhassara Brahmā was not of much help. This is when it hit me to step out of the box.

I had been familiar in general terms with the Buddha's view of a cyclical universe, but here it was staring me in my face. The pair *saṃvaṭṭa* and *vivaṭṭa* appearing in the segment is, then, what took me into the labyrinth of Westernscience. I wanted to put my own labyrinth, the inner ear, closer to the Buddha's voice.

My first step was to look at the term Ābhassara itself, analytically but literally, when I came up with ***'hither-come-shining-arrow'*** as a translation. There already was a shine on my face! Ābhassara Beings are also, in the text, 'self-luminous' as also 'sky-flying'. This was when it occurred to me that my real step outside needs to be into Westernscience, well-known for its cosmic explorations. Thinking along these lines, there now came to be an intuitive leap - this 'hither-come-shining-arrow' is perhaps a *photon*, a 'quantum of energy'. Now I found myself opened up! My task then was to trace the steps of how these photons of Ābhassara Beings eventually end up as females and males in passion, as in # 16, over billions of years.

But personally, I was hardly qualified for the task. My love for Biology in Grade 8 had not led me into any formal training in Science. However, I seem to have always had a fascination for it. For the longest time, e.g., I've had the medical standard reference, *Gray's Anatomy*, on my bookshelf, even though medicine was only what I saw being practiced on patients! Issac Assimov's 'Trilogy' on 'Understanding Physics' has also been staring at me from the shelves, although I rarely returned the gaze. Darwin, Freud and Piaget have been luckier. They have enjoyed more of my company over the years than Marx and Adam Smith, and Einstein and Neils Bohr in their never ending disputes, and understanding not much. A more recent reading was *The Conscious Universe*, by Menas Kafatos and Robert Nadeau. This I found to be encouraging. I found the authors stepping out of the box so to speak, questioning some of the sacred cows of science orthodoxy.

But my conviction of the scientific basis, and the empiricism, of the Buddha's Teachings seems to have had its beginnings much earlier. My first academic exposure may have been Prof. K N Jayatilleke's *Early Buddhist Theory of Knowledge* doing a Master's Degree in Moral Philosophy in Canada in the late sixties. Another eye-opener, teaching Buddhist Psychology at the Vidyodaya University in Sri Lanka in the early seventies, was Dr. W F Jayasuriya's *The Psychology and Philosophy of Buddhism*. It was still later that I had come to discover *Buddhism and Science* (1984), edited by Prof. Buddhadasa P. Kirthisinghe.

Doing my graduate studies, all of them in the West, beginning in 1964 in Linguistics, I was to take many an other course in diverse disciplines – Psychology, Philosophy, Education, Literature,

Economics, Politics, Sociology, Religion and Development Theory, to name a few. And the more I studied and read, the more I came to be convinced of the scientific and empirical basis of the Buddha's Teachings. This only came to be confirmed in my informal readings. A case in point was reading Darwin's Theory of Evolution which confirmed for me, e.g., the validity of the Buddha's term *sattā* to cover both humans and animals under the same phylogenetic scale.

Two other works, by Western writers, may have brought me closer to looking at Buddhism from a Westernscientificpoint of view. One was Prof. Fritjof Capra's *Tao of Physics*. Though Prof. Kuhn's *The Structure of Scientific Revolutions* was not exactly a comparative study, it took me a bit higher in the ladder of knowledge in the area of Westernscience.

But it is working on my own *You're What You Sense: Buddha on Mindbody* (2001), however, in an attempt to present the Abhdhamma in a popular format, that such informal explorings found a tangible home, taking me also into Cell Biology. The preparation for this could have been my Master's Degree on Religion, focusing on 'Buddhism as a Scientific Study', an outcome being my paper (1995), "Whole Body, not Heart, the Seat of Consciousness: the Buddha's View," in *Philosophy East and Wes*t. The Buddha's 'pancorporeal theory' (as I have now come to call it) was, in my view, an advance on not only the traditionally Buddhist 'cardiac theory' (Ven. Buddhaghosa being its best known proponent) but also the contemporary western 'encephalic theory' (both labels again my own).

Taking to meditation later, I also came to see how the Teachings were just as they were said to be - personally verifiable (*sandiṭṭhiko*). And so it is in meditation methodology, as explored in my paper, "'Against Belief': Mindfulness Meditation (*satipaṭṭhāna bhāvanā*) as Empirical Method" a decade later that I found, ironically, the most concrete evidence of empiricism in the Buddha's Teachings.

But it is only in this study, however, that I make bold to look at the Teachings from the perspective of Westernscience.

This comparative streak in me can be said to have had its academic beginnings early in my studies, taking a course on Psychology at the

University of Michigan (1965-6). While there is no trace of the paper now, "Tovil as Psychotherapy" was a look at the exorcistic healing ceremony of the Sinhala people in Sri Lanka - for a serious illness, safe(r) child-birth, etc. It identified four critical ingredients as serving the healing function: 1. efficacy of the healing method, 2. confidence in the healer, 3. centrality of the patient and 4. community support when the entire village would show up for the all-night event. All but the last matching well with contemporary Psychotherapeutic practice, the Professor thought it deserved an A. It is in my doctoral thesis in Canada much later (1978), however, that my multidisicplinary thrust comes to blossom. The title speaks for itself - *Humanistic Nationism: a Language- and Ideology-based Model of Development for Post-Colonial Nations*.

Ironic as it may sound, funny enough, and perhaps even odd, as it may appear to be, it would be remiss here if I were not to talk of my Novel. Did it possibly provide a hidden hand in my research, even insight? As noted in passing, and will be seen in detail later (see Chap. 15 and Appendix), the *Aggañña Sutta* is of the 'story within story' structure. Here, then, is the structure of my novel, *Untouchable Woman's Odyssey* (2010), written two years prior to the present study, and never having read the Sutta earlier.

> Story Present I, Interlude, Story Present II, Story Past and Postlude. Clearly, 'Story Present' (I and II) and 'Story Past' take us to the Jātaka structure. But then there is the 'Interlude', just after Story Present I, as *ex abrupto* as in # 10-16 of the Sutta, baffling many a reader and critic of the novel. Just as in the Sutta, again baffling many a scholar, it is totally unrelated to the main story line, and has no connection to what immediately follows either. The subject matter that makes up the Interlude comes to be resolved only at the very end, in the Postlude, again as in the Sutta, when the Buddha says, at the very end, that Dhamma is the best.

So while I cannot lay my hands on just what my Novel has got to do with my gaining an insight into the Sutta, the similarity of structure seems most intriguing. Does this speak to the unfathomable way the mind works? Did the template of the novel planted in my mind surreptitiously provide a perceptual angle towards understanding the Sutta segment? If so, it must have been at a deep, deep down level, for it is only at this very point in writing that the parallel in the structure even comes to my mind.

Amazing mind!

It was with all this under my belt, then, that I came to this study, with the hypothesis that the Buddha was indeed talking about the universe unfolding. My task then was to find the evidence, confirming it or otherwise.

And it was in order to get enough of a handle on what I was exploring, then, that I began reading up on Western Cosmology and brush up on Darwin. As I began to translate segment # 10-16 of the Sutta, a light would flicker here, and a light would flicker there. But while there were still dark and dingy corners awaiting closer and deeper scrutiny, there was enough light to see the way ahead. It was the exercise of annotating the translation that sharpened my tools of inquiry even more, taking me also to the domains of creative thought, of which, you will see plenty here. But, as in all creative research I believe, what was relevant sometimes came quite unexpectedly, i.e., when I was not even looking for it.

I had completed a first draft to my satisfaction. Yet I was not sure I could convince anyone to read it. Buddhism and Science said in the same breath seem to prompt many to raise eye-brows if not shudder, on both sides of the camp. And so it was with some trepidation that I sent the manuscript to Ajahn Punnadhammo, a Canadian monk ordained in Thailand, who kindly agreed to read my draft. A Pali scholar, as I had known him to be, I was hoping that he would comment on my translation and annotation. But to my great surprise, what I got back from him was far more than what I had expected. He commented on my Science, and actually thought that my interpretation of the segment as speaking to evolution was right on! Not only did he see validity in the picture I had drawn, as captured in the 'Cosmic Narrative' (see I.5), but also provided additional material and references that would strengthen the argument.

It was a colleague, Dr. Bryan Levman, who actually responded the way I had expected. A scholar of not only Pali and Sanskrit, but also Prakrits, his close scrutiny of my translation and the annotation helped me toe the Pali line closer!

And how happy I was by the end of the exploration, after multiple revisions, of course, that I had come to hear the Buddha's voice in my inner ear, loud and clear. But it is not just understanding the content of the segment, baffling as it has been to many a scholar that may be the contribution of this study. It is also in relation to Buddhist research methodology - first the fruitfulness of stepping out of the box, and second, the advantage of comparative study in relation to Westernscience. A third may relate to language usage – to encourage easing up on the style of writing in the Academy by way of opening up knowledge to a wider community.

Part I of this book first appeared in the form of an article in the *Canadian Journal of Buddhist Studies* (2013), under the slightly different title, "Devolution And Evolution in the *Aggañña* Sutta: # 10-16, in Relation to Westernscience". It was encouraging that the initial reception of the research was generally positive. A respected Western Scholar Monk, e.g., noted, "Very interesting, and no doubt it will be a bit provocative among academic scholars." A Scholar Monk of Sri Lankan origin resident in the west commented that "Until now, I think we have tended to interpret this part of the sutta in a symbolic way, but you have produced a new and original point of view." (personal email). The paper also seems to have spurred some discussion on the internet and reproduced on some websites as well.

On the other side of the coin has been the stance that the Buddha considered the question of the beginnings of the Universe to be unimportant. The classical position here is presumably drawn upon the Cūlamālunkya Sutta (MN, 63), one of the sixteen 'undeclared' (*avyākata*) being whether 'The world is eternal' or '…not eternal'. In this context, the Buddha explains very clearly why they have been left 'undeclared'. Simple: "Because it is unbeneficial, it does not belong to the fundamentals of the holy life, it does not lead to disenchantment, to dispassion, to cessation, to peace, to direct knowledge, to Enlightenment, to Nibbāna." (Ven Bodhi tr. (1995, 2001, 533-536)).

The Buddha's very reason itself for leaving them undeclared, however, seems to provide the background for outlining the unfolding of the universe in the Aggañña Sutta. As argued in Ch. 12 of this study, the Buddha is addressing not the Bhikkhu collectivity sitting at a distance, but the two intelligent, inquisitive minds in the persona of Vāseṭṭha and Bhāradvāja. Having abandoned their inherited tradition and left the household life, they are exploring alternatives, which is why they have come to the Buddha. Abandoned their Brahminic heritage they may have, but the Vedic views about the beginnings of the universe (as critiqued in Ch. 11) are still fully intact in their minds. So dislodging the Vedic worldview was the one sure fire way of bringing to the two young seekers a more realistic, and alternative, understanding of the universe. In that sense, then, clarifying the issue can be said to be not only not 'unbeneficial' as in relation to Mālunkyaputta, but contrariwise, 'beneficial', and leading to 'peace' for the obviously discontented minds of the two seekers. That the message did bring them to a realistic world may be evidenced from the fact that both Vāseṭṭha and Bhāradvāja not only enter discipleship under the Buddha, but also eventually attain to Arahantship. So the Buddha can be said to have dispensed with knowledge wisely in a sound educational practice of what may be called selective teaching – to each according to one's need! And in the context of the learning potential of the listener.

Indeed it is relevant to note that the Buddha seeks to explain the Universe, though not totally as in the Aggañña, in two other Suttas as well. The educational principle as above may be seen at play here, too – releasing some information in the Brahmajala, a little more in the Patika and the whole story in the Aggañña. (Fig 8, p. 153) (see Ch. 12 below for a fuller treatment).

One may also be reminded in this context of the folktale of the forbidden fruit. The subjects may not be allowed to taste the fruit of the forbidden tree, but that doesn't mean that it is out of bounds for the Ruler!

Another example of the Buddha's wise selective praxis is when at his last meal, Cunda is advised to serve the *sūkara maddava* (leaving it untranslated) only to himself, and to bury the rest in a pit, serving the Bhikkhus "the remaining hard and soft food". Why? "I can see none .. who .. could thoroughly digest it" (Mahāparinibbāna Sutta, DN ii. 127).

What all this suggests, then, is that it may perhaps be a lack of clear understanding that may have prompted a negative reading of my research in some quarters.

Another criticism of my research is around the issue of why Westerscience can needed to establish the Buddha's Teachings. First let me say right upfront that one only needs oneself to work one's way towards liberation as shown by the Buddha. But the issue in this study is not salvific, but cognitive - getting an understanding of the Teachings. If anything, the present study should show beyond a measure of doubt how a comparative stance in relation to Westernsciencecan only be helpful. It has helped unravel the intricacies of the Buddha's advanced pedagogical methodology, and shown how the Buddha's view is not only scientifically defensible, but is an improvement on the view of Westernscience. We can think of the cyclical nature of the universe, and the relationality of the multiple phenomena – the physical universe, plant life, human sentient life in terms of both physical growth and the acquisition of unskilled states of mind, and social and political growth, providing another example of the Principle of Conditioned Co-origination. Indeed it may be conjectured that it may have been the exclusive internal perspective brought to the study of the Discourse that has rendered its meaning beyond the grasp of students of the Teachings all these many years.

If that speaks to the advantages of comparative study in the direction of Buddhism, it is also to begin to appreciate the contributions of science to world knowledge. So in the final analysis, what a comparative study can do is allow us to give

Science its due, if warts and all, and the Buddha his due. Personally, it allows me to salute Westernsciencefor its contributions, just as I salute the Buddha more.

Part II of the Book seeks to respond to some of the issues raised by the discussion – the influence of the Vedas on the Sutta, audience, intent of the Buddha in delivering it and the structure, seemingly, though unintentionally, speaking to the public response of the published material as well. The study ends with raising a few methodological issues, with an invitation to the Academy to adopt 'Trust in the Buddha' as a Methodological Imperative, welcoming the Buddha as a 'Friend of the Academy'. And the invitation goes to practicing Buddhist scholars to 'come out' and declare their Buddhistness openly, engaging in an 'Academically Engaged Buddhism'.

While, as noted, AS has been seen as 'satire' and 'parody', it is hoped that our discussion confirms our hypothesis – that indeed the Buddha is presenting the universe, and that he could not have been more serious!

If the title of the book, *Dhamma Aboard Evolution*, gives a sense of motion and flight, the imagery behind it seeks to capture the Buddha's intent. I see the Buddha taking us on a ground trip in # 1 to 9, then taking us aloft up into the cosmos and down in # 10 to 21, continuing the journey on the ground beginning in # 22. It is as if we go on board a train on the first part of the Dhamma journey, then go on board a space shuttle, and then, returning to Earth with vistas opened, continues the journey on board a train again, as if to see for ourselves which is better – the temporary space travel or the continuing Dhamma travel.

If the title thus catches the *intent* of the Sutta, as in Ch. 13 and 14 of this study, it also resonates with the style of writing in the book which you will find to be somewhat different from most academic writing. If this possibly reflects my creative writing experience as a Novelist and Poet, and as a Newspaper Columnist (*Toronto Star)*, it may also serve to be my own humble attempt to keep in step with the ethos of language usage of the Buddha, the maestro language user as I find him to be in the Suttas – precise and simple, but rich in meaning, a strength you'll find me openly appreciating.

Now to a few acknowledgements.

My first thanks go to Ajahn Punnadhammo and Bryan Levman for their critical input. In our world of specialization, it is not easy to find scholars who would have much enthusiasm for an unconventional cross-disciplinary treatment. It would be even more difficult to find those with the needed training and background relating to the comparative perspective from which the writer has come to the present study. So I thank them for their kind and critical input. Without them, this study would have been the poorer. Of course, I alone am responsible for any errors in translation, fact, interpretation and judgment.

To Professors Collins and Gombrich I owe much gratitude for prompting me to take the plunge. It is with gratitude and respect that the writer acknowledges that he has immensely benefited not only from the translation and commentary by Collins, but also the translation by Dr Walshe in his Digha Nikaya translation. Prof. Gombrich's critical take on it was another helpful source. As will be seen, however, the writer will also have had the occasion to disagree with all three of them. Naturally, any errors in translation and interpretation are, again, the writer's alone.

This research can be seen as my humble gift to Buddhist scholarship and scholarship in general to mark 50 years of my life in North America, arriving on the campus of the University of Pennsylvania, Philadelphia, USA, on a Fulbright-Smith Mundt Scholarship to study Linguistics. "Buddhism in the modern world is a multi-faceted mosaic that is being shaped as much by technology as it is by Western ideas. To the rich heritage of classical texts, monastic institutions and traditional rituals that have been practiced for centuries, one must add …., the re-interpretation of traditional texts for modern contexts with modern analytical tools, the questioning of traditional philosophical, institutional or ethical frameworks …." My study I hope will then be seen as speaking to these words of Ken McLeod (2014), writing under the title, "How is the Medium Changing the Message?: thoughts on technology in relation to modern Buddhism" (*Insight Journal*, March 2014, Barre Centre for Buddhist Studies, Barre, Mass., USA).

Wishing you the best in health and happiness!

FOREWORD I

Prof. Victor Bruce Mathews

(Dean of Arts and C.B. Lumsden Professor of Comparative Religion, Acadia University, Nova Scotia, Canada)

Whatever else might be said about the historical background and setting of the *Aggañña Sutta* of the *Digha Nikaya* (3.80-98), the work presents one of the best known synopses of what purports to be Gotama Buddha's understanding of creation and evolution. It does so succinctly within the compass of just a few verses, and although there are somewhat parallel discussions of evolution elsewhere in the Pali Canon (e.g., *Ambattha Sutta*, D.1.88), the *Aggañña* brings the topics of geological, biological, social and even political formations into one interesting analytical sweep.

In his book, Suwanda H. J. Sugunasiri has provided a novel perspective on this ancient text. His central argument is that the *Aggañña Sutta* is a genuine utterance of Gotama, and must be seriously regarded as a factual summary of his world-view. In this regard, he takes exception to Pali scholars who see in the *Sutta* a take-off on the *pañcatantra* genre common to Gotama's cultural period (a fable-like story designed to make a point); or the *Aggañña Sutta* as a fanciful description of evolution, caste and rulership (with "a good-humoured irony", as notes T.W.Rhys Davids); or as a satire (Steven Collins), or as a parody of a earlier Vedic creation myth (Richard Gombrich). Rather, for Sugunasiri, the *Aggañña Sutta* is as much a sincere scientific exhortation as it is a teaching on the ultimate primacy of following a *dhamma* or instruction based on the moral 'norms' of conduct associated with human society.

Sugunasiri urges us to see how the Buddha's views on cosmological and evolutionary topics are not contradictory to what he calls 'Westernscience'. Thus the *Sutta's* description of the origin of the cosmos, the creation of proto-human life forms (*Abhassara* beings), the unique force of human craving (*Taṇhā*, in due course a key element of the Second Noble Truth or source of painfulness), and what the author describes as "a characterization of the flow of nature" or evolution – all these are, in the author's opinion, to be regarded as a serious attempt to explain reality.

Others have similarly emphasized a compatibility between Buddhist teaching and modern notions of scientific reality (e.g., W F Jayasuriya, K.N. Jayatilleke, Buddhadasa P. Kirthisinghe). Sugunasiri's point of view is perhaps best distilled in the title of his monograph, *Dhamma Aboard Evolution* - in other words, Buddhist teachings traveling compatibly alongside of modern evolutionary concepts.

An added strength is that he writes very well.

His thoughtful study will be welcome by students of Buddhism and the Indian Religious Tradition in general.

FOREWORD II

Ven. Ajahn Punnadhammo Mahathero

(Abbot, Arrow River Forest Hermitage, Thunder Bay, Ontario)

The Aggañña Sutta, Digha Nikāya 27, is one of a few texts of central importance for elucidating the cosmological vision of early Buddhism. In this dialogue the Buddha lays out his vision of the origins and natural history of life on Earth, and the beginnings of human society and the state. This is the basic message Dr. Sugunasiri seeks to convey in this study.

In recent times most scholars looking at this text have focussed on the socio-political aspects which are most evident in the later sections where the Buddha describes the origins of private property, the state, kingship and the division of human society into separate castes. It has been suggested that the primary purpose of the Aggañña was to critique and satirize the brahminical claims of a special origin. This was certainly one aspect of this multi-layered text. There is also the intriguing way in which the Buddha anticipates Locke and postulates a social-contract theory of human politics. In the Aggañña version, the state and kingship are necessary evils, which only appear after a long period of gradual moral degeneracy from a primal state of innocence.

However, in this work the author has focussed primarily on the early part of the sutta which describes the origin of life at the beginning of a world-cycle. This is an aspect which has been neglected by modern students of the text.

The problem of origins is one which is common to all religions, and from another angle, to scientific inquiry as well. The Buddhist version differs radically from the creation myths of other religious traditions in that it is not a creation myth at all. Buddhism is non-theistic and there is no creation because there is no creator. Causality has always been a central axiom of Buddhist philosophy. Things arise due to causes and conditions and never randomly or arbitrarily. Although the Buddha himself refused to be drawn into speculations about the ultimate origins of the world, the logical conclusion drawn by most of his followers in later centuries has been that the world is, in fact, beginingless. No matter how far back in time you go, there must always have been a previous moment as a condition to set up the causes for the present moment.

Buddhism, and Indian thought generally, has always seen the vast sweep of time as cyclical. There is a long period in which the universe unfolds, or "rolls out", a period in which the many worlds and their diverse inhabitants come into being. This is followed by a period in which the world folds up, or "rolls back", in which the various worlds are destroyed. This cycle has always existed and always will exist. There is no final beginning or ending. This is the broadest understanding of samsāra, the cycle of conditioned existence. To the beings caught in it, this cycle is both fascinating and terrifying. It is also ultimately futile and it is the promise of the Buddha's third noble truth that we can transcend it altogether by realizing the unconditioned.

It is important to put the tale told in the Aggañña Sutta into this broader perspective. This is not a story of ultimate beginnings, because such a story cannot be told. It is only a description of how the world unfolds after a new cycle begins.

In the western world there are two competing stories of the origin of things. The older version is the religious vision of creation by an omnipotent deity, either in its literal form as found in the book of Genesis, or in more liberal interpretations that see a divine hand, an "intelligent designer", behind the arising and evolution of the world. Since the nineteenth century there has been a competing model, that of natural science, which dispenses with the need for a creator. The Buddhist vision takes a third, or middle position, between the two. For the Buddhist, both of these models, which are so much opposed to each other, share a crucial failing. Both creationism and scientific materialism end up breaking down in a denial of causality. Both have an arbitrary element; either the arbitrary will of a creator or in the case of scientific materialism, the inescapable factor of random arising.

Consider why one being is born strong and healthy and another sickly and weak. Theistic religions have to rely on the idea that somehow that was God's will and thus the perennially insoluble problem of theodicy; "why do bad things happen to good people?" Science can tell us the "how" and can speak about genetic or environmental factors but does not even attempt to address the "why." To ask why this person was born with a defective gene instead of another person is a question that is not even meaningful in the scientific model, but remains a troubling human issue all the same.

Buddhism is not, we have said, theistic. But neither is it materialist. It differs from the materialist paradigm by admitting

Mind as an independent, non-physical factor. Science itself is advancing toward this position; the most straightforward way of interpreting quantum mechanics is to see the world as an unformed field of potential until acted upon by consciousness; the act of observation collapses the wave-function. Mind is not material, but neither is it an exception to the laws of causality. One of the laws which has a profound bearing on the story told in the Aggañña is that of karma. This is best understood as a natural law operating ultimately on the microscopic level of mind-moments; a skillful moment of action produces at some future moment a pleasant moment of experience and an unskillful moment produces an unpleasant one. On the macroscopic level, this means that our actions determine our future conditions and our future births. Indeed, the entire world which unfolds at the beginning of a cycle does so because of the accumulated karma of beings from the previous cycle.

Thus, Buddhism adds not only consciousness but also a moral dimension as integral elements necessary for a complete explanation of the world. This does not contradict any scientific principle, however much it diverges from the currently accepted paradigm. On the contrary, many currently insoluble problems might have light shed on them if we take this broader view. What caused the big bang? How did life originate? How can we explain problems in morphogenesis like protein folding? (Rupert Sheldrake's non-local pure information fields are very much like Mind.)

There is no longer any rational basis for saying that evolution does not occur. The fossil record demonstrates continuous change in Earth's organisms over a billion years.

But is natural selection among random mutations a sufficient explanation? Creationists are good at finding the problems in the standard Darwinian model. How could a complex organ like the eye arise, when each part must work in sync with many others? (What good would a mutation producing a lens be without rods and cones, an optic nerve and appropriate processing sectors in the brain?) How did flowering plants arise in a mutual dance of symbiosis with the insects, or human intelligence for that matter, which goes far beyond what is needed for simple survival? The materialist interpretation refuses to allow for any element of teleology or purposeful direction to evolution. But what if we see the evolution of life as mind progressively experimenting with new and more sophisticated physical vehicles? Not intelligent design, but purposeful direction.

The critical point in the origin story of the Aggañña is when the "mind-made" beings first ingest physical food out of desire or curiosity and end up becoming entangled in gross material forms. The rest of the story is one of their very slow and gradual descent into embodied existence as we know it today. A superficial reading of the text in translation makes the unfolding story appear very different from what we know of the history of the Earth.

Dr. Sugunasiri's contribution in the present work is to apply an exacting scholarship to the Pali text itself and to tease out many fascinating and unexpected parallels to the modern scientific account of Earth's long history. When looked at through the lens of linguistic analysis, as he does, the Aggañña no longer seems like a naive fairy-tale, which I fear is how most modern educated readers will have judged it at first reading. When reading any ancient text, there is always a gulf of understanding; we cannot help but filter the words through our own experience, education and assumption. It is a challenge to try and tease out what those words meant to the speaker and his first listeners. The approach in this book is to attempt to do just that, and to guide the reader along the way to the same vision as the Buddha's listeners twenty-five centuries ago. Paradoxically, the result more often than not seems surprisingly modern.

Translation of a text can never be perfect; languages are not isomorphic systems but idiosyncratic vehicles for expression of ideas. The problem of translation is all the more difficult when we are dealing with an ancient language from a very different cultural milieu. To attempt to understand what an ancient text actually means, or in other words what its author was trying to convey or its original audience took from it, may be a task that can never be definitively and perfectly accomplished. We cannot avoid reading through the filters of our own background and education, and the ancient context cannot never be fully known. Dr. Sugunasiri is well aware of these problems and his attempt at a solution is to bore down with minute attention to the original words. He provides twenty pages of careful notes for just six stanzas from the original sutta. The reader is led into a close examination of the text almost word by word, which uncovers nuances of meaning that could never be conveyed by a simple translation.

The difficulty of dealing with a text like this is doubly tricky. One the one hand, we have to strive to understand the Buddha's words in their original context, as spoken to an audience of intelligent, educated, iron age Indians. On the other hand, we cannot unknow what we now know about the natural history, geology, astronomy and biology of the Earth as twenty-first century people.

The reader can judge for herself how well the current author handles this dilemma. At the very least, this is a bold opening to a new area of investigation. He begins with the original text, and proceeds by considering that the Buddha meant what he said to be taken not just as a parody, but as a serious exposition. He then makes the attempt to understand it both in the original context, and in light of our modern scientific knowledge. Holding these two contexts in mind is a challenge not only for the author of this book, but for the reader as well.

FOREWORD III

Ven. Mahathera Madawela Punnaji

(Former Abbot of the Toronto Mahavihara)

It was a great pleasure to read Prof. Suwanda Sugunasiri's research paper on the Aggañña Sutta, which I believe is a monumental presentation of a generally ignored part of the teachings of the Buddha. Scholars seem to have neglected a very important part of the Buddhist account of Genesis, which other religions seem to consider the most important section of their dogma.

Many scholars have thought that the Buddha was ignorant about the origin of the world, or at least avoided the subject. When the question comes up, they fall back on the Culamalunkyaputta Sutta, saying that the Buddha considered the question to be unimportant, and instead spoke only of the Four Noble Truths. In this study, Prof. Sugunasiri shows that the Buddha was not only discussing the important subject of genesis, but also that he was ahead of modern science.

Astronomers who have been observing the stars through many generations have discovered that the space between the stars are gradually widening. So they came to the conclusion that the universe is expanding. Then they began to think that if it was expanding there must have been a time when the universe was very small or may be even absent. That took them to their religious dogma of Creation. So they must have conjectured that the world could have started with a big bang, and then began to spread out, possibly as in the imagery of fireworks. This may have been how the astronomers came up with the big-bang theory to explain why the universe was expanding. Were they only using guesswork based on their religious dogma about the creation of the world?

The Buddha, on the other hand, was pointing out, more than twenty five centuries ago, that the universe was not only expanding, but goes through a constant cycle of expanding and contracting, without beginning or end. He has pointed to this not only in the Aggañña Sutta, but also in several other Suttas, as well captured in Chap. 12 of this book.

Researchers led by John Sutherland at Manchester University have demonstrated the mechanism that led to the first living, breathing creatures – a process attributed to an unexplained primordial soup by generations of evolutionary theorists, including Charles Darwin. A careful examination of the Aggañña Sutta reveals a wonderful description of a phenomenon similar to the above. Bringing this to the notice of the modern world is a magnanimous feat of Prof. Sugunasiri. I wish to express my great appreciation of his work.

1

Introduction

Aggañña Sutta (AS) (D III 27) has been translated into European languages by many a scholar (see Prof. Collins[1], 1993, 338, for an overview). Dr. Walshe (1987) and Collins are the two latest, Collins making a very valuable contribution to scholarship showing how much of the content of AS is drawn from the Vinaya . The critical study by Prof. Gombrich (1988) gives us another insight, namely, the parallels with the Vedas and the Upanishads.

While, of course, both Walshe and Collins have provided excellent translations of the entire discourse, this writer's task is far more modest, providing a translation of only # 10 to 16. In the *Anguttara Nikāya* (A II 142), the Buddha identifies two phases of the universe, namely, Devolution and Evolution[2]. Our reading of the AS tells us that it is these two phases, the latter in detail, that come to be outlined in # 10 to 16, using here the numbering as in Dr. Carpenter, 1992, as also done by Collins (1993, 338).

And as with Collins, this writer is translating the segment not for the sake of offering another rendition, but to look at it from the particular comparative perspective he brings to it, namely, in relation to Westernscience[3]. Yet, it is not the translation itself, which is not very different from others except at some critical points, that speaks to the contribution of the study, but the interpretation (see 4 and 5).

In this study, we shall seek to show (1) how # 10-21 (Carpenter,

---

[3] The label 'Westernscience' is used here to distinguish it from Science in other civilizations such as Indian and Chinese.

1992) of the Discourse (i.e., going beyond the translated segment), suggest the following:

1. That the universe goes through a cycle of Devolutionary[4] (*saṃvaṭṭa*) and Evolutionary (*vivaṭṭa*) phases[5].

---

[4] To the extent that in Westernscience, the cosmic process is characterized only in terms of 'Evolution', the term 'Devolution' in the current context may raise eyebrows. However, not only is it very much part of the Buddha's view of a cyclical cosmic process as noted and shall see more of later, 'devolution' is very much part of the vocabulary of Westernscience, too, as e.g., in Biology where it comes to be used in the same sense, meaning 'opposed to evolution' and 'degeneration' (Webster's).

[5] While 'contracting universe' and 'expanding universe' may be a standard use, we opt for 'Devolution' and 'Evolution' for three reasons. It is (1) less wordy, and in that sense captures the spirit of the single word usage of the Buddha (*saṃvaṭṭa*; *vivaṭṭa*) (2) more technical and context-specific than 'expanding' and 'contracting', terms applicable to many an other context (as e.g., 'expanding horizons'), but (3) most importantly, descriptively captures the complex process entailed, as also in Westernscience, as e.g., in Biology (see fn 4 above).

2. That there was sentient life in the universe prior to the existence of the Earth.
3. That the origins of such sentient life vis-a-vis the Earth of the *present* evolutionary phase was in space!
4. That with the appearance of the Earth there came to exist conditions conducive to sentient life.
5. That over time, to be counted in billions of years, sentient life culminated in human life and society.

Following this brief introduction that begins Part I[6], we provide an Outline of the Discourse (2), in order to place our translation in perspective. In 3, we present our translation of # 10–16 followed by Notes to the Translation (4) providing some comments. This is followed by what has been titled, 'AS # 10-21 as Cosmic Narrative' (5).

Having understood the segment in Westernscientificterms, we deal with two Chronological Paradoxes (6) generated by the discussion, or has not been dealt with adequately. First (6.1) we deal with how Beings could have had 'fingers' when human beings only appear at a much later phase, placing the discussion within the context of sources of food that appear on Earth. Next dealt with is the issue captured in the header, "*Lingua* Precedes *Linga*" (6.2).

Having now arrived at a comparative understanding of the segment, we now accommodate the traditional understanding of Ābhassara Beings (7, 8), first explaining how they come to find 'a Footing on Earth'. But this generates a new 'Spiritual Paradox' (8) - how *Kāma-taṇhā*-jettisoned Ābhassara Beings Engage in Sex! In this context is introduced a possible new strand of life we call *'Navaka Sattā'*. Towards closure, we revisit the issue of how, based in Westernscience, the 'Primordial Being' ends up as a Human Being (9), Part I ending with 'A Concluding Overview' (10).

---

6 Part I of this book is a slightly modified version of an article first published in the *Canadian Journal of Buddhist Studies*, number 9 (Sugunasiri, 2013b).

If Part I dealt with the selected segment of # 10-21, in Part II , we look at the total Sutta, linking the 'story of the primeval' of Part I, and deal with some related issues emanating from observations made by Gombrich ("Cutting through the Vedic Myth" (11) and Collins ("Intended Audience" (12)). Next we seek to explore the Buddha's intent in delivering the sermon, the next two chapters coming to be titled, "Unfolding the Primeval as Buddha's Intent" and "'Dhamma is Best' as Buddha's Real Intent" (13, 14). Part II ends with an overall look at the Sutta in terms of its structure and quality (15).

In Part III, 'Concluding Reflections', we take up a few issues relating to methodology in the context of the study (16), also proposing 'Trust in the Buddha as Methodological Imperative' (17), with an invitation to the Academy to adopt the Buddha as a 'Friend of the Academy', and to practicing Buddhist scholars to 'come out' and declare their Buddhistness openly, engaging in an 'Academically Engaged Buddhism'. The study ends in a 'Closure' (18).

The Appendix seeks to show that the Buddha is the Originator of the Story within Story literary genre as contained in the Beast Fable of which Pañcatantra is the best known.

2
Outline of Aggañña Sutta

Our translation, as noted, relates to only # 10-16 of AS, and so we provide an outline of the Discourse by way of contextualizing the segment. It would also help us in Part II in which issues relating to the total text are explored.

The Discourse begins with the Buddha, coming out of his afternoon meditation in the mansion of *Migāra Mātā* in the *Pubbārāma* monastery, and begins to pace back and forth in the shade of the mansion.

Vāseṭṭha and Bhāradvāja are two Brahmin seekers interested in becoming ordained under the Buddha, and are sitting among some Bhikkhus (# 1). Seeing the Buddha pacing, Vāseṭṭha suggests to Bhāradvāja that they approach the Buddha: "Perhaps we may get to listen to a Dhamma talk (*dhammiṃ kathaṃ*) from the Blessed One". Having approached him, and paying obeisance, they join the Buddha in pacing back and forth (# 2).

Now the Buddha addresses Vāseṭṭha[7] and asks "You (in the plural *tumhe*)[8] are indeed Brahmin-born, of Brahmin high caste and have gone forth into homelessness from a Brahmin family. Don't the

---

[7] As we shall see in detail later (Part II.12), we may note with relevance, that throughout the Discourse, it is only Vāseṭṭha that is adressed by name by the Buddha.

[8] This suggests that even though the Buddha is addressing only Vāseṭṭha by name, his words are ostensibly intended for Bhāradvāja as well. See again II.12.

Brahmins revile and abuse you?" (# 3).

Saying that they indeed do, Vāseṭṭha expands upon it – that the Brahmins claim to being of the highest caste and the only pure ones, "the true children of Brahma, born from his mouth..." (*brahmuno puttā orasā mukhato jātā*) (# 3). In response says the Buddha, "Surely, Vāseṭṭha, ... Brahmin women, the wives of the Brahmins, can be seen to menstruate, become pregnant, have babies and give suck." And yet "these womb-born Brahmins" talk of being born of the mouth of Brahman! (# 4).

In the next two paras (# 5-6), the Buddha points out how any one of the four classes (*vaṇṇa*), namely, *Khattiya, Brāhmaṇa, Vessa* and *Sudda*[9], can equally be in violation of the Training Principles, (more popularly Precepts[10]), and coming to be 'despised by the wise' (*viññū garahitā*), or be 'praised' by them (*viññuppasatthā*) if upheld. To be distinguished then are the Arahants 'Worthy Ones', also from all four classes, who alone are indeed the 'best' (*aggaṃ*)[11], and this "in accordance with the Dhamma and not in non-accordance" (*dhammen'eva no adhammena*). And now he hones in: "Dhamma, Vāseṭṭha, is the best (*seṭṭho*) for people, in this life and the next" (*Dhammo hi Vāseṭṭha seṭṭho jane tasmiṃ diṭṭhe c'eva dhamme abhisamparāyañca*) (# 7).

As if to substantiate his point, the Buddha now says how King Pasenadi Kosala, who comes to be respected and paid obeisance

---

9 It may be noted that the Buddha begins the list with Khattiya as if to reiterate that he has no use for the claims of the Brahmins.

10 'Training Principle' is the literal translation of *sikkhāpada* (thanks are due to Bhante Punnaji of the Toronto Mahavihara for this translation). 'Precept', a borrowing from Judeo-Christianity, by contrast is, as in Webster's, a "commandment or direction meant as a a rule of action or conduct" , a concept alien to the Buddha's intent and the Buddhist ethos of self-restraint.

11 We translate *agga* here as 'best' to suit the context, in contrast to 'primeval' elsewhere, as e.g., in # 13 (see I.3 later) .

to by the people comes in turn to respect and pay obeisance to the Tathāgata, thereby, in fact, respecting the Dhamma. And it is for this reason, then, that, repeating the line as if for emphasis, "the Dhamma is indeed the best for people" (# 8).

As a sequel to the argument, the Buddha now emboldens Vāseṭṭha and Bhāradvāja to acknowledge, when asked who they are, that "We are Wanderers (*samaṇā*), sons of the Sakyan"[12]. And further, still addressing Vāseṭṭha by name, it is said, "of one who has faith in the Tathāgata which is firm….., of him it is fitting to say" (*kallaṃ vacanāya*) "I am the Blessed One's own son, born from his mouth, born of the Dhamma, produced by the Dhamma, heir to the Dhamma" (*bhagavato putto oraso mukhato jāto dhammajo dhammanimmito dhammadāyādo*)[13]. Why? Because these are the [very] epithets of the Tathāgata: "the Dhamma-body, Brahma-body, Dhamma-become, Brahma-become" (*dhammakāyo itipi brahmakāyo itipi dhammabhūo itipi brahmabhūto itipi*) (# 9)[14].

At this point the Buddha, with no forewarning, and with no apparent link to what was said before, dwells on what will be shown, in our understanding, to be the phases of the universe, namely, **Devolution** and **Evolution** (#10-16)[15].

Humans appearing, now the Buddha deals with social

---

[12] There seems to be here a wordplay in the use of the term *samaṇā*. One is the generic sense of a class of spiritual seekers who have opted out of the received tradition of Brahmanism . The other is in the sense of a disciple of the Buddha (for not all Samanas were the Buddha's disciples).

[13] This, of course, is a word to word play on the Brahmin claim of being born of Brahma's mouth. It may be noted that this is a line used by the Buddha in characterizing, e.g., Ven. Sāriputta as well. See Anupada Sutta (M iii.29).

[14] If, at the surface level, this is to make fun of the Brahmins by turning on its head the qualifications they claim, at a deeper level it may be seen as a honing in of the point that the ***Dhamma is the best*** as in # 5- 6, and elsewhere. See later II.14.

[15] For an in depth treatment of this summarizing para of # 10-16, please see Sections I. 3 and I.4.

organization (# 17-21), which ends with the election of the 'Great Choice' (*mahāsammata*) (# 20) in order to deal with the violation of basically the Training Principles.

Significantly, each of the last three paragraphs (# 23-25) ends with the line, "Dhamma, Vāseṭṭha, is the best for people, in this life and the next".

While # 26 also ends with the same line, it is preceded by a line repeated in connection with all four classes "when a Khattiya [Brāhmaṇa, Vessa, Sudda], disavowing his own, leaves home for homelessness, in order to become an ascetic". Pointing out that that was exactly how the Sangha had come to be made up of all four social classes[16], the Buddha continues, "Of just these Beings, no others, of similar (Beings), not dissimilar", and in "in accordance with the Dhamma and not in non-accordance".[17]

Next the Buddha points out how one who misbehaves in body, word and mind ends up, at the break-up of his body and following death, in the hells (*apāyaṃ duggatiṃ*) while one who is upright in them ends up in the heavenly world (*saggaṃ lokaṃ*). And one who does both " ... experiences [both] happiness and suffering" (# 27-29).

Further, a Khattiya [Brāhmaṇa / Vessa / Sudda] who, restrained in body, speech and mind, cultivates the seven 'factors intrinsic to Enlightenment' (*bodhipākkhiya dhamma*), attains Nibbana in this very life" (# 30).

"Of these four classes, Vāseṭṭha, one who becomes a monk, becoming worthy (i.e., Arahant) with defilements jettisoned, ... in whom the fetters of becoming are destroyed ... indeed is properly called the best (*aggam akkhāyati*) (# 30, l. 1) among them"[18], this "in

---

[16] This again may be seen as serving as an encouragement to the two young seekers.

[17] This then seems intended to put to rest any misgivings that Brahmins are of a special class, and that indeed they are no different from any other, and as well put by Gombrich (1988, 167), that "We're all the same under the skin".

[18] Here again it seems to be to specifically encourage the two to go for ordination.

accordance with the Dhamma and not in non-accordance". Again the closure: "Dhamma, Vāseṭṭha, is the best for people, in this life and the next." (# 31).

In the concluding section (# 32), we surprisingly find the Buddha seeming to seek, as if he were not authority enough, some external validity:

"This verse has been recited by the Brahmin Sanaṃkumāra[19]:

For those who rely on clan, the Khattiya
the best among people.
Likewise one with knowledge and good conduct
the best among devas and people[20].

This verse was well-sung by the Brahmin Sanaṃkumāra, Vāseṭṭha, not ill-sung, well-spoken not ill-spoken, salutary (*atthasamhitā*)[21] not unsalutary (# 32)."

Then saying, "I too, Vāseṭṭha, say so", the lines are repeated.

AS ends with the words, "So said the Blessed One. Vāseṭṭha and Bhāradvāja were pleased, and rejoiced in the Blessed One's words." (# 32).

---

[19] Sanaṃkumāra has been translated as 'Forever youthful' (Ven. Bodhi (Tr.), 2000, 439-440) and 'Ever virgin' (Walsh, 1995, 580).

[20] The same lines appearing in the Samyutta (S I 6 (II.11)), it is a further mocking of Brahmins to have these words come from a Brahmin.

[21] This seems to be the sense here rather than 'meaning' (Collins) or 'connected with profit' (Walshe). Clearly the issue is one relating to the well-being of the people, not about whether it is meaningful (which, of course, it is), although 'with profit' seems to capture a bit of the sense.

While this brief outline helps us understand the context, our task in this study, to repeat, will be focussed just on # 10-16 (Section 3), but drawing upon # 17 to # 21 as well. Here, then, next is the translation of the segment, from a perspective of *the cyclical phases of the universe* that we see in it, and adduced to by the Buddha elsewhere as well, as e.g., in the Pāṭika and the Brahmajāla Suttas[22].

This translation, as also is the case in Collins, is going to be as literal as possible, perhaps making it stylistically poor, although on occasion we go figurative. In this, we hope we have the kind understanding of the reader.

[22] See the discussion around Fig. 11 for a fuller treatment.

3

Original Pali Text and Translation of Aggañña-Sutta, # 10-16

3.1 Original Pali Text

What is shown in the next pages under this header is the original Pali text as in the PTS Edition downloaded (see Acknowledgement in the opening pages). Every paragraph as in the dowload has been left untouched, except changing the font size of the footnote numbers. Anyone facing any issues in going through the Translation (next) is kindly invited to check against the printed version, thank you.

10. 'Hoti[7] kho so Vāseṭṭha {samayo} yaṃ kadāci karahaci dīghassa addhuno accayena ayaṃ loko saṃvaṭṭati. Saṃ- vaṭṭamāne loke yebhuyyena sattā Ābhassara-saṃvaṭṭanikā honti. Te tattha honti[8] manomayā pīti-bhakkhā sayam- pabhā antalikkha-carā subhaṭṭhāyino ciram {dīgham} addhānaṃ tiṭṭhanti. Hoti kho so Vāseṭṭha samayo yaṃ kadāci karahaci dīghassa addhuno accayena ayaṃ loko vivaṭṭati. Vivaṭṭamāne loke yebhuyyena sattā Ābhassara-

---

7 Cp. D. i. 2. 2, ante, vol. i., p. 17.

8 K omits.

kāyā cavitvā itthattaṃ āgacchanti. Te ca honti manomayā pīti-bhakkhā sayam-pabhā antalikkha-carā subhaṭṭhāyino, ciraṃ dīgham addhānaṃ tiṭṭhanti.

11. 'Ekodakī-bhūtaṃ kho pana Vāseṭṭha tena samayena hoti andhakāro andhakāra-timisā. Na candima-suriyā paññāyanti, na nakkhattāni[1] tāraka-rūpāni paññāyanti, na rattin-divā[2] paññāyanti, na māsaddha-māsā paññāyanti, na utu-saṃvaccharā paññāyanti, na itthi-pumā[3] paññā- yanti. Sattā sattā tv eva saṅkhyaṃ gacchanti. Atha kho tesaṃ Vāseṭṭha sattānaṃ kadāci karahaci dīghassa addhuno accayena rasa[4]-paṭhavī udakasmiṃ samatāni.[5] Seyyathā pi nāma {payaso} tattassa[6] nibbāyamānassa upari santānakaṃ hoti, evam evaṃ[7] pātur ahosi. Sā ahosi vaṇṇa-sampannā gandha-sampannā rasa-sampannā, sey- yathā pi nāma sampannaṃ vā sappi, sampannaṃ vā navanītaṃ, evaṃ vaṇṇā[8] ahosi; seyyathā pi nāma khudda-madhu[9] anelakaṃ[10] evam assādā ahosi.

12. 'Atha kho Vāseṭṭha aññataro satto lola-jātiko, "Ambho kim ev'; idaṃ bhavissatīti?" rasa-paṭhaviṃ aṅguliyā sāyi. Tassa rasa-paṭhaviṃ aṅguliyā sāyato acchādesi, taṇhā c'; assa[11] okkami. Aññatare[12] pi kho Vāseṭṭha sattā tassa sattassa diṭṭhānugatiṃ āpajjamānā rasa-paṭhaviṃ aṅguliyā sāyiṃsu. Tesaṃ rasa-paṭhaviṃ aṅguliyā sāyataṃ acchādesi, taṇhā ca tesaṃ {okkami}. Atha kho te Vāseṭṭha sattā rasa-paṭhaviṃ hatthehi ālumpa[13]-kārakaṃ upakkamiṃsu paribhuñjituṃ. Yato

---

1 Bmr nakkhatta-tāraka-. 2 Bmr rattidivā.

3 So SS Bmr; K -purisā. 4 Sct rasā; Sd rasāya.

5 K samantāni (and in 18).

6 So Sdt Bm Sum; Sc payasotakkattassa; Br pāyāsotakkassa; K payatatt-; Dt payattatassa.

7 Bm eva; Br eva kho. 8 So Sdt K; Sc Bmr vaṇṇo.

9 SS khuddaka; Bmr K khuddamadhuṃ; Sum-Scd khuddaṃ madhuṃ. See 14.

10 Bmr K aneḷakaṃ.

11 So Bmr; SS omit ca; K p'; assa.

12 So Sct; Sd aññataro; Bmr K aññe.

13 So SS Sum-Scd; Bmr Sum-Br K āluppa (and in 18)

86 AGGAÑÑA-SUTTANTA [D. xxvii. 12.

kho[1] Vāseṭṭha sattā rasa-paṭhaviṃ hatthehi ālumpa- kārakaṃ upakkamiṃsu paribhuñjituṃ, atha[2] tesaṃ[3] sattānaṃ sayam-pabhā antaradhāyi. Sayam-pabhāya antarahitāya candima-suriyā pātur ahaṃsu.[4] Candima- suriyesu pātu-bhūtesu, nakkhattāni tāraka-rūpāni pātur ahaṃsu. Nakkhattesu tāraka-rūpesu pātu bhūtesu, rattin- divā paññāyiṃsu. Rattin-divesu paññāyamānesu, mā- saddha-māsā paññāyiṃsu. Māsaddha-māsesu paññāya- mānesu, utu-saṃvaccharā paññāyiṃsu. Ettāvatā kho Vāseṭṭha ayaṃ loko puna vivaṭṭo hoti.

13. 'Atha kho te Vāseṭṭha sattā rasa-pathaviṃ paribhuñ- jantā[5] tam-bhakkhā tad-{āhārā} ciraṃ dīgham addhānaṃ aṭṭhaṃsu. Yathā yathā kho te Vāseṭṭha sattā rasa- paṭhaviṃ paribhuñjantā tam-bhakkhā tad-{āhārā} ciraṃ dīgham addhānaṃ aṭṭhaṃsu, tathā tathā tesaṃ[6] sattānaṃ[7] kharattañ c'; eva kāyasmiṃ okkami, vaṇṇa-vevaṇṇatā ca paññāyittha. Ek'; idaṃ sattā vaṇṇavanto honti, ek'; idaṃ[8] dubbaṇṇā. Tattha ye te sattā vaṇṇavanto, te dubbaṇṇe satte atimaññanti, -- "Mayam etehi vaṇṇavantatarā,[9] amheh' ete dubbaṇṇatarā ti." Tesaṃ vaṇṇātimāna-paccayā mān- ātimāna-jātikānaṃ rasa-paṭhavī antaradhāyi. Rasāya[10] paṭhaviyā antarahitāya sannipatiṃsu, sannipatitvā anut- thuniṃsu, -- "Aho rasaṃ, aho rasan ti." Tad etarahi pi manussā kiñcid eva sādhu[11] rasaṃ labhitvā evam āhaṃsu, "Aho rasaṃ, aho rasan ti." Tad eva porāṇaṃ aggaññaṃ akkharaṃ[12] anupatanti,[13] na tv ev'; assa atthaṃ ājānanti.

14. 'Atha kho tesaṃ Vāseṭṭha sattānaṃ rasāya[14] paṭha-

---

1 Br adds te. 2 Br adds kho. 3 Br adds Vāseṭṭha.

4 So SS Sum-Scd; Bmr Sum-Br K ahesuṃ, and below, 18.

5 Scd paribhuñjitvā. 6 Br adds Vāseṭṭha.

7 Br adds rasapaṭhaviṃ paribhuñjantānaṃ.

8 Br adds sattā. 9 Sc -vantarā; Sd -vanta.

10 So Sc Bm; Sdt rasā; Br K rasa-; SS Bmr agree below in rasāya.

11 Dt Br su. 12 K omits.

13 So Scd; St apatanti; Bmr Sum-Br anussaranti; Sum - Scd K anupadanti. 14 K rasa-.

D. xxvii. 15.] THE EVOLUTION OF MAN 87

viyā antarahitāya bhūmi-pappaṭako[1] pātur ahosi. Seyyathā pi nāma ahicchattako, evam evaṃ pātur ahosi. So ahosi vaṇṇa-sampanno gandha-sampanno rasa-sampanno. Sey- yathā pi nāma sampannaṃ vā sappi sampannaṃ vā navanītaṃ, evaṃ-vaṇṇo ahosi. Seyyathā pi nāma khuddaṃ[2] madhuṃ aneḷakaṃ,[3] evam assādo ahosi. Atha kho te Vāseṭṭha sattā bhūmi-pappaṭakaṃ upakkamiṃsu paribhuñjituṃ. Te taṃ[4] paribhuñjantā tam-bhakkhā tad- āhārā ciraṃ dīgham addhānaṃ aṭṭhaṃsu. Yathā yathā kho te Vāseṭṭha sattā bhūmi-pappaṭakaṃ paribhuñjantā tam-bhakkhā tad-āhārā ciraṃ {dīgham} addhānaṃ aṭṭhaṃsu, tathā tathā tesaṃ sattānaṃ bhiyyoso-mattāya kharattañ c'; eva kāyasmiṃ okkami, vaṇṇa-vevaṇṇatā ca paññāyittha. Ek'; idaṃ sattā vaṇṇavanto honti, ek'; idaṃ sattā dubbaṇṇā. Tattha ye te sattā vaṇṇavanto, te dubbaṇṇe satte atimañ- ñanti, -- "Mayam etehi vaṇṇavantatarā, amheh'; ete dubbaṇ- ṇatarā ti." Tesaṃ vaṇṇātimāna-paccayā mānātimāna- jātikānaṃ bhūmi-pappaṭako antaradhāyi. Bhūmi-pappaṭake antarahite badālatā[5] pātur ahosi. Seyyathā pi nāma kalambukā,[6] evam evaṃ pātur ahosi. Sā ahosi vaṇṇa- sampannā gandha-sampannā rasa-sampannā. Seyyathā pi nāma sampannaṃ vā sappi sampannaṃ vā navanītaṃ, evaṃ-vaṇṇā ahosi. Seyyathā pi nāma khudda-madhu- aneḷakaṃ, evam assādā ahosi.

15. 'Atha kho te Vāseṭṭha sattā badālataṃ upakkamiṃsu paribhuñjituṃ. Te tam paribhuñjantā tam-bhakkhā tad-āhārā ciraṃ dīgham addhānaṃ aṭṭhaṃsu. Yathā yathā kho te Vāseṭṭha sattā badālataṃ paribhuñjantā tam- bhakkhā tad-āhārā ciraṃ dīgham addhānaṃ {aṭṭhaṃsu}, tathā-tathā tesaṃ sattānaṃ bhiyyoso-mattāya kharattañ c'; eva kāyasmiṃ okkami vaṇṇa-vevaṇṇatā ca paññāyittha.

---

1 So SS; Bmr K pappaṭiko; K (note) bhūmipappaṭako ti pāṭho. Cp. 18. 2 So SS; Bmr K khudda.

3 Sc Br anel-; Sdt anīl-; Bm K aneḷ-.

4 So SS Bmr; K omits.

5 So Sc Sum-Scd; Sd bhaddālata; St badāḷatā; Bmr padālatā.

6 St kaladukā; K kalabakā.

88 AGGAÑÑA-SUTTANTA [D. xxvii. 15.

Ek'; idaṃ sattā vaṇṇavanto honti, ek'; idaṃ sattā dubbaṇṇā. Tattha ye te sattā vaṇṇavanto, te dubbaṇṇe satte atimañ- ñanti, -- "Mayam etehi vaṇṇavantatarā, amheh'; ete dubbaṇṇatarā ti." Tesaṃ vaṇṇātimāna-paccayā mān- ātimāna-jātikānaṃ badālatā antaradhāyi. Badālatāya antarahitāya sannipatiṃsu, sannipatitvā {anutthuniṃsu}, -- "Ahu vata no,1 ahāyi[2] vata no1 badālatā ti." Tad etarahi pi manussā kenacid eva[3] dukkha-dhammena puṭṭhā[4] evam āhaṃsu: "Ahu[5] vata no, ahāyi vata no ti." Tad eva porāṇaṃ aggaññaṃ akkharaṃ anupatanti, na tv ev'; assa atthaṃ ājānanti.

16. 'Atha kho tesaṃ Vāseṭṭha sattānaṃ badālatāya antarahitāya akaṭṭha-pāko sāli pātur ahosi, akaṇo athuso6 sugandho taṇḍula-pphalo.[7] Yan taṃ sāyaṃ sāyam-āsāya āharanti, pāto taṃ hoti pakkaṃ paṭivirūḷhaṃ. Yan taṃ pāto pātar-āsāya āharanti sāyaṃ taṃ hoti pakkaṃ paṭivirūḷ- haṃ, nāpadānaṃ paññāyati. Atha kho te[8] Vāseṭṭha sattā akaṭṭha-pākaṃ sāliṃ paribhuñjantā tam[9]-bhakkhā tad- āhārā ciraṃ dīgham addhānaṃ aṭṭhaṃsu. Yathā yathā kho te Vāseṭṭha sattā akaṭṭha-pākaṃ sāliṃ paribhuñjantā tam-bhakkhā tad-{āhārā} ciraṃ dīgham addhānaṃ aṭṭhaṃsu, tathā tathā tesaṃ sattānaṃ bhiyyoso-mattāya kharattañ c'; eva kāyasmiṃ okkami, vaṇṇa-vevaṇṇatā ca paññāyittha. Itthiyā ca itthi-liṅgaṃ pātur ahosi, purisassa purisa-liṅgaṃ. Itthī ca sudaṃ[10] ativelaṃ purisaṃ upanijjhāyati, puriso ca itthiṃ.[11] Tesaṃ ativelaṃ aññam aññaṃ upanijjhāyataṃ[12] sārāgo udapādi, pariḷāho kāyasmiṃ okkami. Te pariḷāha- paccayā methunaṃ dhammaṃ paṭiseviṃsu. Ye kho pana te Vāseṭṭha tena samayena sattā passanti methunaṃ dhammaṃ paṭisevante, aññe paṃsuṃ khipanti, aññe seṭṭhiṃ

---

1 Dt me, and below. 2 Sd apāyi, here and in repetition.
3 Bmr kenaci, omitting eva. 4 Bmr phuṭṭhā.
5 So Bmr K; Sc aha; Sd aho.
6 Bmr K add suddho and so SS, 18. 7 Dt -pphasso.
8 So SS; Bmr K omit. 9 So Bm; Scdt taṃ; Br K tab.
10 Bmr omit; K suraṃ. 11 K adds ca.
12 K upanijjhāyantānaṃ.

D. xxvii. 17.] THE EVOLUTION OF MAN 89

khipanti, aññe gomayaṃ khipanti, -- "Nassa asuci,1 nassa asucīti. Kathaṃ hi nāma satto sattassa evarūpaṃ karissa- tīti?"2 Tad etarahi pi manussā ekaccesu janapadesu va- dhuyā3 nibbuyhamānāya4 aññe paṃsuṃ khipanti, aññe seṭṭhim khipanti, aññe gomayaṃ khipanti. Tad eva porā- ṇaṃ aggaññaṃ akkharaṃ anupatanti, na tv ev'; assa atthaṃ ājānanti.

3.2 Translation

10. There comes a time, Vāseṭṭha [1][23], when somehow or other, at times (*kadāci karahaci*) [2] after the passage of a long time beyond (*dīghassa addhuno accayena*), this world devolves (*ayaṃ loko samvaṭṭati*) [3]. In this devolving world, as is the norm (*yebhuyyena*) [4], there come to be Ābhassara-devolving-Beings [5] (*sattā ābhassarasamvaṭṭanikā*). (Or, 'There happens to be existing in this devolving world (or phase) Ābhassara-Beings'.) [6]. There they remain mind-based (*manomayā*) [7], feeding on rapture (*pītibhakkhā*), self-luminous (*sayampabhā*), moving through space (*antalikkhacarā*), continuing in glory (*subhaṭṭhāyin*), for a very long stretch of time (*ciraṃ dīghaṃ addhānam*) [8]. Somehow or other, after the passage of a long time beyond, Vāseṭṭha, this world evolves (*vivaṭṭati*). In this evolving world, as is the norm, having passed away from their Ābhassara-bodies (*ābhassara-kāyā cavitvā*), Beings come into the present state [9]. Here they remain, mind-based, feeding on rapture, self-luminous, moving through air, continuing in glory, for a very long stretch of time.

11. At that time, there was just (one vast mass of) water [1]. All darkness, (just) blinding darkness. Not known were moon or sun [2] nor constellations and stars, nor night and day, nor months and fortnights, nor years and seasons, and nor females and males [3, 4], beings reckoned just as beings [5]. Then (*atha kho*), somehow or other, after the passage of a long time beyond [6], a savoury-Earth (*rasapaṭhavi*) spread itself (*samatāni*) over the waters [7]. It looked just like a cobweb-like layer (*santānakaṃ*) [8] that forms itself over hot milk as it cools down [9]. It was endowed with colour, smell and taste [10]. Its colour [11] was like that of fine ghee or butter / cream [12], and its taste was like fine, pure honey (*khudda*) [13].

12. Then, Vāseṭṭha, a certain Being of a greedy nature [1],

---

[23] Please see Section I.4 for an elaboration of items shown in square brackets.

wondering [2] 'What exactly will this be?' (*ambho kim ev'idam bhavissatīti)*, tasted the Earth-savour [3] with its finger [4]. As it [5] tasted the Earth-savour all over its finger, craving came upon it [6]. [Now] in imitation of that Being, Vāseṭṭha [7], other Beings, too, tasted the Earth-essence [8] with their finger(s). They, too, were taken with the flavour, and craving came upon them. Then, Vāseṭṭha, these Beings started to devour the Earth-essence, taking them in lumps with their hands. As they did so, their self-luminosity came to disappear (*antaradhāyi*) [9]. As their self-luminosity disappeared [10], the moon and the sun made its appearance [11]. As the moon and the sun appeared [12], the constellations and the stars came to make their appearance. As the constellations and the stars appeared, night and day came to show up (*paññāyiṃsu*). As night and day showed up, the months and the fortnights came to show up. As the months and the fortnights showed up, the seasons and the years came to show up. Thus, Vāseṭṭha, does the world evolve again (*loko puna vivaṭṭo hoti*) [13].

13. So those Beings, Vāseṭṭha, continued for a very long stretch of time, enjoying (*paribhunjanti*) [1] the Earth-essence [2], partaking of it as their food. To the extent they continued for a very long stretch of time, partaking of it, they became coarser and coarser in their bodies (*kharattaṃ c'eva kāyasmiṃ okkami*) [3, 4] and differences in (skin) colour (*vaṇṇavevannatā)*) came to show [5] to that extent. Now some Beings came to be good-looking [6], others ugly. Those who were good-looking despised those who were ugly: "We are better-looking than they are; they are uglier than us!" [7] [Beings coming to be] class-conscious to a fault [8] and conditioned (*paccayā*) [9] by their colour-pride, the *savoury*-Earth came to disappear [10]. When it had disappeared, they came together and lamented, "Oh (*aho*), the savour!" [11, 12]. So nowadays, when people have tasted something good, they say "Oh, the taste; oh, the taste!" (*aho rasam*) [13], they are only falling in line with a very ancient expression, without actually realizing it [14, 15].

14. Then, Vāseṭṭha, when the savoury-Earth had disappeared [1], there appeared for those Beings ground-*pappaṭaka* (*bhūmipappaṭako*)

[1], that looked like mushrooms (*ahicchattaka*) [2, 3]. It had colour, smell and taste. The colour was like fine ghee or butter / cream, and its taste was like fine, pure honey. Then, Vāseṭṭha [4] the Beings approached (*upakkamiṃsu*) the ground-pappaṭaka [5] and set to eating, ravishing on them. Those Beings spent a very long stretch of time eating it, a living on it as their food [6]. To the extent that these Beings kept enjoying eating it, taking it to be their food, for a very long stretch of time, Vāseṭṭha, to that extent did they become coarser and coarser in their bodies, the variation in skin colour coming to be manifested, too. Some Beings were good-looking, others ugly. "We are better-looking than they are; they are uglier than us!" [Beings coming to be] class-conscious to a fault, and conditioned by their colour-pride, the ground-pappaṭaka came to disappear [7]. As they disappeared, a kind of creeper by name *badālatā* [8], bamboo-like, came to appear [9]. It had colour, smell and taste. The colour was like fine ghee or butter / cream, and they were very sweet, like pure clear honey.

15. Those Beings, Vāseṭṭha, now approached the badālatā creeper (crop) [1] so they could enjoy it. Thus they spent a very long stretch of time ravishing on the creeper crop, living on it as their food. To the extent that these Beings kept enjoying eating it, taking it to be their food, for a very long stretch of time, Vāseṭṭha, to that extent did they become coarser and coarser in their bodies, and the variation in colour / appearance come to be manifested [2]. Some Beings were good-looking, others ugly. "We are better-looking than they are; they are uglier than us!" [Beings coming to be] class-conscious to a fault, and conditioned by their colour-pride, the creepers came to disappear [3]. When it had disappeared, they came together and lamented, "We had it all, but now we've been done in (i.e., the creeper has given out on us)!". So nowadays, when people are touched by some hardship, they say "We had it all, but now it's given out on us!", they are only falling in line with a very ancient expression, without actually realizing it'.

16. Then, Vāseṭṭha, when the creeper had disappeared, there appeared for those Beings rice [1], fully grown without stalks [2], free from a coating of red powder and free from chaff [3], sweet-

smelling and 'fruit-of-the-seed'. Whatever the amount they gathered in the evening for their evening meal had come to grow back again [or, 'against all [seeming] odds'] (*paṭivirūḷhaṃ*) [4], by the morning. Whatever the amount they had gathered in the morning for their evening meal had come to grow back ripe [against all [seeming] odds] by the evening, there appearing no diminishment (*nāpadānaṃ paññāyati*) [5]. Thus, Vāseṭṭha, they spent a very long stretch of time ravishing on the fully grown without stalks, living on it as their food. To the extent that these Beings kept enjoying eating it, Vāseṭṭha, taking it to be their food, for a very long stretch of time, to that extent did they become coarser and coarser in their bodies, and the variation in colour (and/or appearance) come to be (further) manifested. The female *linga* appeared in the female, and the male *linga* in the male [6, 7]. The female looked at the male just so long as did the male at the female. Looking at each other for long, passion arose in them, *burning all round* entering their bodies (*pariḷāho kāyasmiṃ okkami*) [8]. Because of this burning, they indulged in sexual behaviour [9]. Those other Beings, Vāseṭṭha, seeing them indulging in sexual behaviour, threw Earth (at them), some ash, others cow-dung, (saying) "Away with your filth, away with your filth!", [and] "How could a Being do such a thing to another Being?" So nowadays, when people in certain areas throw dirt, ash or cow-dung when a bride is being led out [10], they are only falling in line with a very ancient expression, without actually realizing it.

4

Notes to the Translation

10.1 This writer is not entirely convinced by Collins' baffling decision to replace Vāseṭṭha with 'Monks' here (as in 'Monks, you were (both) born brahmins..') and throughout, even as he notes that "Buddha's words (here and throughout) use the vocative singular Vāseṭṭha"[24].

10.2. Collins translates *kadāci karahaci* as 'eventually' and Walshe 'sooner or later', both correctly, as in PED, and as referring to time. But, immediately following *kadāci karahaci* is another reference to time: *dīghassa addhuno accayena* 'after the passage of a long time beyond' as translated by this writer, taking 'after the passage' to capture both the process as well as the end of the process. Our translation 'Somehow or other', by contrast, refers to a process. Hence our preference, suggesting that the Buddha intended to say something like *yena kena ci ākārena* (not in the text) 'in one way or another'. But why then didn't he actually use *yena kena ci ākārena*? Perhaps it is because *kadāci karahaci* is onomatopoeic, of the 'struggle' (itself onomatopoeic?), to evolve / devolve (see # 10-16). In *kadāci karahaci*, there occurs the 'rough-sounding' voiced /d/ and /r/ and the shorter vowels /a/, /i/, as compared to the repetition of the 'softer' 'n' and the longer vowel 'e' in the hyopothesized *kena yena.* I grant that this is a license on the part of this writer, but hoping to capture the spirit of the sentence though perhaps not the letter.

To seek out the spirit going beyond the letter may be to give the

---

24 See II.12 for a more detailed treatment.

text a more realistic presence. To give an example from our own Sutta, we may take the term *sāyaṇhasamayaṃ* (in *atha kho Bhagavā sāyaṇhasamayaṃ patisallānā vuṭṭhito pāsādā orohitvā.*, # 1). As in PED, it has been rendered literally as 'evening' by both Collins and Walshe. But, of course, even though 'evening' in English has, as a localism (e.g. 'in rural areas'), the primary meaning of 'the period from noon through sunset' (Webster's), as it is in vogue today, 'evening' is the 'period between sunset ... and bedtime'. But the Buddha is pacing back and forth *in the shade* of the mansion. So clearly, the sun was still up. Thus the translation that better captures the reality would be (late) 'afternoon' (*aparaṇha*). The reason why *sāyaṇha* seems to occur in the text is that it is "usually opposed to *pāto* (*pātaṃ*) 'in the morning'" (PED). In English, and in contemporary culture, the 'afternoon' is a functional category which is why 'afternoon' would be a better translation of *sāyaṇha* than 'evening'. So while sticking to the letter seems to give us a less accurate picture, seeking out the spirit seems to bring us closer to reality and the Buddha's likely intent.

10.3 To repeat, we opt for 'devolve' in the context of the overall framework of a devolving and evolving universe. We may note that Ven. Dr. Bodhi's translation, 'dissolves' (Bodhi (Tr.), 2012, 521) does not seem to capture the idea of the complex process involved since it can apply to any number of other contexts such as e.g., the soap dissolving in water. It is to be noted in passing that *saṃvaṭṭa* and *vivaṭṭa* are translated in PED with a reverse meaning.

10.4 *Yebhuyyena* has the meaning of 'mostly' (PED), with even a clarification as by Ven. Bodhi (Tr.), 544, "for a great multitude, with the exception of noble individuals (*ariyapuggala*)". However, the meaning here seems to be "as it happens, usually, .. as a rule" (2nd meaning in PED), or, 'as is the norm' as opted for here, for otherwise it would suggest that there would be times when the process of Devolution (taking *yebhuyyena* as qualifying *loke* that precedes), or the process of Beings (taking it as qualifying *sattā* that follows) 'coming into the present state', doesn't take place. That would be to negate the entire cyclical evolutionary process. It is for this reason that we have opted for the 2nd meaning in PED, 'as is the norm'.

10.5 To repeat, we have used 'Beings' with a capital letter to emphasize the presence of consciousness, as is the case with all *sattās* as in Buddhianscience, given the characterization that it is mind-based (*manomayā*) (see next).

10.6 Collins translates *sattā ābhassarasaṃvaṭṭanikā* as 'beings devolve as far as the Ābhassara world' and Walshe as 'beings are mostly born in the Ābhassara Brahma world'. But both 'Ābhassara world' and 'Ābhassara Brahma world' clearly show a following of tradition (as e.g., in the Abhidhamma analysis (see Bodhi (Gen. Ed.), 1999) more than a license, on the part of the translators, for there occurs not the word *loka* or *Brahmaloka* in our Sutta. There is also nothing in the original that suggests the qualifier 'mostly' before 'born' either, remembering here that this writer is trying to be as literal as possible in his translation.

10.7 Introducing Ābhassara Beings, they are immediately characterized as being mind-based (see 10.5). This, then, tells us that these beings may be characterized as being mindbodies (*nāmarūpa*), mind, of course, being 'the forerunner' (*mano pubbangamā dhammā …*) (*Dhammapada 1*).

10.8 Note again the reference to 'a very long stretch of time', undoubtedly, as calculated in Westernscience, counting in terms of millions if not billions of years though within the same eon. Thus it is that this writer has sought to capture the idea of 'a very long time' by fortifying it with the words 'stretch of'.

10.9 While both Walshe and Collins translate '*itthattaṃ*' in *itthattaṃ āgacchati* as 'this world', we have opted for 'into the present state', to be more authentic to the original, literally meaning 'the state of being here'. It is not that 'this world', possibly contrasting with the conventionally taken 'Brahma world' (10.6), is wrong. But it is just that 'this world' occurs in the line preceding (*ayaṃ loko vivaṭṭati*) to mean the universe as a whole, rather than a particular dimension of it.

11.1 Here, the Ābhassara Beings can still be said to continue to be moving through space, given that there is as yet no 'footing' for them to walk on, 'Earth' appearing later (see 11.7).

11.2 While English diction dictates 'sun and moon', the text gives us 'moon and sun' *(candimasuriyā)*. 'Not known' (*na paññāyanti*) here does not imply that they didn't exist. Only that there was no evidence of them[25]. This is understandable. If the Earth were covered by a thick gaseous cloud, the surface would indeed have been "all darkness." This would be supported by modern science, which posits that the early Earth had a very dense atmosphere:

> Part of the ancient planet is theorized to have been disrupted by the impact that created the Moon, which should have caused melting of one or two large areas. Present composition does not match complete melting and it is hard to completely melt and mix huge rock masses. However, a fair fraction of material should have been vaporized by this impact, creating a rock vapor atmosphere around the young planet. The rock vapor would have condensed within two thousand years, leaving behind hot volatiles which probably resulted in a heavy CO2 atmosphere with hydrogen and water vapor. Liquid water oceans existed despite the surface temperature of 230 °C (446 °F) because of the atmospheric pressure of the heavy CO2 atmosphere. < http://en.wikipedia.org/wiki/Hadean>.

11.3 While the listing, namely, 'darkness' to 'seasons' to 'females-males', may appear to be just that – a mere listing, an insightful reading may reveal another point embedded in it. It is a confirmation that this is the end of the Devolutionary phase. If the darkness is a marker

---

[25] The writer thanks Ajahn Punnadhammo (personal communcation) for this interpretation, providing a valuable reference (next), too.

of it, the absence of the variations of night and day, etc., confirms that this is still an era of no change, characterized by the Buddha as a 'stand-still' evolutionary phase (*vivaṭṭhaṭhāyī*). Secondly, the absence of 'females and males' suggests that no other sentient life has emerged as yet either, just the evolving-Ābhassara Beings. It is also of interest to note that it is *pumā* that the Buddha uses here and not *purisā* as in *purisa-linga* (# 16). Should this not confirm that no gender distinction was present at this stage, while later it does? (See Section 6.2 for a discussion.)

11.4 *Itthi-pumā* has been translated here as 'female and male', and not as 'men and women' as by others. This is primarily for the reason that the Pali words given for 'man' are *manussa, nara, manuja* and *macca* (Buddhadatta, 1979), more generic. Distinct from them are *puma* and *purisa* for 'male', the latter, however, with an association with '*purisa'* – *porissa* as in 'manliness' and *purisocita* 'man-like' The order in which we come to list 'females and males' in that order, it may be noted, conforms to the original '*itthi-pumā*' while both Walshe and Collins place males / men before females / women, just as indeed Ven. Buddhaghosa himself does (*Visuddhimagga*, XIII, 51, 418). In the case of the western translators, it is reasonable to opine that this may have been to stay within the English usage and diction. But what needs to be remembered is that this primacy of males over females is of Judeo-Christian origins, as e.g., Eve being created out of Adam's ribs, as in the Bible story. In the case of Ven. Buddhaghosa, the guiding hand seems to be his former Brahminical religion, again with male-dominance.

If the reversing of the order by the three is to be inauthentic to the text, it does injustice as well to the English reader with no familiarity with the original Pali. It is to misrepresent the Buddha himself who consistently gives primacy to females. Two examples would: *mātāpitaro* (D III.36), and *mātāpitū upaṭṭhānaṃ (Mahamangala Sutta)* (K 2 Sutta Nipāta (Sn 2.4)). In terms of practice, paying homage to the parents, in Sinhala Buddhism, the oldest and the longest living Buddhism in the world, it is to mother that homage is paid first (see

Sugunasiri, 2012, 26). The listing of females first is also, of course, for reasons of commonsense, since sentient beings come to be born of mother! Additionally, to make an outlandish argument, it is not unlikely that the Buddha was reflective of the reality that females constituted, to put it in contemporary statistical terms, 51% of the human population, and further that if a given human population were to perish in a disaster such as a Tsunami or heavy floods or hurricane or heavy thunder and lighning, but with a handful of survivors, the randomization would ensure that there will remain at least two females more than males, with at least one of them (hopefully!) impregnated before the death of the last male, ensuring the continuity of the species[26]. The Buddha beginning with females and then coming to males does not, of course, mean that the Buddha's view is that males originated from females, as if presciently countering later Christianity! His view more likely could have been that the two genders co-evolved, i.e., were mutually conditioned, as under the Conditioned Co-origination (*paticcasamuppāda*) Principle[27].

11.5 This confirms that there is already consciousness, *sattā* literally 'state of' (*-tā*) + being (*sat-*). That is to say that the Ābhassara is a conscious Being, the capital letter, as noted, suggestive of 'life'. Collins' translation of this, incidentally, 'Beings just have the *name* 'Beings'' (italics added) seems to be somewhat misleading, the point being precisely that the Being in question has no name!

---

[26] This, of course, would not be applicable in the case of the cataclysmic process entailed at the end of a Devolutionary phase, the Ābhassara Being in AS (# 10), an obvious survivor of the process, being of no gender, or rather of both genders which come to manifest alternately in due course.

[27] A classic example from Westernsciencewould be in relation to the DNA, the basic foundation of a cell, when amino acid needs protein to grow while protein needs amino acid to grow (see Olomucki, 1993, 58).

11.6 Here again, from our evolutionary perspective, Collins seems to have missed the point. His translation, "Then (on one such occasion)" ignores the significant emphasis on the passage of time.

11.7 Our translation, 'spread itself', as also in Walshe, relating to 'Earth', well captures the automatic process. *Samatāni* (< *sama* 'equality') also suggests 'in equal measure'; so perhaps the term is intended as a *double entendre*?

11.8 Here *santānaka* has the meaning of 'cobweb' (V I.48, in PED), suggesting a structure made of thin strips. The cobweb (or creeper) simile is significant since it suggests not a *continuous* solid layer of Earth, but allowing for the presence of cracks and stretches of water in between – rivulets, rivers and oceans, etc., which can be said to be a more realistic picture of the topography of the Earth, emerging from 'all water', sustaining sentient life. However, strips of solidity also suggest a *gradual* formation of the Earth, ***not*** all water suddenly turning all Earth.

11.9 Here 'as it cools down..' is a significant hint as to the stage of the evolving universe, which had begun hot and is now cooling down, preparing the conditions for an increasingly complex sentient life to begin to emerge.

11.10 The Abhihamma characterizes colour, smell and taste not as 'sensitivity' inherent to the senses (*pasāda rūpa*) such as eye, ear, etc., which are part of a sentient being, but as 'stimuli' (*ārammaṇa*) (see Ven. Bodhi (Gen. Ed.), 151 ff.). The presence of colour, smell and taste in nature may then be considered the source of the origins of the senses - visual, olfactory and gustatory as here, in a sentient being. We may also in passing note that, in the text, smell comes after colour, even though in the literature, the aural sense (with sound as stimulus) comes to be listed folowing the ocular sense – *cakkhu, sota, ghāna, jivhā, kāya* 'eye, ear, nose, tongue and body', in that order.

11.11 Even though the examples are shown as being for colour only, it has to be assumed that they speak to smell as well, given the earlier line referring to smell following colour.

11.12 Here, 'butter' as in Walshe and 'cream' as in Collins both acceptable, we have adopted both.

11.13 Collins points out that the word *khudda* (not in PED in this sense: see PTS and Childers) can refer to both honey and bees. If so, does it suggest that by now, animal life, too, had come to be? (See Section 5 for an elaboration.)

12.1 In 'greedy nature', we may note the emergence of 'sense thirst' (*kāma taṇhā*), one of the three characteristics of sentience. A metaphorical interpretation here would be that the tasting of the nutritive essence may be taken as representing the first engagement of mind into coarse materiality at the beginning of a new cycle[28].

12.2 Our term 'wondering' here seems closer to Collins' term 'thinking' than Walshe's 'said', this latter possibly guided by how the line "*Ambho kim ev'idam bhavissatīti*?" is shown in the Romanized Pali edition, with a capital at the beginning and a question mark at the end and within double quotes, all added by Europeon editors. The term 'said' suggests the emergence of spoken language, which is highly unlikely at this stage of evolution. Without wanting to be seen to be splitting hairs, it may be said that Collins' term 'thinking' suggests a more sophisticated level of mental activity than 'wondering' which is suggestive more of a surface level mental activity, and possibly more reflective of the early stage of evolution. From a Linguistic point of view, perception precedes linguistic formation precedes speaking. This seems to resonate with the sequencing of steps two and three of the Noble Eightfold Path, where 'harmonious language' (*sammā*

---

[28] This observation comes from Ajahn Punnadhammo.

vācā) comes to be preceded by 'harmonious conceptualization' (*sammā saṃkappa*)[29].

12.3 It is the same term *rasa paṭhavi,* as in 11, that occurs here in the text. However, it is clear that while the first occurrence seeks to capture the idea of the appearance of a *physical* form of 'Earth' replacing an earlier state of 'all water', it is equally clear that here the term refers to the *quality* of the Earth, with an emphasis on the *rasa* component. That is, in the first occurrence of the Adjective + Noun phrase *rasapaṭhavi* (# 11) the emphasis is on the Noun, while in the second, it is on the Adjective. An example showing the difference would be: 'Yesterday there was a *heavy* ***rain***. But soon, the ***heavy*** *rain* gave way to a **light** rain'. Thus we change the translation here, from 'savoury-Earth' (in 11) to 'Earth essence' as with Collins (357-358), with an emphasis on the *paṭhavi* component.

12.4 Eating with fingers can be said to be indicative of a significant stage in evolution. It shows that the Beings have now, noting that this is *'after the passage of a long time beyond'* as in the earlier paragraph, evolved into a Beings with limbs, fingers here, and as we see later, hands (next sentence). (See also later for a different interpretation in relation to Westernscience.)

12.5 We continue with the neutral 'it' here, since the Beings are still just Beings (see # 11), even though it is mind-based and thus a conscious sentient being. 'She' and/or 'he' would be not appropriate since no gender division has taken place as yet.

12.6 The Buddha now tells us up front that 'sense-thirst' has emerged.

---

29 While *saṃkappa* (in *sammā saṃkappa*) is generally translated as 'intent', this writer's Linguistics background suggests 'conceptualization' as a better rendering, which may include 'intent' (though not vice versa). (See Fig. 3 for some more details.)

(See 12.1 above.)

12.7 It is as if here the Buddha is saying to Vāseṭṭha, 'No surprise there, is there now?'

12.8 Here we translate the same *rasa paṭhavi* as 'Earth-essence' to capture the idea that now, it is not merely a matter of just tasting it, but eating chunks.

12.9 We use the clause 'came to disappear' here as translation of *antaradhāyi* to capture the idea of a *gradual* process. It is to be noted that there are at least two other forms in Pali - *vigacchati; adassanaṃ yāti*, that cover the same semantic range as *antaradhāyi*. So the choice of *antaradhāyi* , literally 'placed [-*dhāyi*] in between [*antara*-]' seems to be the Buddha's way of suggesting a stepwise process. So e.g., the first step in the change could be seen to be from luminosity to luminosity^{-1} (minus 1) to luminosity^{-2} to luminosity^{-3} to luminosity^{-4} to luminosity^{-nth}, along a series of steps.

12.10 We opt for 'as' here to again show a continuing process and a co-conditionality, as distinct from 'when', as in others, suggestive of a particular temporal point in time.

12.11 'Made its appearance' again is to indicate a process, as opposed to 'appeared' – with a sharp and sudden implicit finality.

12.12 'Appeared' is used here to capture the idea that now the process, or at least a phase of it, has been completed, suggesting finality.

12.13 The literal translation here would be 'There is evolution in this world again' (*loko puna vivaṭṭo hoti*). Note the term *puna* 'again' here, this suggesting a *sub*-phase of the longer Evolutionary phase, making a beginning of the 'stay put' stage.

13.1 The Buddha's use of *paribhunjanti* < -*bhuj* 'to eat', + *pari*-

'total', here, meaning 'enjoy', in preference to *khādanti* 'eat', seems to suggest a full-fledged enjoyment, ravishing on the newly discovered food and nourishment, also reflecting the fact that craving had now arisen.

13.2 It appears that what is meant by *rasapaṭhaviṃ* here is material food but with a suggested gustatory sense.

13.3 The bodily changes in terms of coarseness could be explained in terms of the differential body cells growing, getting to be solidified[30] into different shapes, in response to the refinement in food. The result could be the bodies getting more variegated, and coming to be more differentiated from each other. We may consider here such differential and variegated growth in an embryo, when the different parts of the body – eyes, ears, sex organ, etc. coming to be formed over time as a result of nutrition and cell division (mitosis) and, with the cell clusters becoming solidified into particular shapes – as eyes, fingers, heart, brain, etc. It may be noted that *kharattanc'eva kāyasmin okkami* 'became coarser and coarser in their bodies' (literally, 'coarseness entered their bodies') is followed with *vaṇṇavevaṇṇatā ca paññāyittha* 'came to show differences in (skin) colour' (literally, 'discolouration of colour appeared'). Of course, '*vevaṇṇatā*' literaly means 'state of skin dis-colouring' (< *vi-* + *vaṇṇa* + *-tā*). Indeed Monier Williams shows '*nānāvaṇṇah*' (Sanskrit) as meaning 'variegated' with '*nānāvaṇṇatā*' meaning 'variety. This seems to suggest, then, that it is the dual change, in skin colour and physical appearance, that bring about differences between and among Beings – fairer or darker skin; a longer nose, wider mouth, more protruded chin, and well- or ill-balanced positioning of features of the face, etc., as a result of the changing differential cellular structures as reflected in the term 'coarser'. This can easily result in some being pretty (in particular, the proportionality of the facial features) and others ugly. In the changing body cells looking for more specific nutrition, what

---

30 It may be noted that *khara* 'solid' has the meaning of being 'opposed to *drava*', 'liquid' (Monier-Williams, 337).

we have again may be characterized as a co-conditionality.

13.4. In terms of etymology, *kharatta* can be said to be from Sanskrit *kharatva* 'the state of an ass' (Monier-Williams, 1993, 37), the suffix semantically similar to Pali *bālatta* '(state of being) foolish' (Ven. Buddhadatta, 1979, 207). So again, the choice of the term by the Buddha seems intended to capture both a 'fall' in terms of body as well as mind (remembering that the Beings are 'mind-based' (# 10)). Here also can be seen an implication of the beginnings of *moha* 'ignorance', one of the three characteristics of sentience, 'thirst', an aspect of *rāga*, already present (see 12.1 and 12.6). 'Anger' / 'hatred' (*dosa.*) is yet to show up.

13.5 *Vaṇṇavevaṇṇatā*: While literarally this means 'state of the discolouring of colour' (see 13.3), it may also have an association of class, as the fairer ones claim superiority, as in the case of the Brahmins (see Collins, 361, for a detailed look at the term). The Buddha can be said to be hinting here at the beginnings of the *caste system,* on the basis of appearance, gradually leading to a hierarchical social structure, social class and finally caste – Brāhmaṇa at the top, followed by Kṣatriya, Vaiśya and Śudra, to give the Sanskrit terms in the context of Brahmanism . By extension, however, it can be seen as the beginnings of *racism* and *ethnocentrism* in human populations as well, based in skin colour, as if returning to the original basis as in the Sutta.

13.6 Here we may note the association of fairer skin colour with good looks and social class.

13.7 We note here the beginnings of *mamaṃkāra, ahaṃkāra* 'I-ness' in sentient beings, another dimension of *moha*.

13.8 While 'to a fault' is no more than to use a standard idiomatic expression in English, it does unintentionally happen to speak to the message in the Sutta - that to be class-conscious as the Brahmins are, is to be at 'fault'!

13.9 We may note here the direct reference to conditionality, as e.g., in the first link in Conditioned Co-origination, 'conditioned by ignorance are the forces' (*avijjāpaccayā saṃkhārā*).

13.10 It is *not* that the physical Earth disappears, but that there now came to be changes in the quality of the Earth (see 12.3) in terms of physical changes as well as its flavour, taste and essence. This also becomes clear from the next line when the Being laments the loss of flavour. For otherwise, we will have to be thinking of an unexplainable loss of Earth that had earlier replaced water (as seems to be implicit in Walshe's translation when he uses the same term 'savoury Earth' in all instances), signalling another sub-phase of evolution as earlier captured in the line, *puna vivaṭṭo hoti.* (# 12). But the text gives no such indication.

13.11 Note that by now, i.e., at the next stage of evolution during the Evolutionary Phase (note again '*puna vivaṭṭo hoti*' (# 12)), language seems to have emerged, if earlier only there was just 'wondering' or perhaps even 'thinking', both still in the mind domain. The words of the lamenting Beings, '*aho rasam ti*', could still be, as earlier, in the thought domain. (See later, Fig 3, for a discussion.)

13.12 It is significant to note here that 'linguistic manifestation', as represented by language, seems to have preceded 'sex manifestation' as represented by the appearance of the female and the male *linga* (# 16). See Section 6.2 for a detailed treatment.

13.13 Implicit here is the presence of 'volition food' (*manosañcetanāhāra*).

13.14 'Falling in line with a very ancient expression, without actually realizing it'. The translation of *anupatanti* (in *poranaṃ aggaññaṃ akkharaṃ anupatanti na tv'eva assa attahaṃ ājānanti*) by Walshe

as ‘repeating’ and by Gombrich as ‘recall[ing]’ both suggest that it is something that has been known to the community sometime in the past but not now. However, since the Buddha’s reference is to a time bya [billion years ago], it is hardly likely that it would be within the memory of any living sentient being (except the Buddha as here). While our translation ‘falling in line with’ also may suggest such pre-knowledge in a literal sense, in its idiomatic sense, also being its literal translation (<anu ‘following’ + pat- ‘to fall’), no such pre-knowledge is implicit. We have taken *poranaṃ aggaññaṃ* to mean ‘very ancient’, since the term *poranaṃ* already suggests ‘ancient’ and *agga* implies a superlative. So it may be seen that by using the phrase, the Buddha is suggesting intensity.
While *akkharaṃ* also allows for several different interpretations (see Collins 362), we opt for ‘expression’, in preference to Walshe’s ‘ancient saying’ or Collins’ ‘primary word(s)’, given that ‘*aho rasaṃ*’ is itself an expression.

13.15 It appears that the Buddha is foreshadowing here the issue of Brahmins seemingly not knowing what they’re talking about when they claim to be superior, not knowing the history of what they’re saying, i.e., as to how their claim of superiority came about, as in # 4 (*poraṇaṃ assarantaā*) (as above).

There also seems to be an implication here that the Buddha is hinting to Vāseṭṭha that the masses (*puthujjanā*), ‘deranged’ as they are (*sabbe puthujjaṇā ummattakā*), don’t understand the reality of the universe, and seems to be saying, “which is why I’m telling you all this”.

14.1 We leave the term *pappaṭako* untranslated, for any translation would at best be a ‘best guess’. As noted by Walshe (604, n. 831), “the exact meaning [of *bhūmipappaṭaka*] is unknown”, Rhys Davids suggesting ‘outgrowths’. ‘Pappadum’ is the interesting Sinhala translation of *pappaṭako*[31], noting the sound consonance, the change

[31] This is drawn this from the Tripitaka Sinhala translation (2006).

of voiceless *ṭ* to voiced *ḍ* being not uncommon in transmission. *Pappadum* 'fritters' are a regular item on the Indian as well as the Sinhala Buddhist menu. It is crunchy when fried, pops up in places, and flat though uneven in other places. This seems to be aptly descriptive of the possible evolution of the land at this stage, flat land giving way to variation, and now crustier than moist as possibly in the first phase following the phase of 'all water'. Whether or not the Sinhala translation is tenable, Davids' rendering 'outgrowth' seems to thus allow the interesting possibility of it being something more solid than 'fungus' (Walshe) and 'mushroom' (Collins) but yet soft and tender enough to eat.

14.2 *Ahicchattaka* is literally 'snake's parasol' (PED).

14.3 While *pappaṭako* and *ahicchattaka* seem to refer to the same item, the latter descriptive of the former, it is tempting to consider *pappaṭako* and *ahicchattaka* standing for plant and creeper, the latter well captured in the literal sense of 'snake's parasol'. The snake analogy suggests thin and long growth, but still along the ground, and the parasol, creepers entwining, either by themselves or around the more solid plants, the *pappaṭaka*. Our conjecture, then, suggests the growth of a mixed vegetation, growing out of land spread over the water.

14.4 Vāseṭṭha, we note, is dropped here by both translators, presumably taking it to be a laborious and a routine repetition, as if in the thought that addressing Vāseṭṭha carries no significance. But the continuous use of it in the text, however, seems to suggest that the Buddha is, possibly, making continuous eye-contact with Vāseṭṭha, in an intimate dialogue, good communication calling for proximity (proxemics) and eye contact (oculesics).

14.5 Here 'approached' suggests that the growth was not all over the total land area, but in some areas only, also hinting at plant life living side by side with sentient beings in an ecological balance. 'Approached' also suggests mobility, and the evolutionary development of 'legs' of some primordial type, given the appearance of hands and fingers as earlier (# 12).

14.6 Beings can be said to have been nourished originally on 'consciousness food' (*viññāṇāhāra*), given that they are 'mind-based'. But with the appearance of the savoury Earth, they can be additionally based in 'volition-food' (*manosañcetanāhāra*) (see 13.11) and 'contact food' (*phassāhāra*). At this point in time, we find 'solid food' (*kabalinkāhāra*), decidedly more complex in nutritonal value than lumps of savoury Earth, emerging as a source of nutrition.

14.7 This also possibly speaks to supply and demand. The disappearance of ground-pappaṭaka as Beings become coarser as a result of feeding on them speaks to the natural process as between animals and food supply. As the food supply grows, a given species grows in number, and as the number in the species increases, the food begins to be in lower and lower supply - too many mouths to be fed, too little food available. A similar phenomenon can be envisaged here: as Beings continue to feed on the *ground-pappaṭakas* as the staple diet, the healthy diet resulting in fewer untimely deaths and the birth / arrival of more Beings. But soon, the *ground-pappaṭakas* begin to be in short supply. This is what we may understand by the term 'came to disappear'.

14.8 The morph *-latā* in *badālatā* means 'creeper'. So is it possible *badālatā* is from *baddhālatā* 'bound-creeper', with the conjoint consonant *-dh-* getting elided over time, and 'bound' meaning a creeping growing around another plant. *Badālatā* could also be from *bhaddhālatā* 'excellent creeper' (Sanskrit *bhadra*), 'excellent' here in the several senses of 'lucky', etc. (see PED for similar meanings), but also, contextually. 'life-giving' or 'wish-fulfilling'.

14.9 Also here, if earlier what had come to appear were emblematic creepers – snake-like and crawling-like, now 'bamboo-like' suggests we finally have fully fletched creepers shooting up.

15.1 *Badālataṃ* here may be taken to mean a collective singular.

15.2 Here we may envision another evolutionary step, namely, a possible higher complexity of the cellular structure, with new nutrients feeding the mindbody.

15.3 In addition to the supply and demand condition, there may also be a suggestion here of going to extremes on eating. Unmindful of the outcome of their excess, due to craving, they might have kept eatin' n' eatin' (to add a spoken, and folksy, touch) until nothing more was left, and with no new offshoots, not allowing enough time for the plant to regenerate. And there may also be a suggestion of the exacerbation of the 'sense-thirst' (as in note 12.6) into a 'grasping' (*upādāna*).

16.1 If the vegetation of 'rice' seems like a refinement of the early plants and creepers, signaling another ecological sub-phase, it also signals a further refinement of sentience, given that the food is now in the form of seeds, more flexible (in the sense of being able to be stored in a way that a plant and creeper cannot be). A parallel in the economic sphere may be currency exchange replacing material exchange (of e.g., animals). It also brings the characterization to the contemporary times, rice being a staple of the time, the Buddha's first meal being 'milkrice'.

16.2 The term *akaṭṭha-* < *a* + *kaṭṭha*, is tricky. PED gives three meanings for *kaṭṭha*: (1) 'ploughed', (2) 'bad, useless' and (3) 'piece of wood, esp. a stick used as fuel, firewood'. While the second meaning, with the added negative suffix *a-*, 'not bad', 'not useless', is not improper, it hardly seems to add anything specific. If the intended meaning is the first, 'unploughed' or 'uncultivated', the Buddha can be thought to be seeking to explain that unlike in his own time (and as even today) when rice comes to be associated with ploughing and cultivation', a conscious human activity, this rice was of a natural growth. Though certainly descriptive, it again does not seem to add explanatory much to the narrative. How could one expect rice to be cultivated when Beings were just beginning to emerge? What else but natural growth could we expect in this early phase of the Earth?

Rejecting the first two, then, the third meaning, 'piece of wood, esp. a stick used as fuel, firewood', seems to be descriptive. Could the term mean 'without stalks', suggesting a growth just off the ground, as contrasted with rice seeds on stalks of today? In other words, they were seeds growing right off the ground with no supporting stem, may be seed on seed.

This seems to find some confirmation in the last characteristic of rice in the text - '*taṇḍulapphalo*'(<Sanskrit *taṇḍula* 'grain' (Monier-Williams)), literally meaning 'fruit-of-the-seed'. What this seems to suggest is that once the seed on top is harvested, the supporting base seed on which it grew now comes to be pushed out by another, new, seed just beneath, each of them, of course, without a stalk. The new top seed then continues to mature over the next half day, and comes to be ready for harvesting. It is thus that we opt for meaning three. (Please see also 16.5.)

16.3 The rice of today comes with two coatings: an outer chaff, thicker, and an inner red coating, thinner. But in this early growth, the rice is said to be without them, perhaps because there was no time for the elements (sun, wind, chemicals in the air, etc.) to act upon the seed, since only half a day passes before the next crop.

16.4 *Paṭivirūḷhaṃ*: *paṭi* 'against' + *virūḷhaṃ* < *ruh-* < Sanskrit *rūḍha* 'grown' or *ruḍḍha* 'obstruction'. So there seems to be a word play here again. Thus we have given both 'come to grow back' .. and '[or, against all [seeming] odds'], the latter, not taking away anything from the former, seeking to take account of the, to us, unbelievably unreal half-day growth.

16.5 *Nāpadānaṃ* could also be from *na* + *āpadā (naṃ)* 'with no [apparent] damage', here possibly meaning with no great harm done to the growth by the quick harvesting. It may also mean that the early strain of rice came to spring fast, nature providing for a faster maturational process[32].

---

[32] It is with interest that we read some research relating to the *pigeonpea* with origins in India. Prof. Rupert Sheldrake, a Zoologist, notes in relation to them, "*regenerative* growth, now the basis of a new cropping system involving *multiple* harvests" (Sheldrake, 1990, xii) (italics added). This sounds intriguingly close to what we seem to have in AS. Re 'regenerative growth' and 'multiple harvests', we read: "Whatever the amount they gathered in the evening for their evening meal had come to grow back ripe" and "there appearing no diminishment". If that is in relation to *regenerative* growth, in a joint paper, Sheldrake and two colleagues talk of "Environmental and cultural factors" affecting "growth and short-duration" of pigeonpeas and its "potential for multiple harvests" (Chauhan, Venkataratnam and Sheldrake, 1987).

The paper also makes reference to the issue of the "effect of location, soil type". Then there is a finding about the impact of "a lower temperature", suggesting how this might have also contributed to "the decreased *dry-matter* production at this location." While this writer is not sure what 'dry-matter' refers to, what may be noted is that in AS, the rice is said to be "free from a red coat of powder and free from chaff". Does it have anything to do with 'dry-matter'?

Pigeonpea cropping now travelling across the globe, to Africa, West Indies and Australia, showing its wider adaptability, as 'rice' would have been in the early era, more recent research notes another factor; "Water deficit significantly decreased the cumulative intercepted photosynthetically active *radiation* (CIR). The relationship between biomass accumulation and CIR was linear and water deficit affected the slope of the relationship (i.e., radiation use efficiency, RUE)..." It is noted that "The results indicated that RUE is critical in determining pigeonpea productivity under well-watered and moisture-deficit regimes." <http://oar.icrisat.org/1698/>.

In yet another study, the researchers identify "1,213 disease resistance/defense response genes and 152 abiotic stress tolerance genes" in the "pigeonpea genome" that make it "a hardy crop", a likely feature of early 'rice' as well. <http://link.springer.com/article/10.1007

16.6 Here, as earlier, the singular needs to be taken to mean a generic meaning the plural 'females' and 'males'. It is also of interest to note that it is *purisā* (as in *purisa-linga*), with its association with sex, that the Buddha uses here and not *pumā* as in # 11, the first reference. Should this be read to mean that while no gender distinction was present at the earlier stage but later it does? (See later 'Chronological Paradox' (I.6.2)).

16.7 The appearance of sex organs 'in the female' and 'in the male' need not be seen as being odd, or as some form of magical development. We, of course, associate the terms 'female' and 'male' as already being with sex organs. However, it may also be taken to mean the *potential* for them. The Abhihamma analysis shows that femininity and masculinity (*bhāvarūpa*) are inherent to sentience as 'alternatives' or 'changeables' (*vikārarūpa*) (see Ven. Bodhi (Gen. Ed.), 239; 262-263). The wording that the female sex appeared "in the female", and the male sex "in the male" only suggests that while Beings had been asexual earlier, beginning with the Ābhassara stage (# 11), individual Beings had by now, i.e., an advanced evolutionary sub-phase, picked the gender of choice, out of the inherent potentiality of femininity and masculinity, this very volitional activity determining, in a co-evolution, the appearance of the corresponding sex organ. (See again later Section I.6.2 for a fuller discussion.)

16.8 *Pariḷāho*, translated as 'burning all round', is made up of *pari-* + *ḷāho* (< root *dah*-to burn', *d* changing to *ḷ*- not uncommon). *Pari-* here is an 'intensifying prefix', meaning 'all over', 'all round',

---

%2Fs13562-011-0088-8>.

While the pigeonpea *per se* may be of no interest to this study, what is relevant is whether the reference to 'rice' in AS may be generic, and refer to a pigeonpea prototype, subject to the impact of the differential conditions – water, soil, photosynthetically active radiation, etc., resulting in multiple crops, regenerative growth and being hardy, etc., as could be expected under the early conditions.

'completely' (PED), as e.g., in *paridhovati* 'wash all round'. Thus, 'burning all round entering their bodies' (*pariḷāho kāyasmiṃ okkami*) could better be captured figuratively in the words, 'the fever of passion consumed their bodies all round', showing the intensity.

16.9 If earlier there had come to appear 'sense-thirst' (*kāma taṇhā*) (# 12), we find here a sharper focus of the sense-thirst into 'passion' (*rāga*). Engaging in sex, then, can be seen as being conditioned by the thirst of passion. Additionally, with 'I-ness' already present (13.7), it would be natural that the Beings would now want to see themselves continuing, in a 'thirst to be' (*bhavataṇhā*)[33], engaging in sex being the *modus operandi* towards the fulfilment of the thirst.

16.10 The hurling of stuff at the couple(s), possibly a practice in Buddha's time, can be based first in a (shocking?) misunderstanding on the part of these others, having never seen a pair in union. Second, it may be jealousy, or anger and hatred (*dosa*) that two people seem to be enjoying in a way these others themselves can't or haven't, this itself stemming from the arising of passion within themselves, and, of course, I-ness. By now then we have the three cankers – passion, hatred and ignorance, coming to be present in these early sentient beings.

---

[33] The 'thirst to be', of course, is inevitably linked with the end of existing life, namely death, i.e., the 'thirst to be not' (*vibhavataṇhā*), without which there could be no rebecoming.

5

Aggañña Sutta # 10-21 as Cosmic Narrative

In our translation of AS # 10-16 and the Notes, we have thus far merely touched on the Buddha's perceived evolutionary perspective. We now seek to expand upon it by way of a narrative, with the help of Fig. 1, drawing upon additionally (the untranslated) #17-21, entailing human and social evolution.

1	2	3	4	5	6	7	8	9	10
CYCLE	**TIME PERIOD**	**EVOLU-TIONARY PHASE**	**ENVIRON -MENT**	**TYPE OF LIFE**	**EXAMPLE OF LIFE**	**REPRODUC-TIVE TYPE**	**BIRTH TYPE**	**LIMBED-NESS**	**NUTRI-MENT**
1	Infinite to the past	Pre-Devolutionary	As in 3 & 2	As in 3 & 2	As in 3 & 2	As in 3 & 2	As in 3 & 2	As in 3 & 2	As in 3 & 2
2	13.5 +bya	Devolutionary	Space	Spatial	Ābhassara Beings	Asexual	Spontaneous	Limbless	Consciousness food
3a	13.5 - bya	Evolutionary	Water	Aqueous	'Post-Ābhassara-Aqueous-Beings'	Asexual; Sexual	Water-born; Moisture-born; Egg-born	Rudimentary Limbs	Volitional food
3b	4.5 bya	Evolutionary	Earth	Amphibious; Land	Tiny-honey; Homo Sapiens Sapiens	Asexual; Sexual	Womb-born	Fully limbed	Contact food; Solid food
4	Infinite into the future	Post-Evolutionary	As in 2 & 3	As in 2 & 3	As in 2 & 3	As in 2 & 3	As in 2 & 3	As in 2 & 3	As in 2 & 3

Fig. 1. Four Phases in the Devolutionary / Evolutionary Cycle of the Universe (speculatively developed based in the *Aggañña* Sutta)

In the AS, the Buddha points to two phases of the universe, namely, 'Devolutionary'[34] (Col. 3, Row 2 in Chart), followed by 'Evolutionary' (3,3). In order to show the cyclical and continuing nature of the cosmic process, the Figure shows two more, namely, 'Pre-Devolutionary' (3,1) and 'Post-Evolutionary' (3,4), each of them 'Infinite', to the past (2,1) and into the future (2,4) respectively, each, of course, having the same characteristics as under Col. 4 to 10, 2.2, and 2.3a / 2,3b. Each of the phases is said to emerge 'after the passage of a very long time beyond'.

We show 13.5+ bya (2,2) as marking the beginnings of the Devolutionary phase, or what in Westernsciencehas come to be called the Big Bang[35]. Likewise we show the pre-Devolutionary phase preceding the present Evolutionary phase simply as 'Infinite to the past' (2,1) but which, on the basis of present knowledge, may be assigned at least another 13.5 to 20 additional billion years. The Evolutionary phase is then shown as beginning 13.5- bya (2,3a)[36], the minus sign simply meaning 'more recent than'. This is the phase during which, in the text, craving comes upon the Beings, and as they begin to devour the Earth-essence, their self-luminosity disappears and the moon and the sun make their appearance and other environmental changes take place (# 12).

---

[34] In this narrative, we give the Pali original only if called for by the context. This is to make the narrative flow easier, referring anyone interested in the original wording to the translation (1.3) and the Notes (1.4).

[35] We may contrast here the theistic connotations of a 'first beginning', the Big Bang, with the Buddha's Teaching of a particular phase in a beginningless and endless cycle.

[36] Though not of any relevance to the discussion, life-spans of Beings are shown in Buddhist cosmology in terms of three kinds of eons – an interim eon, an incalculable eon and a great eon (*antarākappa, kappa, mahākappa* respectively) For a detailed discussion, plcasc scc Ven. Bodhi (Gen. Ed), 198.

There is not much said in AS about the Devolutionary phase. However, we find the Buddha talking elsewhere (A IV 101) of 'seven suns' that seems to suggest the end of the Devolutionary phase, clearly *preceding* the Big Bang of 13.5 bya[37]in Western terms. To give the translation by Ven. Bodhi, 2012, 1071-3,

> There comes a time, Bhikkhus, when rain does not fall for many years, for many hundreds of years, for many thousands of years, for many hundreds of thousands of years. When rain does not fall, seed life and vegetation, medicinal plants, grasses, and giant trees of the forest wither and dry up and no longer exist."[38]

Next he speaks of a 'second sun'[39], again 'after a long time', when

---

[37] While the 'age of the universe', and hence the Big Bang in Westernscience has been estimated to be between 13 to 20 billion years, the most recent estimate dates it to around 13.5 ± billion. Says a Nasa report, "Measurements by the WMAP satellite can help determine the age of the universe. The detailed structure of the cosmic microwave background fluctuations depends on the current density of the universe, the composition of the universe and its expansion rate. As of 2013, WMAP determined these parameters with an accuracy of better than than 1.5%. In turn, knowing the composition with this precision, we can estimate the age of the universe to about 0.4%: 13.77 ± 0.059 billion years!" <http://map.gsfc.nasa.gov/universe/uni_age.html>

[38] The Buddha here is speaking to the point of impermanance: "So impermanent are conditioned phenomena, so unstable, so unreliable....". But we shall skip this as not being relevant to our discussion.

[39] It is interesting to note that in the earlier section as above, there is no mention of a 'first sun'. This speaks to the Buddha's skill in using precise language, as if keeping to a principle of textual editing: cut out, unless absolutely necessary. That he is talking about a 'first sun' in the earlier context comes to be obvious as one comes to the 'second sun'.

'small rivers and lakes dry up and evaporate and no longer exist'.

Moving along through the 3rd to the 6th sun, he eventually comes to the seventh sun:

> With the appearance of the seventh sun, this great Earth and Sineru, the king of mountains[40], burst into flames, blaze up brightly, and become one mass of flame. As the great Earth and Sineru are blazing and burning, the flame, cast up by the wind, rises even [up] to the brahma world...[41]

What the characterization above suggests is the end of the Devolutionary phase of the cosmic cycle, climaxing with the Big Bang in western terms, which nicely leads into the beginnings of life in the Evolutionary phase, but leaving the Brahma world unscathed. But before we move into the Evolutionary phase, let us see what Westernsciencesays regarding the sun:

> The Sun does not have enough mass to explode as a supernova. Instead it will exit the main sequence in approximately 5.4 billion years and start to turn into a red giant. It is calculated that the Sun will become sufficiently large to engulf the current orbits of the solar system's inner planets, possibly including Earth.

Even before it becomes a red giant, the luminosity of the Sun will have nearly doubled, and the Earth will be hotter than Venus is today.

---

[40] This is characterized, at the beginning, as being of the dimensions of 84,000 yojanas each in height, depth into the ocean, length and width.

[41] We add here the term 'up', missing in the original Ven. Bodhi translation, to make the point clear that the scathing stops *at* the boundary of the Brahma world: *yāva brahmalokāpi gacchati*. 'Rises even to the Brahma world' as in the original allows the impression, in this precise writer's understanding, that it goes some ways up the Brahma world, too.

Once the core hydrogen is exhausted in 5.4 billion years, the Sun will expand into a sub-giant phase and slowly double in size over about half a billion years. It will then expand more rapidly over about half a billion years until it is over two hundred times larger than today and a couple of thousand times more luminous. This then starts the red giant branch (RGB) phase where the Sun will spend around a billion years and lose around a third of its mass.

While this is not literally seven suns, but a single sun getting much bigger and hotter, it speaks to much of the effects of the process: "over about half a billion years until it is ... a couple of thousand times more luminous." The increasing heat and desiccation of the Earth will be very gradual[42].

Talking about the 'juvenile Earth', meaning the early stages of our present Earth, Prof. Cyril Ponnamperuma[43] (1972, 51) notes how the sun was "the most powerful source of energy for the Earth. The spectrum of the sun has energy of various wavelengths, from the very shortest to the longest, the shorter-wave-length light being the most energetic." The Buddha's 'seven suns', presumably a metaphor for extremely high levels of energy, may then well be the shorter-wave-length, "the most energetic".

While the reference here is to the sun up there we see now, it is to be noted that "the solar flux about four and half billion years ago may not have been very different from what it is today." Once a star like our sun "reaches this stage in its evolutionary development, it remains stable for several billion years." Given the Buddha's view of a cyclical cosmic order, there is, then, no reason to think that the sun of the past Evolutionary phase was any different from the sun of the

---

42 <http://en.wikipedia.org/wiki/Sun#After_core_hydrogen_ exhaustion>. This expansion and reference are again thanks to Ajahn Punnadhammo.

43 Prof. Ponnamperuma,author of *The Origins of Life*, is Professor of Chemistry at the University of Maryland, and formerly Director of the Program in Chemical Evolution at the Exobiology Division of NASA.

present Evolutionary phase.

Remaining stable in that past Evolutionary phase for several billion years, to put a number on the Buddha's phrase 'after the passage of a long time beyond', the Evolutionary phase can be said to begin to decay, under the principle of 'change' (*anicca*) as also by 'entropy' as in Westernscience[44]. This is when it can be said to begin the Devolutionary phase. The process may be presumed to be a matter of the longer wave-lengths with the lesser energy giving way to the shorter ones with the highest energy, ushering the stage of 'seven suns'. While details may be yet to be worked out, what is significant is that there is a range of energy, long wave-length to short, allowing for a parallel of a single sun to seven suns in the Buddha's perception.

Returning to AS, the Buddha next says, "There happens to be existing in this devolving world Ābhassara-Beings"[45], they being the 'Example of Life' (6,2 of the Figure) at the 'Environmental Stage' of 'Space' (4,2), rendering it a form of 'Spatial' life (5,2). Ābhassara-Beings are characterized as 'moving through the sky'

---

[44] As explained in Westernscience, "…entropy is … a driving force for physical and chemical changes (reactions)" <http://www.science.uwaterloo.ca/~cchieh/cact/applychem/entropy.html > "The quality of energy deterorates gradually over time. How so? Usable energy is inevitably used for productivity, growth and repair. In the process, usable energy is converted into unusable energy. And this process is called 'entropy increase' " (personal communication from a Physicist colleague)

[45] It needs to be noted here that while it is the evidential position in Westernscience that life began on Earth, in the Buddha's understanding, life already existed, as noted, *before* the present Earth was formed. This, then, seems to be in agreement with a recent proposition made by two western Scientists, Richard Gordon and Alexei Sharov, based on a computer modeling <http://www.digitaljournal.com/article/348515#ixzz2R9WpPINk>. See Sugunasiri, 2013, for a brief informal treatment.

(*antalikkhacarā*).

It is interesting that the Buddha uses the term *antalikkha* here to mean 'sky' (or 'air' or 'space'), and not *ākāsa,* also having the meaning of 'sky' (giving us a plausible *ākāsacarā*). Tracing the etymology, *antalikkha* may be drawn upon <*antari* + *kṣa,* to give the Pali source, to mean 'situated between sky and Earth' (as in PED). Or it could be, to give the Sanskrit source, from *antari* + *kṣi* 'dwell between' (Monier-Williams, 1993, 327). But in our context of Devolution, most interestingly, *kṣi* also means in Sanskrit 'decay', decrease', 'diminution', 'wane' (Monier-Williams, 328). Thus *antari* + *kṣi* could well mean, 'in the process of waning', understanding the phrase 'in the process' itself as meaning 'in between'. And that would be between the Devolutionary phase going into the Evolutionary phase, statistics allowing the range between two numbers, say 2 and 1, the range of 1 being ½ to 1½, and the range of 2 beginning at 1½ (extending to 2½).

And that is not all. *Antalikkha* could well be from Sanskrit *antar* + *īkṣa* 'looking between', again *antar* here with two possible meanings: between Earth and sky (spatial), or between Devolution and Evolution (temporal), or of course, both. *Īkṣa* can also mean 'gazing' or 'beholding' and (though not in Monier-Williams), also 'surveying'.

So the usage *antalikkha* could be seen to have been used by the Buddha to capture all of the above connotations to mean something like 'a space between sky and Earth, and in between Devolution and Evolution, during the waning period of Devolution'. If our interpretation has validity, then, by opting for *antalikkha*, as contrasted with *ākāsa*, the Buddha seems to be suggesting that these Beings are between two levels of the sky, and likely at the lower stratospheric level[46], closer to what would eventually become Earth

[46] Stratosphere is defined as
"1.the region of the upper atmosphere extending upward from the tropopause to about 30 miles (50 km) above the Earth, characterized by little vertical change in temperature. 2. (formerly) all of the Earth's atmosphere lying outside the troposphere." <http://dictionary.reference.com/browse/Stratosphere>.

(see later).

Ābhassara-Beings are also said to be 'self-luminous' (*sayampabhā*). We find it extremely interesting that *ābhassara* can be literally taken to mean 'hither-bound-shining-arrow' <*ā-* + *-bhās* + *sara.* Of course, the Buddha is speaking from the perspective of being on Earth, hence 'hither-bound'.

But what is this 'shining'?

It may be noted that the Beings were said to be 'moving through air'. So we have to think of a phenomenon in the sky, what the Buddha terms 'tangle-free space' (*ajaṭākāsa*)[47]. 'And Ābhassaras are said to be 'self-luminous', in both the Devolutionary and the Evolutionary phases. So what could this self-luminous and flying phenomenon be?

Let us now turn to Westernscience to see if we could get some understanding of the sky-born and self-luminous phenomenon called Ābhassara. "Electrons somehow "jump" between specific orbits, and as they do, they appear to *absorb* or *emit* energy in the form of light, i.e., photons", (italics added), say scientists Kafatos & Nadeau (1990, 31) in their book, *The Conscious Universe.* As for 'absorbing', Einstein "argued that the energy of light is …. concentrated in small, discrete bundles … or 'quanta', of energy. … It is the energy of the individual quanta, rather than the brightness of the light source, that matters." (29). So it appears that a case may be well made that **the shine-emitting and shine-absorbing Ābhassaras are 'photons',** defined as a "quantum of light" (Issacs, 1963, 174) or a quantum of energy (Apfel, 1985, 49[48]):

---

[47] This is as contrasted with another kind of space that the Buddha talks of, namely, 'circumscribed space' (*paricchedākāsa*), the fifth of the Great Elements (*mahābhūta*), Earth, heat, wind , water and 'extension', or, as in Bodhi, 'space element' (*ākāsadhātu*) (Ven. Bodhi (Gen Ed.), 241).

[48] "… each time an electron jumps down to a lower energy level, it emits a quantum of energy" (Apfel, 49).

> "If photons could not crowd together in the energy of light, the light energy that fuels quantum mechanical process that lead to the evolution of chemical structures, including what we call life, would not exist" (Kafatos & Nadeau, 33).

So we could take 'the shining one' to be a variation of (a form of) photons, in some primordial version. We may now see the connection between the Devolutionary phase ending up burning under the seven suns (as above) and the shining Ābhassara-Beings. They can be said to be survivors of the burning hot Devolutionary phase, looking for a home in the newly emerging Evolutionary phase. It is of relevance to note that the Abhihamma posits 'heat' (*utu*) as one of the sources of origin for matter (Ven. Bodhi, 1999, 246)[49]. So it may be understood that the Ābhassara-Beings stems from a preponderance of heat. This well matches with the fact that they are survivors of the seven deadly suns that bring an end to the Devolutionary phase.

'Being' (*sattā*), of course, is the Buddha's term for 'sentient being', here in the form of a primordial 'chemical structure', i.e., 'life'. So what the self-luminosity symbolizes, or speaks to, then, can be said to be 'life' associated with matter. In this connection, we may note that Ābhassara-Beings are said to be 'mind-based' (*manomayā*). If this suggests early rudiments of consciousness, an Ābhassara-Being, already made of matter, can be characterized as a composite psychophysique (*nāmarūpa*).

Calling a photon-like primordial form in the sky a psychophysique will undoubtedly raise eye-brows in some quarters. But let us see what the Scientist Olomucki, author of *The Chemistry of Life* (1993, 43-4) says:

> Since the earliest days of the universe, matter has been organizing and evolving toward increasingly complex

[49] To list all four, "Material phenomena originate in four ways, namely, from kamma, consciousness, temperature and nutriment" (*kammam cittam utu āhāro cāti* casttāri *ruūpasmuṭṭhānāni nāma*).

forms. But what drives this evolution? Today[50], everything seems to indicate that it was driven from the very outset by natural selection due to environmental pressures – in short, that the Darwinian scheme can be extended to processes unknown to Darwin himself. This selection is no way teleological (it does not assume a purpose); it naturally eliminates the least stable structures, those least adapted to the environment, and this process of elimination ensures more or less regular improvement of the organization of matter. It must be recognized that such phenomena become apparent even before we begin studying the origin of life when we wonder about the earliest molecules – those formed at a time which could be called the "protochemical" period of the universe by analogy with the proto- or prebiotic period.

Of course, the Buddha knows it! He shows that the process begins earlier - in the Devolutionary phase itself.

So how about that 'arrow' that the Ābhassara was said to be? Light travels at 300 km per second (Kafatos & Nadeau, 24). What better image could indeed the Buddha have found from the culture of the times to capture the idea of speed? Today we could think of a 'shooting star' as an analogy. Ot it could well be an offshoot of a meteorite.

In sum, then, an Ābhassara-Being can be said to be a surviving form of consciousness encapsuled in matter in the form of light from the Devolutionary phase. They are said to be, as noted, mind-based, self-luminous and feeding on rapture (*pīti-bhakkhā*).

But why are they so darned rapturous? Wouldn't you be if you were to survive the seven suns reducing everything to ashes? But that is the mundane explanation. If we were to now fall back on Buddhist texts, there is a very special reason why they would be rapturous. It was noted how the universe goes up in flames under the scorching

[50] It may be noted that he was writing in 1923 when the book was first published.

heat of the seven suns, burning up the entire Earth. However, this stops at the 'boundary' of the '*Ābhassara* Brahma world' (as above)[51]. Now that is the Abode where humans on Earth in a given Evolutionary phase who attain at least the second *jhāna*, end up. So the '*Ābhassara* Brahma world' is literally the safe haven safely out of the reach of the ravenous flames of the scorching heat[52]. So the happiness of Ābhassara Beings can be said to be well-founded. Indeed a survival of the fittest, in Darwinian terms.

The term *pīti*, however, lends itself to further elucidation. It is classed under '*sankhārakkhandha,* not *vedanā*', notes the PED. The fact that it is a 'force' (*sankhāra*) explains why it is given as one of the qualities of the Ābhassara Beings, which then suggests that it is inherent to them. The fact that *sankhāra* immediately precedes *viññāṇa* 'consciousness' in the listing of aggregates (*rūpa vedanā saññā samkhāra viññāṇa*) suggests how it serves as the condition for the emergence of 'consciousness'. In scientific terms, every organism survives on food. In that sense, *pīti* can be said to serve as 'food', i.e., nourishment, the force, to consciousness. This then amply explains the characterization of Ābhassara Beings as *pītibhakkā* 'feeding on rapture'. Ābhassara Beings chracterized as being 'mind-based' (*manomayā*), the term also seems to strengthen the characterization of Ābhassara Beings as sentient beings; they are made up of not only mind (outcome) but also forces (condition).

A final point is how *pīti* immediately brings to the mind of the listener (and the reader in us) the necessary link to the Ābhassara Beings, given that 'rapture' is associated with the 2nd jhāna (D.i.3.22), resulting in a birth after death in the Ābhassara Brahmaloka.

Beings of this stage of evolutionary existence 'moving in the sky', are '*reckoned just as Beings*' with no gender distinction - 'no females and males are known'. What this immediately suggests is

---

[51] See Ven. Bodhi (Gen Ed), 1993/1999, 186, for a characterization of these levels in the sky in Buddhist cosmology.

[52] We may put a little mischievous play on it: spirituality can't touched by the flames of secularism!

'asexual' reproduction (7,2) under 'Reproductive type', which may be specified under 'Birth type' 'spontaneous' (*opapātika*) (8,2), one of four types of generation identifed by the Buddha.

Now "stay[ing] there for a long stretch of time", the Ābhassara Beings are said to 'come into the present state' (*ittatthaṃ āgaccahti*)[53], 'leaving their Ābhassara body' (AS # 10), still mind-based, self-luminous, moving in the sky and feeding on rapture[54].

If each of Devolution and Evolution relates to a total phase, AS allows us to calculate a period of time within the present Evolutionary phase, at the beginning of which 'there was just one mass of water' (# 11). What this suggests is the outcome of the cooling off period past the burning under the seven suns, setting off the *new Evolutionary* phase (3,3a). If in the Abhidhamma, this is when it has begun to rain for long periods of time ceaselessly, in Westernscience, this is when the initial burst of energy comes to be dissipated, gradually cooling off, the sun itself containing 87% Hydrogen (Ponnamperuma, 1972, 41): "Of every hundred atoms in the universe, ninety-three are hydrogen atoms." Further, when "our planet was formed from the primordial solar nebula, the cloud of hydrogen which enveloped it, as it revolved with the dust particles in orbit around the central dense mass, played a vital role in determining the kind of molecules present" (41-42). The oxygen present, interacting with the hydrogen, "would have yielded water" (42).

A new Evolutionary phase can now be said to dawn, with a cooling process begun, ultimately ending up in 'water' as the 'Environment' (4,3a), in which, of course, 'space' continues to exist.

While the Beings have still not been named by the Buddha, it

---

53 The 'present state' (in 'Beings come into the present state') well captures the unknown phenomenon, be it, as interpreted by us as a 'photon', i.e., a material state, and / or a form of consciousness, i.e., a psychological state.

54 In this connection, while not identical, the concept of 'panspermia' may come to one's mind. Proposed by the Swedish physicist Svante Arrhenius (1859-1927), it states "that life appeared on Earth because it was seeded by "genes" from other worlds" (Olomucki, 1993, 17).

may be assumed that the reference is to some form of life, the former Ābhassara-Being not only now abandoning the sky, but also evolving into what we may simply call a 'Post-Ābhassara-Aqueous-Being' (coining the Pali term here **pacchābhassarodaka-sattā* (5,3a; 6,3a). This suggests that enough time, to be counted in billions of years, of course, has gone by to begin aqueous life. Notes Carl Zimmer, in his book, *Evolution: the triumph of an idea* "In the history of life … [n]ine tenths of our evolution took place completely under water" (Zimmer, 2001,70)[55].

Let us see what the Buddha has to say about what happens next, when, following a period of time where all was water, 'savoury Earth spread itself over the waters' (4,3b), giving company to the already existing space and water. We may note here again the phrase, 'after the passage of a very long time beyond', suggestive of the billions of years prior to the forming of the Earth some 4.5 billion years ago (2,3b) as is the current calculation for the age of the Earth[56].

---

[55] Does this also explain why our mindbodies are made up of 70% of water?

[56] And in AS, it is "all darkness, (just) blinding darkness. Not known were moon or sun [2] nor constellations and stars, nor night and day, nor months and fortnights, nor years and seasons". Now this, of course, is right in keeping with the view of Westernsciencewhich posits the Earth as appearing *after* the appearance of the sun. If we were to return to the Devolutionary phase as in Buddha's characterization, there was an Earth prior to the fire of the Seven suns. As in the quote above, 'When rain does not fall, seed life and vegetation, medicinal plants, grasses, and giant trees of the forest wither and dry up and no longer exist.' Then, 'small rivers and lakes dry up and evaporate and no longer exist'. With the appearance of the seventh sun, 'this great Earth and Sineru, the king of mountains, burst into flames, blaze up brightly, and become one mass of flame. As the great Earth and Sineru are blazing and burning, the flame, cast up by the wind, rises …'. Here, then, is indication of the presence of the Earth as the *Devolutionary* phase begins. The mountains bursting into flames clearly suggestive of volcanic activity, the volcanic dust of such a magnitude would surely be enough to cover the sun, rendering it all dark.

This Earth was endowed with colour, smell and taste, noting how in the Abhidhamma, form, sound, odour, taste and touch are shown to be as being inherent in nature, the five senses emerging in the context of them as objects (*ārammana*).

But something else, too. "Its taste was like fine, pure honey." (AS # 11).

Now it is not insignificant that at this critical chronological point in time of 4.5 bya the Buddha says that "the world evolves again" (*loko puna vivaṭṭo hoti*) (# 12).

What this suggests may be that now begin to appear conditions more conducive to complex life that would eventually climax with the appearacne of human life. For, the appearance of the Earth suggests three evolutionary developments in relation to life.

One is the obvious amphibious life (5,3b), though, in a continuing understatatement of the Buddha, it finds no mention in AS, alongside, of course, the already existing Spatial and Aqueous life.

Although there is no seeming mention of Land life (5,3b) either, there is the conjectured Example of Life of land animals (see Note 11.13), namely 'tiny honey' (*khuddamadhu*) (6,3b). If Collins' insight as to the existence of honey bees bya is for linguistic reasons, this writer is encouraged for several other reasons.

First, given that the idea of the presence of taste has already been made by the Buddha in relation to the Earth (*rasa paṭhavi*, # 11), there doesn't seem to be a reason to introduce the idea again, his presentation of the topic being, as elsewhere, quite succinct.

To make a second point, a flower and a bee, as Darwin notes, "become, either simultaneously or one after the other, modified and adapted in the most perfect manner to each other, by continued preservation of individuals presenting mutual and slightly favourable deviations of structure." (in Zimmer, 2001, 192). Even though only creepers and plants are named in AS at the period bya under disscussion, there is no reason to think that the process of 'co-evolution', as Zimmer puts it, would not occur between the bees and plant life that had emerged. Here plant life may, of course, be considered to include flowers, undoubtedly of different colours, given that the Earth is said to be 'possessed of colour' (*vaṇṇasampaṇṇā*), noting here the plural ending *ā*.

To come to a third point, what is of critical importance at this stage towards the continuity of life is the emergence of sexual reproduction (7,3b, as implicit from 7,3a) in its primordial form, in addition to asexual, and a cross between. Interestingly, the bees seems to provide a model.

> A queen makes sons and daughters in distinctly different ways. Males start out as unfertilized eggs, which divide and develop into full-grown insects without any sperm. Because they don't receive any DNA from a father, male honey bees have only one copy of each gene. On the other hand, a queen mates with one of her male consorts and uses the standard Mendelian shuffle[57] to create daughters, each with two copies of each gene." (Zimmer, 248).

This then can be a huge evolutionary step in relation to the emergence of complex life.

Interestingly, strengthening the case of the presence of bisexual bees may be the primordial volvox, although appearing very much later, but as a possible model, "a freshwater alga … found in ponds and ditches, even in shallow puddles", the most favorable place to look for it being "the deeper ponds, lagoons, and ditches which receive an abundance of rain water." < http://en.wikipedia.org/wiki/Volvox>. The "ancestors of *Volvox*" are said to have "transitioned from single cells to form multicellular colonies at least 200 million years ago, during the Triassic period". While this is to pre-date bees by a 50 or million years, the examples given here are to be considered merely indicative, given that the period under discussion is several bya. That is to say that the actual process that have come to mature

[57] See Zimmer, 74-79 for a description.

as bees and volvox could be said to have begun in the very remote past, counting in billions.

When it comes to bisexuality, the volvox seems to provide the prototype again:

> An asexual colony includes both somatic (vegetative) cells, which do not reproduce, and *gonidia* near the posterior, which produce new colonies through repeated division. The daughter colonies are initially held within the parent coenobium and have their flagella directed inwards. Later, the parent disintegrates and the daughters invert. In sexual reproduction two types of gametes are produced. *Volvox* species can be monoecious or dioecious. Male colonies release numerous microgametes, or sperm, while in female colonies single cells enlarge to become oogametes, or eggs.

The example of the volvox pre-dating the bees, again, is merely to be indicative of the forms of life in the earliest period of the Earth, that must surely include amphibious life, with both asexual and sexual reproduction (7,3a).

In an apparent reference to the continuity of the species, it was noted how females and males engage in coitus, bringing us to the 'Reproductive type' in the Figure (Col. 7), calling also for 'Birth Type' (Col. 8). To begin with, the spatial type (5,2) Ābhassara Beings were seen to be asexual, making it an example of 'spontaneous' birth (*opapātika*) (8,2). Literally meaning 'falling near' (<*upa-* 'near' + *pat* 'to fall'), Westernscience understands it this way:

> … when a system is far from equilibrium, or where it is at a much higher temperature than its environment, new types of structures may originate "spontaneously". The result is that new dynamic states of matter, namely, organic life, are created." (Kafatos & Nadeau, 144).

The advent of amphibious life (5,3b), and land life (5,3b) in the evolutionary scene takes us on an etymological detour. A second type of origins of birth the Buddha talks about is *jalābuja, a* term generally translated as 'born from a womb-' or 'placenta-born', i.e., viviparous 'bringing forth living young' (vivi- < vivus 'alive') (PED)[58].

Such an understanding allows for only a mammalian birth in a human (or animal)[59] womb. A closer look at the term, however, allows a more inclusive derivation. *Jalābu* can be taken to be from the Sanskrit *jala* + *ā-brū* < *ā-bruvate* 'to converse with'[60]. So *jalābu* (< *jala* + *ābu*) may be taken to mean 'in conversation with water', 'in association with water' or 'in the context of' water'. J*alābuja* (< *jala* + *ābu* + *ja*) then would mean 'born in association with water', or simply 'born of water', or 'born in water'. Such an interpretation fits equally well with both aqueous life in water as with placental conception in humans, taking the amniotic fluid in the placenta as the human water context.

It gains more credibility when we note that the Buddha has avoided linking the suffix *–ja* in this context to the more straightforward *gabbha* 'womb', resulting in **gabbhaja* (star meaning 'does not exist') and meaning 'womb born', or *jala* 'water', giving us **jalaja* meaning 'water-born'. While the latter would have excluded a placental birth, the former would have excluded an aqueous birth. So it appears that the Buddha, ever the 'language entrepreneur', seems to have opted for *jalābuja* in order to capture both the aqueous and the mammalian contexts under 'water-born' (8,3a; 8,3b as implicit from 8,3a)). And while the term itself is not used in the Discourse, it may

---

[58] This is as opposed to 'oviparous', meaning 'producing eggs which hatch after leaving the body of the female' ('ovi-' from 'ovum') (*Webster's*). See *aṇḍaja* later.

[59] As noted, the Buddha's term *sattā* covers both humans and animals.

[60] We note with interest, but with no comment, that Monier-Williams' Sanskrit Dictionary shows the etymology of *jalābu* as being from *jarāyu* < *jarā* < *jar-* 'to decay' + *āyu* 'age'.

be safely assumed that the Buddha does not exclude water-born form of life in introducing the phase when all was water. Finally, while the human context of *jalābuja* in the context of placental water comes to be sexual, the example of the volvox seems to allow for in-water asexual reproduction as well

A third type of generation the Buddha talks about is 'egg-born' (*aṇḍaja*), relevant to aqueous, ambhibious and land life (8,3a; 8,3b). Here it may be relevant to recall that "Male [volvox] colonies release numerous microgametes, or sperm, while in female colonies single cells enlarge to become oogametes, or eggs."

A final type is 'moisture-born' (*saṃsedaja)* (8,3b), although 8,3a is not to be excluded. The Buddha explains the type as being "born in a rotten fish, .. rotten corpse,…." (Ven. Nanamoli & Ven. Bodhi (Tr.), 1995, 169), although Westernsciencegives it as an example of 'spontaneous' generation (see Ponnamperuma, 13-21). Spontaneous beings, of course, needs to be seen as continuing as well

But a third significant evolution is perhaps the most significant in human terms. Beings are now said to begin to enjoy the 'savoury Earth', this with their 'fingers'. In imitation of the first, other Beings come to taste the stuff with their fingers. Not satiated enough, now they "set to with their hands, breaking off pieces of the stuff in order to eat it." Although legs and toes are not specifically identified, the Beings are said to have 'approached' (*upakkamiṃsu*) (# 14) some food which had by this time come to sprout (see later for a treatment), this clearly suggesting mobility, and the evolution of legs, generating beings with both four legs (quadrupeds) and two legs (bipeds), although 'leg' and 'toes' have to be understood as being of a primordial variety.

But that is not all. While up to now, Beings were non-gender-specific, now we are told that the 'female *linga* appeared in the woman', and the 'male *linga* in the man' (# 16). With this, "The females looked at the males just so long as did the males at the females. As they were looking at each other for long, passion arose in them, and burning all round entered their bodies. Because of this burning, they indulged in sexual behaviour"(# 16). 'Looking', of course, suggests the presence of the visual organ, if also the olfactory organ as they smell each other's odour. At the point of tasting the food, Beings express themselves with the words "Oh, what taste" (# 13), suggesting the presence of gustatory capacity . What we now have then are the prototypes of Homo sapiens sapiens (6.3b), in addition to land animals as exemplified by the tiny honey bees.

Here again, we may see bees as early pioneers of communication when the direction and amount of a food source is communicated at a distance through movement[61], this in Linguistic theory being 'kinesics', entailing synesthesia, namely, "sensation felt in one part of the body when another part is stimulated" (Webster's), as well.

Thus we show this stage as 'fully limbed' (9,3b) under the Column 'Limbedness'. This, of course, is in contrast to that of being 'Limbless' (9.2; 9,3a) as in the case of Ābhassara Beings or being with 'Rudimentary Limbs' ((9,3a), though not mentioned, in relation to aqueous life (5,3a). In this context, it may be noted that the cells of volvox "have eyespots, more developed near the anterior, which enable the colony to swim towards light", suggesting again the early origins of limbedness.

Evolutionary physical change, of course, as seen above, is related to 'Nutriment' (Col. 10 of chart), given that 'All sentient beings are food based' (*sabbe sattā āhāraṭṭhitikā*). We have already encountered Beings tasting the savoury Earth with fingers and breaking up the Earth with hands. Next there comes to be named three types of plant outgrowths – ground-hugging *pappaṭaka*, creepers and rice[62]. All this, then, is what the Buddha calls 'solid food' (*kabalinkāhāra*). (10.3b).

But how did these Earth food types come to be?

---

[61] http://www.polarization.com/bees/bees.html.

[62] In relation to the three types of food Gombrich asks (Gombrich, 171), "Why are there three cycles? True, the Buddhist texts tend to say things three times, but that does not explain the three different kinds of food….". Hopefully our analysis in terms of an evolutionary process of increasingly more complex food types explains the three.

It was noted how the sun was the most powerful source of energy for the Earth. Ponnamperuma (51-61) points out how the varied energy sources - electrical discharges in the form of lightning, radioactivity, heat energy, solar heat, shock waves generated by meteorites passing through the atmosphere, etc., would have been "responsible for much organic synthesis in primeval Earth conditions".

The *pappaṭaka*, creepers and rice could, then, be seen as the early products of such organic synthesis. In this connection, it is interesting to note certain developments in relation to the primitive Earth that are suggestive of the three types.

Ground *pappaṭaka* has come to be interpreted above as being 'crusty'. Notes Ponnamperuma (1972, 44-5), "During the early stages of the Earth's formation, volcanic activity was probably rampant throughout its surface. As the embryonic Earth began to take shape, the gravitational forces caused contractions in the crust." So would it be surprising that the nutritive outgrowths of a crusty Earth would also be crusty? It may be remembered that it was pieces of the ground that the Beings first consumed.

The ground *pappaṭaka* also comes to be associated in the text with the label *ahicchattaka*, meaning 'snake's parasol'. It is with interest, then, that we read about "The strange umbrella-like shape of Kakabekia umbellata which flourished in the Pre-Cambrian era" (Ponnamperuma, 126), understood to be prior to 1.8 bya going all the way back to the formation of the Earth 4.5 bya (see Zimmer, 70-71, again).

Coming now to the second type of plant life in the text, namely, 'bound-creepers' (*badālatā*) we again note with interest "thread-like assemblage of bacteria", the reference being to the fossil algae, said to be two million years old (Ponnamperuma, 124, in the Chapter on 'Molecular fossils'). But there is nothing to say that the beginnings of thread-like plant life did not originate much earlier, when the "earliest evidence of chemical life" appears in 3.8 bya (Zimmer, 70-71). The bound creepers are also said, in AS, to be 'bamboo-like' (14.9), perhaps suggestive of plant diversity. In this context, we are struck by the "rod-shaped bacteria" dating back to two billion years

(Ponnamperuma, 124-126), that "may be related to the modern iron bacteria" (127).

Now, of course, it would be foolhardy to claim that what has been discovered in Westernscienceis the exactly parallel to the food types named by the Buddha. However, it is difficult to ignore two factors – first, that the Westernscientific findings relate to a time of over billions of years, and second, that the similarities of the shapes and features of the various forms of pre-Cambrian organic matter to those of the food types the Buddha provides are too close to be coincidental.

Returning now to the types of nourishment, what we have in sexual behaviour can be said to be 'contact food' (*phassāhāra*) (10,3b), as also in the case of Ābhassara Beings (10,2, though not listed). As females and males were looking at each other for long, passion arose in them, and *burning all round entered their bodies*. It is a Being of the 'greedy' type that begins to taste the savoury Earth, to be followed by others, clearly *greed* setting in. These constitute 'volition food' (*manosañcetanāhāra*) (10,3a). The Buddhist technical term 'Sentient Being', of course, suggests the presence of the fourth type of nutriment: 'Consciousness-food' (*viññāṇāhāra*) (10,2).

Incidentally, it is of significance again that the Buddha does not use the characterization "after the passage of a very long time beyond" here. The reason should be obvious enough. The tasting of food, first by one and then by another and another and another is something that happens instantaneously, by imitation of the first. What it does speak to is a beginning socialization process in a growing sentient milieu.

In contrast to this stage 10.3b, when all four types serve as nutriment, it may be remembered that an Ābhassara Being also came to be seen as being a 'mindbody', suggesting that it was fed on consciousness food (10,2). It is said that Ābhassara Beings 'come to the present state' during the Evolutionary phase. This can be said to entail volition food (10,3a), for, after all, coming 'to the present state' would indicate the Being 'looking' to be elsewhere, suggesting a volitional activity. At this same stage of Earth life, the aqueous and the amphibious, being the result of interacting conditions and physical bodies, we could envision an additional contact food (10,3a).

In summary, then, in AS # 10-16, the Buddha can be seen to be carefully tracing the evolution of life from a Consciousness beginning in the outer space ending with a community of Beings living on Earth and, though not touched on above, coming together towards governance (# 17).

Interestingly again, we find the bees providing the prototype for human social organization, including what would today be called a dictatorial and authoritarian rule of the Queen Bee: "In a honeybee hive, there is a single queen, a few males, and 20,000 to 40,000 female workes" who "spend their lives gathering nectar, keeping the hive in good working order, and feeding the queen's larvae" (Zimmer, 248). The entire colony seems to work to ensure the success of all, including, of course, each of themselves.

The volvox "acting like one multicellular organism", provides the 'back-formation'[63] prototype again. The individual algae in some species being "[I]nterconnected by thin strands of cytoplasm, called protoplasmates", they "are known to demonstrate some individuality and working for the good of their colony".

To summarize, then, having begun with the Devolutionary phase, the Buddha outlines the Evolutionary phase along the following dimensions:

1. Universe: Change cycles;

Moon and sun, stars, night and day, months and half months and seasons (suggesting rain and dry seasons).

2. Ecology: water, Earth, plant life;

3. Sentient life: Ābhassaras, animals and humans.

Let us now re-cap how the banchmarks touched upon by the Buddha measure up against the process of evolution as understood in Westernscience, this with the help of Figure 2:

---

[63] The concept of 'back-formation' is taken from Linguistics, a classical example being the English term 'cherries' from the French 'cerise'. By the rules of English, the singular of 'cherries' comes to be 'cherry' by back formation, dropping the pluralizing suffix. What is envisaged is a similar conceptual take relating to life.

1	2	3	4	5
ERA	**SUB-ERA**	**TIME IN YEARS**	**WESTERN SCIENCE**	**THE BUDDHA**
PRE-CAM-BRIAN	1	13.5 + bya	Big Bang	End of Devolutionary Phase; Presence of Ābhassara Beings in the sky
	2	9 bya	---	Beginnings of Evolutionary Phase / Ābhassara Beings continuing
	3		---	Formation of Water
	4	4.55 bya	Formation of Earth	Formation of Earth
	5	4.4 bya	Condensation of water into oceans	
	6	3.8 bya	Earliest chemical evidence of Life	
	7	2.7 bya	Earliest Chemical Evidence of Eukaryotes	
	8	2.6 bya	Bacteria living on land	
	9	1.8 bya	Oldest multicellular fossils	
CAM-BRIAN	10	575 mya	Oldest animals (Ediacarans)	
	11	500 mya	Plants evolve	Plants evolving
	12	450 mya	Insects and other vertebrates move on land	Plants variegating; Insects evolving
	13	360 mya	Four-limbed vertebrates move on land	
	14	225 mya	Mammals and dinosaurs	
	15	5 mya	Ancestors of humans and chimps diverge	
PLIO-CENE	16	150 kya	Anatomically modern humans	Anatomically modern humans

Fig. 2 Benchmarks identified by the Buddha as against the Benchmarks of Evolution in Westernscience

Legend:

bya: Billion years ago;
mya: Million years ago;
kya: Thousand years ago.

This Chart (Fig. 2), drawn upon Zimmer, 2001, 70-71, shows three Eras (Col. 1) as identified in Westernscience: Pre-Cambrian (4.5 bya to 575 mya) (1-9), Cambrian (535 mya to 5 mya) (10-15) and Pliocene (5 mya – 150 kya) (16) showing no sub-eras. Under Pre-Cambrian are sub-eras 1 to 4 showing the physical cosmic process ending up in Earth, and 5 to 9 the earliest forms of life. The Cambrian Era shows continuing growth of plant and animal life, with humans emerging in the Pliocene Era (16).

In AS, we find the Buddha touching on 1- 4 of the Chart (see Col. 5), first identifying the Devolutionary and the Evolutionary phases, and next, skipping nine billion years, as in the writer's calculation, bringing us to the formation of the Earth. In introducing us to plant life (ground *pappaṭaka, bhaddālatā* and rice) and animal life (tiny honey), he is seen to skip another four billion years, a time period covered in the Chart from 5 to 10 (Pre-Cambrian and Cambrian). In bringing us to the emergence of 'anatomically modern' humans (Col. 4), constituting a mere blip in the history of the present cycle of the Universe – 150,000 years (150 kya) (Row 16), detailing them with fingers (to lick with) and sexual organs, he skips a final four *million* years. So we see the Buddha touching on only the critical stages in presenting his understanding of the universe and its evolution (physical and human).

To take a closer comparative look now, what Westernsciencecalls the Big Bang, the Buddha sees as being the *end of the Devolutionary* phase of burning, followed by an Evolutionary phase of cooling, culminating in the appearance of water, the process plausibly taking nine billion years. To apportion time here, the Big Bang is said to be about 13.5 billion years ago, and the appearance of the Earth 4.5 bya, the difference in time between the two events being about 9 billion years. But in the Buddha's eyes, the period is made up of two phases, Devolutionary and Evolutionary, it may not be unreasonable to assign 4.5 billion years to each phase. Indeed the Buddha does use the line 'This world evolves again' at the point when the Devolutionary phase changes into the Evolutionary phase. Hence, in a refinement, we show 9 bya as the beginning of the Evolutionary phase.

The Buddha's scant mention, of course, comes to be detailed out in Westernscience, following the apearance of the Earth. When it comes to plant and animal life, while in Westernsciencethe latter follows the former, the Buddha shows them as co-evolving. Finally, while humans appear at the tail end in both, Westernscienceshows how the human ancestors go back to 2.7 bya when the earliest chemical evidence of what are called Eukaryotes, "an enormous group of organisms … which include animals, plants, fungi, and protozoans" (Zimmer, 66) comes to be found. .

Stages 5 to 15 are, of course, the details left out by the Buddha: condensation of water into oceans, earliest chemical evidence of life, oldest fossils, earliest chemical evidence of eukaryotes, bacteria living on land, oldest multicellular fossils, oldest animals (ediacarans), insects and other vertebrates moving on land, four-limbed vertebrates moving on land, origin of amniotes and amphibians, origin of mammals and dinosaurs and ancestors of humans and chimps diverging.

While such details, of course, are the bread and butter of the Western Scientist, they play no role for the Buddha. Of critical importance, however, is that the Buddha seems to be not unaware of the evolutionary steps. And he heralds the process leading to the appearance of humans at the end of the formation of the Earth (# 4 in chart, 'Formation of Earth) with four simple words: *loko puna vivaṭṭo hoti* 'The world evolves again'.

Despite the fact that the Buddha is skimpy in his detailing of the stages of evolution as above, it is not that he fails to give a broader outline. This he seems to do using *language* and *food types* as the navigational tools.

Following the proclamation 'the world evolves again', we find 'a certain being' tasting the Earth savour 'wondering', 'What exactly will this be' (# 12). This one word characterization - 'wondering', comes to be followed, after 'a very long stretch of time', by a 'lament' and a self-comparison to others in terms of looks, and a further expression, 'Oh, the taste' (# 13), this in relation to 'Earth savour'. Then, after another 'very long stretch of time', we again have the same comparison and the lament, but this time in relation to ground pappaṭaka (# 14). Then after yet another 'very long stretch of time', the comparison and the lament are repeated, now in relation to *badālatā* (# 14, 15). But, next in relation to rice (# 16), we have the words put into the mouth of Beings, "Away with your filth', the reference being to sexual relations.

We conjecture the progression in a little more detail in the next figure (Fig. 3, next page).

In this figure, we seek to associate the words put into the mouth of Beings by the Buddha, alongside the food types located on Earth, with the Evolutionary phases, this drawn upon Fig. 2. To begin with, we have the beings 'wondering' (Col. II, row 1), a single word, and with reference to none (1, IV) (following laterally). While other Beings are said to also taste the Earth savour 'in imitation of' the Being, 'wondering' is not assigned to them. Thus no communication involved, we assume the language here to be indicative of a mere simple level *mental* activity, i.e., conceptual, thus entailing no speech, or speech mechanism (1, III). As noted, from a Linguistic point of view, perception precedes linguistic formation precedes speaking. This being in the context of 'Earth savour' (I,1, para 12), we assign it to 4.5 bya (1, VI), when 'the world evolves again' (1,V).

So it can be said that while there is likely no interpersonal communication, the first condition for language, namely, conceptualization has begun, given that the Beings, by definition, have consciousness (*manomayā*). So the world evolves again can be said to indicate a critical change from the phase when Earth itself providing nutrition to the beginning of plant life, and by association, organic life.

At Phase 2, still in the context of Earth savour (I, 2), but now following 'a very long stretch of time' (V, 2), what is placed in the mouths of the Beings comes to be slightly more complex. There is

I	II	III	IV	V	VI
PHASE / [PARA] / FOOD	WORDS OCCURING	LINGUISTIC MANIFES-TATION	REF. TO THE OTHER	T I M E STRETCH	EVOLUTION-ARY PHASE
1 [12] Earth savour	"wondering…"	*Single* word; Conceptual; Individual; *No* speech mechanism	*[None]*	'The world evolves again'	**4.5 Bya** [appearance of earth]
2 [13] Earth Savour	"despised"; "We're better looking than they are.." "came together..... lamented" "Oh, the taste!"	*More* words; Conceptual; 'we', 'they': Collectiive; Stage 1 (*primordial)* 'speech mechanism' -cellular	'they' (3rd person) *[None]*	'..a very long stretch of time'	**2.7 Bya** [earliest chemical evidence of Eukaryotes]
3 [14] Ground pappaṭaka	"We're better looking than they are.."; "...lamented"	Same words; Conceptual, 'we' and 'they' [increasing population]; Stage 2 'speech mechanism']	'they' (3rd person)	'..a very long stretch of time'	500 **Mya** [Plants evolve]
4 [14/ 15] Badālatā	"We're better looking than they are.."; "...lamented"	Same words Conceptual, 'we', 'they' [increasing population]; Stage 3 'speech mechanism']	'they' (3rd person)	'..a very long stretch of time'	225 Mya [Mammals]
5 [16] Rice	"Away with your filth.." "How could a Being do such a thing to another Being"	Complex Language proper; Oculesics / kinesics / proxemics	'your' (2nd person)	'..a very long stretch of time'	**150 kya** [anatomicaly modern humans]

Fig. 3 Stages of Linguistic Growth in Beings and Food Type as Indicative of the Evolutionary Phases

first a 'despising' and 'lamenting', inferring 'anger' (*dosa*) and 'unhappiness' (as we could translate *dukkha* in this context). Then, unlike 'wondering' earlier, now we have tactile enjoyment (though not yet lingual), too: 'Oh, the taste' (2, II), a clear advance on sense functioning. There is also a comparing between 'we' and 'they', entailing a longer sequence of words and a reference to the other (2, IV): "We're better looking than they are" (2, II). The fullness of structure here (Noun + verb), the comparison and the variety of expression and emotion - 'despised' (hatred)), 'lamented' (sorrow) and 'oh' (enjoyment), all seem to indicate a relatively mature stage of linguistic evolvement, though still with a 'primordial speech mechanism' (see next), this again after 'a very long stretch of time'. This phase may thus be associated with the 'earliest chemical evidence of Eukaryotes (2, VI), and an evolutionary time of 2.7 bya.

Then (I,3) follows another very long stretch of time (3, V), with just about the same level of linguistic expression (3,II), although there is now no particular mention of 'despising', perhaps to be now taken for granted, having already emerged in Beings. Both this absence, and the presence of the other two expressions, seem to suggest a continuing evolution of language, giving us a 'stage 2' speech mechanism' (3,III; 4,III). At these first three levels, there is actually no speech mechanism as such, the cellular structure beginning to undergo a form of mitosis (i.e., cell division) towards increasingly complexing itself and growing towards such a mechanism. By way of a parallel, we may consider here, as earlier, too, embryonic growth. While it will be several weeks and months before the mouth, tongue, nose, etc, come to be formed, the earlier weeks can be said to be preparatory. Likewise may be understood the first two stages, each following a long stretch of time.

However, stage 3 (I, 3) seems to indicate a dramatic evolutionary development, ushering in a new phase, in that this is when the first plant / food, namely, Ground Pappaṭaka appears. This, then, gives us a second Earth-based phase of 500 mya (3,VI), the 'very long stretch' countable as two billions plus years (2.7 bya to 500 mya).

Just about the same level of linguistic expression continues at the next phase (I, 4) when the second variety of plant / food, namely, Badālatā appears. Here at 'stage 3' 'speech mechanism' (4, III), we see a critical development in the evolution of language. Given that it, too, follows upon another very long stretch of time (4, V), we may associate this with the evolutionary phase of 225 mya (4,VI) when the first mammals appear. Homo sapiens being a mammal, it may be envisaged that the speech mechnism has now come to mature into a physical reality with mouth, tongue, nose, larynx, etc. However unsophisticated and phonemically undiscriminated[64], i.e., 'grunty' as the the sounds may be, mammal communication entails sounds, differentiated pitch levels, etc.[65], suggesting a *coordinated* speech mechanism. Unlike the earlier 'very long stretch of time', now our count drops to millions of years. The Buddha indeed seems to give us a hint as to this drop from billions to millions, the relative shortness of time passed. He brings in Badālatā within the same same paragraph as Pappaṭaka (# 14, 15), unlike when the latter is introduced earlier in a separate paragragh following reference to Earth savour, and rice is introduced in a separate para (# 16) after Badālatā.

It is only in the 5th, and final, phase (I,5), associated with rice, then, it can be said that we encounter actual human communication. The words, phrases and sentences up to now can be said to be how an 'observer' on the evolutionary scene would capture the ideas in the

---

[64] "Human languages are characterized for having a **double articulation** (in the characterization of French linguist André Martinet). It means that complex linguistic expressions can be broken down into meaningful elements (such as morphemes and words), which in turn are composed of smallest phonetic elements that affect meaning, called phonemes. Animal signals, however, do not exhibit this dual structure." http://en.wikipedia.org/wiki/Animal_communication#Animal_communication_and_linguistics.

[65] E.g., "The greater spot-nosed monkeys have two main alarm sounds. A sound known onomatopoeiacally as the "pyow" warns against a lurking leopard, and a coughing sound that scientists call a "hack" is used when an eagle is flying nearby." <http://en.wikipedia.org/wiki/Animal_communication#Animal_communication_and_linguistics>.

mind of the Being in her/his own human language. It is a 'reporting' rather than 'transcribing' actual words. But when we hear the words "Away with your filth…." and "How could a Being do such a thing to another Being?!", what we have is complexity and sophistication of language, noting the question and/or exclamation, as contrasted with the exclusive statements, here and earlier.

The statement and the exclamation also speak to a critical human marker - a *values* system, entailing moral judgment[66].

We may even envisage a final critical component of communication here - the paralinguistic features that render the communication more communicative: *oculesics* (eye-communication), *proxemics* (closeness of speakers to each other) and *kinesics* (gestures). If these paralinguistic features can be said to have been evolving in the earlier phases, now they can be said to be in full gear, when the the speaker comes to address in the 2nd person 'you': 'away with your filth', this as contrasted with amaking reference to a 3rd person in the earlier phases (2,IV to 4,IV). So now, real language! And with a corresponding cortical development. The communication has now moved to a face to face level, the sexual relations that prompt the comments speaking to an intimacy, another paralinguistic dimension. All this, of course, is very different from the personal, and private, 'wondering' the process began with[67].

What we have sought to establish through this Figure, then, is how the Buddha seems to suggest phases of evolution culminating in human life, beginning with a single 'certain being' and ending up with a community of beings, through the use of highly selective, and well placed, language, put in the 'mouths' of Beings, accompanied by food types.

As hopefully additionally supported by Fig. 3, what we see overall,

---

[66] Entailed here may also, of course, be jealousy, and ignorance of reality.

[67] An informal, rough parallel for the evolutionary phases covering billions of years would be a child's first year of growth relating to food and 'language' growth:

as characterized in detail in relation to Fig. 2, then, is the efficient hand of the Maestro of the understatement educating us nevertheless on the reality of the evolution of the physcial universe and sentient beings, culminating in humans. While the Buddha may be short on detail, touching only on the critical stages, his characterization of the flow of nature can be said to be congruent with the understanding in Westernscience. Of course, our thesis has to be considered to be hypothetical, with the current level of knowledge hardly able to confirm or challenge it, leaving that task to future generations.

PHASE	AGE	'WORD' PARALLEL	MIND PROCESS	FOOD
1	Day 1	'oh, how yummy this!'	Conceptual	1st breast milk tastier
2	Day 2 & on	'oh, different kind!'	Conceptual ; Comparative	Regular breast milk
3	6 months	'Here's a different taste'	Conceptual; Comparative	pureed food
4	11 months	'Coarser, this'	Conceptual; Comparative	First solids
5	1 year	'Love it, this mix – solids, liquids, fruits ..'	First language: 'mom'	Regular food

6

Two Seeming Chronological Paradoxes

6.1 Fingers, Food, Humans and Earth

The above discussion still leaves two interrelated issues unresolved. One relates to Beings laying their 'fingers' and 'hands' (as later in # 12) upon the tasty Earth, which in Westernsciencecomes to be dated to be *4.5 bya*. The other relates to the types of food - ground *pappaṭaka, badālatā* and rice, enjoyed by the Ābhassara Beings bya, way before the time of the chemical processes and the photosynthesis conducive to plant life as has been calculated in Westernscience. So how are they to be resolved?

To place the issues in its evolutionary context, we may note that in Westernscience, the appearance of humans is a mere blip in the evolutionary process, countable in terms of *thousands* of years, the last one minute, in fact, in a twelve-hour geological clock representing the age of the Earth (Ponnamperuma, 121-122). This point in time is preceded by chemical evolution and biological evolution, and the beginnings of photosynthesis supportive of plant life in the Pre-Cambrian era, billions of years earlier. This is followed by the Paleozoic, Mesozoic and Cenozoic eras when 'life' begins, the last being invertebrates, fish, land plants, reptiles, mammals, and at the very end, man, now moving forward into the thousands of years.

To begin with 'fingers' and 'hands', then, one possible interpretation is that they may not have been anything like our own, but miniscule, and rudimentary, extensions of a miniscule body, like the pseudopods (Greek: 'false feet') of amoeba[68], more like the thread-like tentacles of sea anemone, immobile plants as they are, that 'capture' any passing food[69].

Even though humans may have been the Johnny-come-late on the cosmic scene, we have the 'Earliest chemical evidence of eukaryotes' 2.7 bya (col. 3, 7 in Fig. 2). Here, then, is what we read in the New World Encyclopedia:

> A **eukaryote** (or *eucaryote*) is an organism with a complex cell or cells, in which the genetic material is organized into a membrane-bound nucleus or nuclei. Eukaryotes comprise *animals* [italics added], plants, and fungi — which are mostly multicellular — as well as various other groups that are collectively classified as protists (many of which are unicellular). In contrast, prokaryotes are organisms, such as bacteria, that lack nuclei and other complex cell structures and are usually unicellular.
>
> Eukaryotes are considered to share a common origin, and are often treated formally as a superkingdom, empire, or domain. The name comes from the Greek ευ, meaning *good,* and κάρυον, meaning *nut,* in reference to the cell nucleus.

---

[68] Thanks again to Ajahn Punnadhammo for this suggestion, and the following reference: "Pseudopods serve two important functions—locomotion and food capture, activities that are often interrelated..." <http://science.jrank.org/pages/301/Amoeba.html>.

[69] "The ornately colored sea anemone (uh-NEM-uh-nee) is named after the equally flashy terrestrial anemone flower. A close relative of coral and jellyfish, anemones are stinging polyps that spend most of their time attached to rocks on the sea bottom or on coral reefs waiting for fish to pass close enough to get ensnared in their venom-filled tentacles." <http://animals.nationalgeographic.com/animals/invertebrates/sea-anemone/>

> The evolution of eukaryotes is postulated to have occurred through a symbiotic relationship between prokaryotes, a theory called *endosymbiosis*. According to this theory, mitochondria, chloroplasts, flagella, and even the cell nucleus would have arisen from prokaryote bacteria that gave up their independence for the protective and nutritive environment within a host organism. Analogous to the symbiosis between algae and fungi in lichens, this process would have conferred a tremendous adaptive advantage upon the combined organism. This type of evolution would be far more powerful and far-reaching than the conventional process whereby change occurs in small increments due to accumulated mutations.
>
> The fact that the cells of protozoa, algae, fungi, plants, and animals are eukaryotes, combined with the evolutionary connectedness of eukaryotes and prokaryotes, reveals a commonality of all life—a connectedness from the simplest organism on the microscopic level, with a rudimentary ability to sense its environment, to the complexity of the thinking and loving human being. <http://www.newworldencyclopedia.org/entry/Eukaryote>.

Here, then, we seem to have the connection. While humans as we know them may appear late on the chronological scene, their primordial 'good nut' (eukaryote) foreparents can be seen to have made their presence way back then. While the origins of the Earth may be 4.5 bya, it is not out of perceptual reality to consider that it was not before two more billions would pass before plant life suitable for more complex being would appear[70]. On this basis, then,

[70] One possible reading here, as Ajahn Punnadhammo points out, is that we have "an early Earth covered in dense clouds and warm oceans full of amino acids and other organic compounds, but as yet no living beings. Beings from the higher realms fall to the new Earth level, becoming already somewhat coarser and more material in the process. At some point, they engage directly with the oceanic medium and

we may place the greedy 'Beings' who 'tasted' the savoury Earth, not to the pre-Earth times of the Ābhassara Beings, but the post-Earth time of the Eukaryote superkingdom, noting that it includes not only "protozoa, algae, fungi [and] plants," but also 'animals', the Buddha's term *sattā* capturing not only four legged animals and the two-legged us, and indeed no-legged or multi-legged ones, but also 'atom-sized ones' (*aṇuka*), and 'those who expect to become' (*sambhavesī*) (*Karaniyametta sutta,* K 1.9). This then allows the possibility that the fingers and hands may have been not what we think them to be but a primordial version. The reference to 'fingers' and 'hands' by the Buddha may then have been to both help visualize, and could you believe, perhaps dramatize, as a good playwright of today would assuredly do!

Now when it comes to the issue of food, it is interesting in this connection that the verb used by the Buddha to describe the activity of the greedy Beings is *sāyi* (from *sāyati*) meaning 'taste', associated also with honey (two lines later). Although the PED does give the meaning of 'eat' as well to the term, the verb stem with more associative meanings of 'eat' would be *khād-,* associated with 'solid food' (*khādaniya*), 'teeth' and even 'javelin', suggesting biting into the solid food. So the use of *sāyi* by the Buddha suggests not so much eating as such, but making contact with the crusty (as suggested by *pappaṭaka*) 'savoury Earth', clearly 'tasteable' rather than 'eatable'. In a continuing semantic thrust, when it comes to

---

take a very great fall; mind entering into the organic soup sparks the beginning of life in the form of simple one-celled organisms. From that point on, life evolves into ever greater complexity eventually arriving at the human form. This may, however, suggest a teleological element, not sitting well from a strict Darwinian point of view - mind seeking always to find a more perfect vehicle for its physical expression."

To add this writer's own comment, it could also be simply seen as a co-evolution, with the evolving Being, with a 'thirst to be', continuing to be in search of that which helps maximize continuing existence and increased complexity. This, of course, would be a good Darwinian fit of the survival of the fittest.

badālatā 'bound' or 'wish-creepers', and rice (*sāli*), the Buddha interestingly uses the verbs *paribhunjituṃ* and *paribhunjantā,* from *bhuj-* (with *pari-*), meaning 'enjoy' ('all around'). Again there is no 'eating' per se. While again today it is something to be eaten, it may be again taken to mean some primordial type, the Buddha himself making the point that they were 'free from a coating of red powder and free from chaff', but 'fully grown'.

Further, while *sāli,* is translateable as 'rice', it may very well be that, "'rice' is meant simply as a synecdoche for 'food' generally, just as in English idiom we say, 'our daily bread' meaning our food"[71]. By extension, then, *pappaṭaka* and *badālatā* could also have been understood to mean some kind of food, without necessarily knowing, or wanting to know, what they actually were. So the Earth food, called *sāli* by the Buddha may not have been anywhere close to what we understand by 'rice' today (see above fn. 32 re pigeonpea)[72], the same way *anguli* may not have meant 'finger' as understood today.

---

[71] Ajahn Punnadhammo who makes this point, also kindly offers an example from an Asian culture: "I know that in Thai, the word for rice, *khao*, is often used almost as a synonym for food generally, as in the expressions, 'to take rice' meaning 'to eat a meal', or 'with 'rice' meaning 'curries'".

[72] In a further research, *sāli* could well have been 'finger millet', http://www.agridept.gov.lk/index.php/en/crop-recommendations/890 (*kurakkan* in Sinhala) which seems to be "wheat Free" which could be taken as meaning 'chafe free' as in our text. It is "high in nutritional value", a panacea "to ward off all ill effects of heat during the summer months." Of "medicinal value", it is "a popular food among diabetic patients. ..., [and] for infants." In North-west of Vietnam, it is used "as medicine for women when they are born.", and its flour used to make alcohol among the H'mong minority. <http://www.wellsphere.com/healthy-cooking-article/ragi-finger-millet-and-its-health-benefits/352804. Being heat-resistant, finger-millet could have been an advantage in those early years of the Earth's hot surface, and for its nutritinal and medicinal value as well. Its use for alcohol seems to suggest that the craving of the early Beings included drinking!

Last in the list of food types, the Buddha may have used the familiar term *sāli* so his listeners could relate to it, by linking it to the food of the day.

By extension, then, *pappaṭaka* and *badālatā* would also come to be 'understood', by association, to mean some kind of food, without necessarily knowing, or wanting to know, what they really were. In that sense, then, *pappaṭaka* and *badālatā* and *sāli* may be seen to be referring to the outcome or product of some primordial chemical processes, the three different types showing diversity as per the emerging and different conditions in a process of co-evolution. Now it may be noted in this connection that the reference to the three food types come in separate paragraphs (# 14, 15 and 16), as if to suggest billions of years between each of them (see discussion in relation to Fig. 3), also suggesting nutritional diversity.

So while both the Earth food types and the fingers and hands may not have been anywhere close to what we understand by them today, it can be said, "They did the trick" of making sense to the Buddha's two listeners.

The text allows another resolution of the issue. The Buddha talks of Ābhassara Beings in relation to the stage of coming 'to be in the present state' when the sun and the seasons were yet to manifest. But it is 'a certain Being' (*aññataro satto*) that first comes to taste the Earth with fingers, and it is 'other Beings' (in the plural) (*aññatare sattā*) that follow suit. This, then seems to suggest that by then the Ābhassara Beings had come to evolve alongside the evolutionary changes in relation to the material universe.

Yet another way of looking at it may be that the Buddha is speaking only figuratively. The references to them simply may be to be indicative of the earliest Evolutionary phases.

One more explanation may be that even though the Earth appeared 4.5 bya, the reference by the Buddha is to a period much ***later***, billions of years later, in fact, when the first humans appear. In other words, while the Earth may have appeared, it was barren for billions of years. The first chemical evidence of life appears 3.8 bya, the first plants 500 mya, and 'anatomically modern humans'

150 kya. So the reference in AS may indeed be to a much later time period, including the time period as identified in Westernscience. We may read such a fast forward in the fact that the humans with fingers tasting the Earth come not in the same paragraph as when the Earth appears but in the next paragraph.

The fact that the standard 'when somehow or other, at times' (*kadāci karahaci*) line doesn't occur here may appear to be unsupportive of this interpretation. However, what is interesting is that at the end of the very same paragraph come the words, 'Thus, Vāseṭṭha, does this world evolve again'. So the Buddha seems to be capturing the idea that while the Earth continues, with life evolving, there come to be changes in the skies as the moon and sun appear along with night and day, seasons, etc.

Such an interpretation also suggests a continuing evolution of the 'good nuts' into 'complex nuts', with primordial fingers and hands emerging in the context of the variety of food, the eventual products being the 'thinking and loving human being'.

Clever Buddha!

While one or more of the above assertions may be seen to be not quite in tandem with Westernscience, could it be possible that Westernscienceitself is yet to dig deeper to find primordial human life dating earlier than the 150 kya?

6.2 Lingua Precedes Linga

The AS text seems to imply that there were already quite advanced beings with fully formed complex bodies and even the power of speech before they began to differentiate into two genders. This, of course, is baffling to us humans. But is there a secret or two that the Buddha knows that are out of reach for us average humans? Let us then spend some time to explore the issue, beginning with a revisit to the relevant lines in the text:

> "# 12. Then, Vāseṭṭha, a certain Being of a greedy nature, wondering 'What exactly will this be?', tasted the Earth-

> savour with its finger ...".
>
> # 16. "To the extent that these Beings kept enjoying eating it [the reference here being to 'rice'], Vāseṭṭha, taking it to be their food, for a very long stretch of time, to that extent did they become coarser and coarser in their bodies, and the variation in colour (and/or appearance) come to be (further) manifested. The female *linga* appeared in the female, and the male *linga* in the male."

In # 12, then, we have language usage and in # 16, the appearance of *linga* (still retaining the original term for reasons that will come to be clear presently) chronologically later than language.

The Pali term *linga* here can be taken, as in Sanskrit, with which the Buddha was not unfamiliar with having had the education worthy of a prince, undoubtedly in the sense of 'pudenda' (< sg. 'pudendum') (in one of its meanings in Monier-Williams), meaning 'the external genitals of either sex' (Webster's), i.e., 'organ of generation' In Pali, it is rendered as a 'sexual characteristic', 'male as well as female' (2nd meaning in PED). That this sense of 'organ of generation' seems to be intended in # 16 comes to be clear two lines later when the females and males, burning in passion, "indulged in sexual behaviour" (*methunaṃ dhammaṃ paṭiseviṃsu)*.

But is that, or is that all, that the Buddha was seeking to convey, in opting for *linga*? Let us, then, see what terms he has opted out of.

There is first of all the gender-specific term *itthinimitta* meaning 'vagina' or 'vulva' (Ven. Buddhadatta, 1979), in relation to females, and in relation to males '*pullinga'* < *purisalinga*, with the meaning 'membrum virile', 'penis' (PED). Then, there is the term *yoni* in relation to females, with associations of, again among others, 'womb', 'place of birth', etc. (PED). There is again the gender non-specific term *indriya,* as in *itthindriya* / *purisindriya,* "often interpreted as 'organ'" (PED), reminding us of *cakkundriya* 'eye-organ', *sotindriya* 'ear-organ', etc., and understood in the Abhidhamma as *pasādarūpa* 'sensitive matter' (Ven. Bodhi (Ed.), I 8, p. 41). Then there is also the pair *itthatta / purisatta* in the Abhidhamma characterized as the 'material phenomena of sex: femininity and masculinity' (*bhāvarūpa*) (*itthattaṃ purisattaṃ bhāvarūpaṃ nāma*) (Ven. Bodhi (Ed.), VI.3, p. 237).

If what the Buddha wanted to convey was just the meaning 'organ of generation' and nothing more, then there were these other terms as well. Does the fact that he doesn't use any of them, then, tell us that he may be seeking to capture an additional nuance or shade of meaning, too, associated with the term *linga*?

What could this, then, be?

We may begin by noting another meaning of *linga*, in relation to females: 'female quality' (PED, under *itthi*[73]). Then there is the meaning 'characteristic' (as above), and 'sign, attribute, mark, feature' (PED). While the term *indriya* has been noted (above) to have been often 'mistaken' as an organ, *itthindriya* and *purisindriya* are used, "in Buddhist psychological philosophy and Ethics", in the sense of 'womanhood' and 'maleness' respectively, as a '**controlling principle, directive force**' (PED). E.g., they are among twenty two 'controlling principles' (*bāvīsati indriyāni*)[74] that include clearly non-physical items such as *saddhā, sati, upekkhā* etc.[75]. Is it possible then this - is a shade or nuance intended by the Buddha in addition to the physical - that while the Beings had differentiated sex organs, they had no sense of sexuality?

---

73 The other meanings shown alongside it are 'sign of a woman' and 'female sex'.

74 The *Visudhimagga* includes these among the 22 indriya which Ven. Nanamoli (1975, 559 f.) translates as "faculties". Most of the list makes clear that non-material attributes are intended, not organs: "[the function] of the femininity faculty and the masculinity faculty is to allot the modes of the mark, sign, work and ways of women and men." (VM XVI 10).

75 In their complete form, it would be *saddhāindriya, satindriya, upekkhāindriya.*

To understand this, we need only to fall back on our common knowledge. A human being is born with what we call a 'sex organ '. But, functionally speaking, it would only be accurate to call it an 'elimination organ'. Of the two functions of the said organ, it is used, at birth, only for a single function - the urinary And it is only at puberty that the sexual function comes to mature.

In psychoanalytic theory, Freud posits four developmental stages in the child - oral, anal, phallic and oedipal, "relatively fixed in time", "that are determined by the interaction between a person's biological drives and the environment" <http://www.answers.com/topic/psychosexual-development-2#ixzz2lxb4uTdd>. If the preoccupation of the newborn is the gratification of the mouth through suckling, enjoying the taste of milk and other liquids and basically meeting one's nutritional needs, at one year or so, elimination comes to be, in the Freudian analysis, the focus of attention. At the next phallic stage, "the immature penis" comes to be "the libidinal object of infantile sexuality in the male" <http://www.answers.com/topic/phallus#ixzz2lxboE1tP>, *libidinal* meaning "the psychic and emotional energy associated with instinctual biological drives" and the "manifestation of the sexual drive" <http://www.answers.com/ topic/libido#ixzz2lxcjnzRJ>. The same, of course, should be applicable to the female. It is the oedipal stage, then, that marks the full maturation of sexuality.

To understand it all in Abhidhammic terms, let us see how the cognitive process takes place, taking the eye as an example. For the manifestation of eye-consciousness (*cakkhuviññāṇa*) in the mindbody, there are four essential conditions:

1. 'sensitive matter' *(pasādarūpa*), namely the physical eye organ (*cakkhupasādarūpa*);
2. an 'object' (*ārammaṇa*) (e.g., this page);
3. a 'facilitative condition' (*upatthambakapaccaya*)[76] of light; and

[76] Both the English and the Pali terms under no. 3 are of my own concoction to cover the variables given against each sense in the

4. attention (*manasikāra*)[77].

While, of course, *linga* is not a 'sense' organ in the classical sense (such as eye, ear, nose, tongue, body and mind), it can certainly be said to be a *pasādarūpa* 'sensitive matter', in the sense of 'a sensitive physical part of the body' to put it more descriptively. A *pasādarūpa* is explained by Ven. Bodhi (1993, 41) in the following words:

> "Eye-consciousness arises based upon eye-sensitivity (*cakkhupasāda*). Its function is to see, to cognize directly and immediately, the visible object. The other types of sense- consciousness also arise based upon their respective sensitivity, and their function is simply to cognize their respective objects -. sounds, smells, tastes, tangibles."

In that sense, then, we may think of a *lingapasādarūpa* (this writer's term again) '*linga*-sensitivity'. Beginning with puberty, then, there comes to be of the organ *linga*, '*linga*-sensitivity' (condition 1) in relation to the object of sexual desire, namely the opposite sex (condition 2). This is conditioned by the facilitative condition of the availability of a partner (condition 3). Indeed the Buddha points to this in the AS text: "As they were looking at each other for long, passion arose in them..." (# 16). Then, there is also an 'attention' to a maturing sexuality (condtion 4). So only at puberty can it be said, *functionally speaking*, that a human (or animal) has a 'sex organ' or 'generative organ', in the context of "biological drives and the environment" in Freudian terms. That indeed is when the *linga* doubles up both as organ and sexual sensitivity, maturing up to the libidinal and oedipal stages.

Abhidhammatthasangaha - 'light' re the eye, 'space' re the ear, 'air element' (nose), 'water element' (tongue) and 'Earth element' (body) (Ven. Bodhi (Ed., 1993) 151-152).

[77] See Ven. Bodhi (Ed., 1993), IV 4 for details.

Such a stage-wise maturation can be understood in embryonic terms as well. To begin with, the different organs in the fetus come into shape as it grows in the womb, immediately suggesting a chronological order. Any *given* organ is a cluster (*khandha*)[78], made up of composite and complex elements, both in terms of structure and function, including the interconnections between and among the neurons. Not all dimensions of a cluster, i.e., an organ, in the womb, can be said to develop, or function, equally or equally well, or at the same pace or time.

So while the physical organ of *linga* comes to manifest itself in all its *external* features at birth, not all of its cellular and hormonal features come to be in place. Over time, the cellular structure comes to be formed in tandem with the psychological structure in reciprocity, the genitalia eventually doing the intended double duty, the 'eliminating organ' now ending up also as 'sex organ'. This indeed seems to be what is intended by the Buddha, when we read the line, 'passion arose in them (*tesam … sarāgo udapādi*), burning all around entering their bodies (*pariḷāho kāyasmiṃ okkami*)' (# 16). Here we have both the psychological and the physical dimensions, indicative of the maturation of sexuality and the intended double meaning of *linga*.

In Abhidhammic, Freudian and embryonic terms, then, we could say the Buddha was using the term *linga* as a *double entendre*, meaning both in the literal and the nuanced senses of the term.

The Buddha's wording, "The female *linga* appeared in the female, and the male *linga* in the male" (*itthiyā ca itthilingaṃ pāturahosi, purisassa purisalingaṃ*), indeed, then, can be said to speak to these practical and theoretical observations. What they, then, suggest is that while the 'females' and the 'males' (or 'femaleness' and 'maleness') were already there in their full physical armour, it is only at the point in question that sexuality comes to express itself in full force, as a sexual *controlling principle* and *directive force.*

This, of course, is no different from saying, "Menstruation and

---

[78] Cf., the 'five aggregates' (*pañcakkhandha*).

breasts appear in girls upon attaining puberty". The girl was there for puberty to materialize just as the female and the male were there for sexuality to materialize.

Let us then see how our new understanding of the Buddha's nuanced intent in using the term *linga* can help resolve the perceived chronological disconnect of language use preceding the *linga* in females and males.

Take a quick look at the growth of language in the child. Just as a human being is born with both the capacity for sex as well as the 'sex organ', they are also born, not just with the *capacity* for language, this being a species imperative, but 'language organs' as well – mouth with lips, teeth, tongue, palate and uvula, and nasal canal, not to mention the air supply organ, namely the lungs. However, a given language comes to be 'learned' *following* birth[79]. It would be a year or so before mom gets excited about hearing the first sounds of the tiny tot – likely /əm/ or /əmma/[80] or a variation thereof such as /ma/, /mama/, etc. It will be another six years before a child becomes a 'linguistic adult' when she comes to be able to express any and every idea of her own world in full grammatical if simple sentences[81].

So while the inborn capacity for language of a child matures by age six, it will be another four to six years when she menstruates and comes to be sexually energized, i.e., when sexuality comes to be a 'directive force' and 'controlling principle'.

---

[79] There is even the possibility, as some recent research seems to suggest, that the learning of the mothertongue may have begun in the womb itself, with the growing embryo directly privy to the mother's sounds, intonation patterns, semantic nuances, emotions, and so on, in their most rudimentary terms.

[80] This may be regardless of culture, /m/ being the automatic nasal sound produced when the two lips come together and the air naturally flows out of the nasal passage, with /ə/ as the opening resting position of open lips and /a/ the final closing position.

[81] Of course, complex structures, creative uses of language and vocabulary come in due course.

Quick then. Which comes first – language or sexuality? We could simply say, "Of course, (wo)man speaketh before she sexualizeth!" So then, it should no surprise that in the AS, the maturation of speech precedes the maturation of sexuality.

But the claim, it may rightly be objected, is still made from a theoretical point of view, in the context of contemporary homo sapiens. But what about the historical and the evolutionary context where it rightly belongs?

First it may be noted here that it was in the context of his Brahminic audience, Vāseṭṭha and Bhāradvāja, that the Buddha *instructively* opts for the term *linga*. In Brahminic thought, the term refers to the sex organ of Śiva, in the context of *yoni* of his consort (Umā/Pārvatī) (Monier-Williams)[82]. So when *linga* is used first in relation to females, the two youth could be said to have immediately grasped that the Buddha means something both other than a physical limb as well as also an organ. How so?

Instructively, it was said, that the Buddha used the term. While, in AS, as elsewhere[83], the Buddha always refers to female first and then only male, in this context it would have been for an additional reason: to intentionally create cognitive dissonance in the listeners so

[82] "Shiva, the lord of erect Phallus (*urdhvalinga*), is traced to the ithyphallic figure of Indus Valley civilization or to the phallic images found more generally in prehistoric India. The epics and Puranas tell how a great fire appeared from the cosmic waters, and from this flame Linga Shiva emerged to claim supremacy and worship over Brahma and Vishnu, when he was castrated because he seduced sages' wives in the pine forests of Himalayas. He castrated himself because no one could castrate the Supreme Lord. Thus fallen phallus of the Supreme Lord destroyed all the worlds until it reached the Yoni of Uma/Parvati and cooled down. All procreation of worlds started after the worship of Yoni-Linga was restored and all Gods, including Vishnu and Brahma accepted supremacy of Lord Shiva." <http://www.vepachedu. org/linga.htm>.

[83] An example would be *mātāpitaro* 'mother and father' (D III.66), *mātāpitū upaṭṭhānaṃà*, 'attending on mother and father' (*Mahamangala Sutta*, K 1.5).

as to drive home the point. Upon the association of the term *linga* in relation to females first (where by tradition it should have been *yoni*), indeed we can envisage the neurons in Vāseṭṭha and Bhāradvāja firing, immediately giving the insight, 'So it is not in the traditional sense of the term the Blessed One is using it', but immediately realizing, upon hearing it used in relation to both, that it is in the traditional sense, too. We can even envision the Buddha pausing, as is natural in speaking, after saying *itthiyā ca itthilingaṃ pāturahosi,* allowing the two listeners to mull it over, before proceeding to say *purisassa purusalinga,* allowing a return to cognitive 'assonance'.

So the term could be said to have been used instructively, but also because no other term could have done the double duty as effectively as the term *linga* does. None of the terms *nimitta, indriya*, or even the Abhdhammic – *atta* as in *itthatta / purisatta*, *pasādarūpa*, *bhāvarūpa* could be said to capture the double-acting *linga*.

In summary, then, what happens at the critical phase (para # 16) is not the emergence of the physical form of sex p*er se*, but sexuality, in the sense of sexual consciousness or sex-awareness[84], and the attendant feelings of passion, shame and desire for privacy[85].

It may even be possible to consider the remote possibility that the two phases of sex, meaning the physical presence and the psychological presence, if we could call them so, as understood here, may not even refer to the same genre of Being. There was clearly no

---

[84] Again, the embryonic stage allows us an early peak at this evolving life process when even the rudiments of sex organs do not appear until about the fifth week of growth (Gray, 1994, 157), although gender choice, of course, has already been determined at the point of conception.

[85] Another little insight from Ajahn Punnadhammo: "Are we reminded here of the Christian account in Genesis where Adam and Eve come to be suddenly aware of their nakedness after eating the apple? Animals, e.g., dogs who [yes, who, and not that, since in Buddhist thought, they fall into the same pylogenetic class, *sattā*] have no compunction whatsoever about mating in plain sight may help us with the distinction being suggested here."

gender distinction in photonic life[86].

That it is a nuanced sense that is intended by the Buddha also finds some confirmation in the fact that the sex-related psychological change in the text is accompanied by a corresponding body-related physical change: "…taking it to be their food, for a very long stretch of time, to that extent did they become coarser and coarser in their bodies, and the variation in colour (and/or appearance) come to be (further) manifested." (# 16, as also earlier). What it suggests, then, is that the implicit psychological change in females and males comes to be a natural outcome of cellular change as reflected in the changes in the coarseness of the body, co-evolving with a new type of food source and nutrition. So the intended second sense of the Buddha is indeed a 'psychobiological' change as in the Freudian view. And, such a change, of course, doesn't happen overnight either, as a literal *first* reading of the words, "The female sex appeared in the female, …", may suggest. It is after taking their new food, "for a very long stretch of time" that the change takes place, the line repeated twice in the same paragraph, meaning same context.

Just how long is 'a very long stretch of time'?

The evolutionary change which finally ends in the 'directive force' and 'controlling principle' of the sex organs can be said to have taken place over the three phases as in AS, and also in Freudian terms. In the first phase, the concern was on food (oral, but also anal, given that elimination is a fundamental characteristic of all cells), when the Earth savour appears:

> Then, Vāseṭṭha, a certain Being of a greedy nature, wondering 'What exactly will this be?', tasted the Earth-savour….

---

[86] In support, notes Ajahn Punnadhammo, "Even among primates, of relatively recent origin, female and male chimps are hard to tell apart. Even though female and male baboons, also primates, are quite distinct, as are male and female humans, what this suggests is that the morphological differences may not have been pronounced enough to matter in the early phases."

It is the same focus we find in the second evolutionary phase when ground-*pappaṭaka* and *badālatā* appear. And it is in the third phase (libidinal and oedipal[87]) that the focus comes to be on sex.

It is, of course, not that Beings had no limbs in the very first phase; they devour the Earth savour with 'fingers' and 'hands'. Thus it can be conjectured that they had sexual organs as well. This may also be confirmed from the fact that in terms of evolution, non-human life had come to be both asexual and sexual (see Fig. 1). It was, however, in the third phase, to repeat, that sex evolves as a 'controlling principle, directive force'.

This evolution seems to be directly linked to the evolution of the food chain, as in Fig. 3, from a bare 'Earth-savour' to rice. The Buddha seems to indicate the critical nature of this last stage of evolution by way of a detailed description. In the case of the first two phases, the description of each of the food types (Earth savour, ground-*pappaṭaka* and *badālatā*,) comes to be not only brief, but identical, too: "It had colour, smell and taste. The colour was like fine ghee or butter / cream, and they very sweet, like pure clear honey." (# 11, # 14 (twice)). However, when it comes to rice, as if to signify the new evolutionary stage – abundance, wider spread, wider impact and a wider condition for the co-evolution of, among others, sexual life, we have a detailed description:

> # 16. Then, Vāseṭṭha, when the creeper had disappeared, there appeared for those Beings rice, fully grown without stalks, free from a coating of red powder and free from chaff, sweet-smelling and ready to be eaten. Whatever the amount they gathered in the evening for their evening meal had come to grow back ripe, against all [seeming] odds, by the morning. Whatever the amount they had gathered in the morning for their evening meal had come to grow back ripe against all [seeming] odds by the evening, there

[87] Here, of course, without necessarily implying all the associations of the oedipus complex.

appearing no cultivation (obstacle?).

The Buddha seems to be here cleverly making symbolic use of language, as a creative writer would[88], to reflect the changing reality. It would be natural that there would be only a few Beings at first, namely during the first phase. These were the Ābhassara Beings who had come from the Brahma world. Almost by definition, it is only the very few – the spiritually evolved ones, from among the human population of the earlier cycle that would have ended up in the Brahma world. Even out of them, only a few can be said to have come back to the Earth during the harsh conditions of the opening phase – others still continuing to be in the Brahma world, their life-span and merit-span yet to mature. However, as the environmental conditions come to be more sentient–friendly, an increase in the population can be expected. It may also be conjectured that good times could have provided the conditions for *new* 'beings'[89], to be 'spontaneously' born, co-evolving with the friendly natural environment. Whatever the explanation of origins, there is no doubt that the sparse population of the first two phases come to be transformed into an increasingly denser population. So it is that the first two sparse phases come to be given a terse single liner, with the increasing population getting a more robust, right royal linguistic treatment. Should we, incidentally, see a symbolism in the single sentence expanding into several lines - being reflective of the process of expansion, i.e., namely evolution?[90]

Our exploration above on the basis of theory, text, evolution, language usage and communication, then, hopefully resolves the

---

[88] In Indian esthetics, this is called *vyangya*, meaning "that which is manifested or indicated or made perceptible..; (in rhet.) indicated by allusion or insinuation, implied, suggestive" (Monier-Williams).

[89] A lower case is used here to suggest that the reference is *not* to the spiritually higher Ābhassara Beings (who, it may be noted was also characterized as being 'spontaneously' born' (as above). See later '*Navaka sattā*'.

[90] See also the discussion around Fig. 3 for how the language could be said to have evolved.

seeming paradox of *linga* showing up at the textual podium after *lingua*! If we may understand 'lingua' here as meaning "a tongue or organ resembling a tongue" (Webster's), it needs to be noted that each of *linga* and *lingua,* as structure, also stand for function.

7

Going Traditional: Ābhassara Beings Finding a Footing on Earth

The writer has thus far doggedly stuck, apologies, to the position that AS # 10-16 is unmistakably a treatment of the cosmic cycle by the Buddha, and that the Ābhassara Being is nothing but a primordial photon-type. The stance seeking to look at it purely in relation to Westernscience can be explained as an attempt to make sense of # 10 – 16 which seems to have eluded scholars of Buddhism. It is hoped that, after our lengthy treatment, that comparative stance is no longer in question.

Having hopefully made the breakthrough, this writer is, nonetheless, not unwilling to now concede validity to the interpretation of the Ābhassara Being, as by Walshe, Collins and Gombrich, *in relation to the Ābhassara Brahma world*. While this has been hinted at above, the writer now seeks to incorporate the traditional interpretation with the Western Scientific, with some help from the Abhidhamma. This, of course, is not to abandon the position of the study in favour of the traditional. Rather, it is to bring the two together, benefiting from both, hopefully allowing us, again, to see the benefits of cross-disciplinary research.

We begin with our earlier interpretation of an Ābhassara Being being a primordial photon-type, its characterization of being 'self-luminous' allowing for this. This means that it is, as noted, a form of matter, out there in free space, and moving in the sky. If that is the physical characterization, we are also told, however, that it is mind-based and feeds on rapture. This means that in its mental manifestation, it is a conscious being, i.e., with consciousness, as of course, captured in the Buddha's label *Ābhassara sattā* 'Ābhassara sentient being'. Having 'consciousness', of course, is to be conscious of something. So it is the body that consciousness can be said to be conscious of[91]. To put it in a lighter vein, it means, no matter no mind, no mind no matter, no matter which way you look at it!

The question then is how this celestial (used in its literal sense) form of matter has come to entail non-matter, namely, consciousness. This, of course, is where the Abhidhamma explanation proves instructive.

In the Abhidhamma analysis, humans who have cultivated the mind to the extent of experiencing the second *jhāna* come to be reborn, at the break up of the body following death, in the Ābhassara Brahma Realm (see Ven. Bodhi (Gen.Ed.), pp. 186-187). This, clearly, can hardly be in human form. 'Matter' or form, in human life comes to include external manifestation of not just eyes, ears, etc., the five senses, but also arms and legs and sex organs. However, being born into the Ābhassara Brahma Realm (literally, 'world of form' (*rūpaloka*)) means giving up all this. Living up in the air, free floating (*antalikkhacarā*), doesn't allow for the weight of any external baggage, namely, hanging limbs. It is thus that they can be said to settle for the comfort of being a photon, or cluster of photons, of different degrees of lustrousness[92], or some other form of energy.

---

[91] Here we have in mind the Conditioned Co-origination formula, 'conditioned by consciousness is mindbody; conditioned by mindbody is consciousness' (*viññāṇapaccayā nāmarūpa; nāmarūpapaccayā viññāṇa*). Here, *viññāṇa* is be understood as a sub-set of *nāma*- in *nāmarūpa,* one of the mind trio, the other two being *mano* and *citta.*

[92] It would be worth noting how Brahma beings are characterized as being of lesser or more lustre in relation to others (D 18, Janavasabha Sutta).

So it is this externally limbless being that we understand to be the Ābhassara Being as characterized by the Buddha.

Lost its physical attributes may be, but the mental attributes of an Ābhassara Being can be said to be intact, healthy and vibrant. Sentience comes to be characterized by the Buddha as being of the three thirsts – sense-thirst, thirst-to-be and thirst-to-be-not (*kāma-, bhava-, vibhava- taṇhā* respectively). But an Ābhassara Being, by definition freed from of the first thirst, can still be said to be of the other two.

Reborn in the Ābhassara Brahma Realm means arriving at (more accurately, experiencing), the second *jhāna* level during the preceding human existence. But only. Bent on liberation, the Being can be said to now thirst for the next and next levels. It may be a natural, understandable and worthy a desire for a carpenter at the second rung of a ladder to want to get to the next and the next and next rungs, in order to be able to work on the roof. Yet, for the spiritual seeker, in the liberative context of the *jhāna* ladder, wanting to be at the next level of 'being of form' (*rūpabhāva*) constitutes a fetter (*saṃyojana*), a samsaric pull factor. That is to say, achieving the higher *jhāna* levels calls for continued existence, or what may be characterized as a thirst-to-be (*bhava taṇhā*).

However, this thirst-to-be is not simply to continue to live in the Ābhassara Brahma Realm, but to be re-born, more accurately, re-become[93], into a human life, for in a human existence only can one actively work oneself up *jhānically*, if a coinage may be pardoned. But the necessary condition for getting reborn in a human realm is to die out of the celestial realm. Dormant it may be while alive, in the Ābhassara realm or the human realm, but there is no gainsaying that wanting to die remains a thirst - the thirst-to-be-not (*vibhava taṇhā*). The thirst-to-re-become, by definition, then, can then be said to piggy-back on thirst-to-be-not.

The Ābhassara Brahma Realm may be out of harm's way of the

---

[93] The Buddha's term is *punabbhava*, and never **punaruppatti*.

fury of fire of the Devolutionary heat of the Seven Suns. However, it can be said that the Ābhassara Beings are nevertheless burning from the fires of the double-thirst, with apologies for the contrary imagery, and for that reason, 'thirst' may be replaced in translation with 'attachment'. And it is this double thirst, with the thirst-to-be-not as the proximate cause, then, that can be said to prompt an Ābhassara Being to 'come into the present state' (# 10), leaving their Ābhassara body (*ābhassara kāyā cavitvā*), at the expiry of the life-span and merit-span.

Being reborn in a human world may be the condition for a continuing liberation thrust for the Ābhassara Beings. Yet, there is no longer a human world to be born into! The conditions conducive to human survival no longer exist either, both human world and conditions destroyed in the Devolutionary phase-terminating fire. So now it is not a question of a Being looking for a new (if also the past) home. It is that the Being is faced with the colossal, and unimaginably long, task of building up itself, i.e., evolving, eventually, into a human being, even as an environment conducive to human life (water and Earth as in AS) continues to evolve in the very same process. That is to say that the Beings themselves have to be the contributing architects and builders in a co-evolutionary process. A classic case of this in Westernscienceis the embryonic growth, beginning with mitosis (division) of the first cell into two, four, etc., a cluster eventually coming together to form a nose, eye, hair, etc.

What may be envisaged, then, is that a surviving Ābhassara Being, serving its time in the Ābhassara Brahma Realm, comes to somehow, *kadāci karahaci,* make the trip from way up 'there' in the Ābhassara Brahma World to be close to where Earth would evolve. And it is this primordial Being, then, that is introduced to us by the Buddha.

Westernsciencehas long battled with the notion of 'spontanoeous generation' (see again Ponnamperuma, 1972, 13ff.). While it eventually comes to be rejected as an explanation of the origin of life, it is precisely of a 'spontaneous generation' (*opapātika*) that the Ābhassara Beings can be said to come to be. Only, the term is not understood by the Buddha as a 'first' generation. It may be said to be of spontaneous generation simply by exclusion - since it is not born of parents (*mātāpettika*), i.e., not 'water-born' (as in our translation of *jalābuja*) or egg-born (*aṇḍaja*) or 'moisture-born' (*saṃsedaja*).

Having introduced to us the Being up in the sky, the Buddha seeks to explain how the rudimentary form of life works its way, over billions of years, into the eventual human beings, passing through the phases of water, amphibious life (as suggested in this study, and in keeping with the Darwinian theory as well) and land life. The process ends with the once-upon-a-time Ābhassara Beings ending up as humans with sexual maturation.

If this means a change from asexual birth to sexual reproduction, it also means the emergence of a human population, the context which would allow a once-upon-a-time Ābhassara Being to fulfill its ambition of continuing to cultivate oneself towards the higher *jhānas* towards liberation, in this very life time or over time through several rebirths.

8

A Seeming Spiritual P̲aradox? *Kāma-taṇhā*-jettisoned Ābhassara Beings Engage in Sex!

Our title could well have been a steaming headliner in a Brahminic tabloid of ancient India! It would be even today. But the question appears to be prompted by the text of AS itself. Here is what we first encounter:

> Then, Vāseṭṭha, a certain Being of a greedy nature, wondering 'What exactly will this be?', tasted the Earth-savour with its finger. As it tasted the Earth-savour with its finger, it was pleased, and ***craving came upon it***. (*taṇhā ca tesaṃ okkami*) (# 12).

We also note the beginnings of *mamaṃkāra, ahaṃkāra* 'I-ness' in sentient beings, another dimension of 'ignorance' (*moha*) behind the thirsts:

> Now some Beings came to be good-looking, others ugly. Those who were good-looking despised those who were ugly: "We are better-looking than they are; they are uglier than us!" [Beings coming to be] class-conscious to a fault and conditioned by their colour-pride, the savoury-Earth came to disappear (# 13).

Then, at the end of the Section under discussion in this study, we read,

> The female *linga* appeared in the female, and the male *linga* in the male. The female looked at the male just so long as did the male at the female. Looking at each other for long, passion arose in them, burning all round entering their bodies (*pariḷāho kāyasmiṃ okkami*). Because of this burning, they indulged in sexual behaviour (# 16).

It may be remembered that the Buddha's account begins with Ābhassara Beings transferring over from a Devolutionary to an Evolutionary phase (both in the initial para # 10). So here, then, we seem to have, by association, Ābhassara Beings, who, by definition, are freed of the sense thirsts (*kāma taṇhā*), ending up, billions of years later as it may be, in sexual relations, steeped in passion (*rāga*), a specialized and deepened version of it, the burning so intense that it envelops the Beings all round.

But is this not contradictory? If 'sense thirst' has been jettisoned, how could this be?

8.1 Ābhassara Beings: a Heretical View

One way of resolving the impasse is to take another look at the phrase 'having passed away from their Ābhassara bodies' (# 10). While it may be seen to be just a matter of the Buddha talking about the move from the Devolutionary to the Evolutionary phase, it may also suggest a spiritual 'fall' in the sense that 'passing away' from the Ābhassara body may also entail a 'passing away' from the spiritual status, given the necessary relationship between mind and body. But, could the downgrading of spiritual attainement be that automatic?

So another way is to consider the possibility that the path to liberation for Brahma world expatriates is via, heresy here alright, a *temporary* foothold in *kāma taṇhā* without which there could not have been human life! Even though *kāma taṇhā* comes to be exterminated, the Ābhassara Beings, as noted, are not free of the 'thirst to be' (*bhava taṇhā*). There thus remains the possibility of *traces* or *strands* of *kāma taṇhā*, infinitesimal as it may be, continuing in the *bhava taṇhā*, given the neuronal interconnections in the primordial parallel of the central nervous system between and among the two varieties of thirst[94]. Such a change may indeed be implicit in the lines in the text to the effect that the Beings, "having passed away from their Ābhassara bodies and come into their present state" (*ābhassara kāyā cavitvā itthattam āgacchanti*).

But there is a stronger reason – inheriting it from the parents[95] who by definition would be in the full heat of *kāma taṇhā* (pun not unintended). Evolving back into humanness, then, may mean sense thirst coming to be 'resuscitated', if only temporarily, and enough to allow for survival in human life, accompanied by new cellular growth.

However, during a given new lifetime, in an 'era of a Buddha's birth' (*buddhuppāda* (J I.59)), one may take to the spiritual practice of meditation and mind cultivation such that the habitual and in-built spiritual strengths gained in the pre-Ābhassara lifetime(s), locked in the mindbody, again in terms of cells, DNA, etc., come to gather spiritual momentum, now underdeveloping[96] the parent-inherited

---

[94] In humans, and other mammals, it is the central nervous system, through its neuronal interconnections, that keep the system going. Even though at the earliest phase that we are talking about, there may not be a 'central nervous system' *per se* of the complexity that comes to be evolved over time, it could be reasonably conjectured that the *seeds* of such a system, by whatever name it is called, needs to be present in earlier organisms, too. An acorn tree can come out of only an acorn seed. Hence the qualification 'primordial'.

[95] While, of course, the 'devolving Ābhassara Being' begins the life process as a photon, over time, it would have to evolve into (egg-born and) womb-born Beings in order to have life as a human being. See next for a more detailed treatment.

[96] The term 'underdevelop' is introduced by Frank (1966) to explain the process of how the income divide comes to widen as the poor (individuals, cities, countries) becoming poorer *in the very same process* as the rich getting richer.

sense thirst or one's own nanoscopic remnants captured in the 'thirst to be'[97].

Of course, this process, as noted, takes place over billions of years. AS begins with the Devolutionary phase, immediately changing over to the Evolutionary phase when the Ābhassara Being comes to be in the present life. To recap, then, while it is 'all water' at this time, next the Earth spreads over it. Now each of these transitions, it may be noted, comes to be associated with two key characteristics: first, the status quo continuing 'for a very long stretch of time', which then, coming to be followed by 'the passage of a long time beyond' (# 10; # 11). Thus 'devolving Ābhassara Beings' remain in that original state 'for a very long stretch of time', and then, 'after the passage of a long time beyond' (# 10), they come to be in 'the present state' when 'this world evolves again'. Again, they remain in the present state 'for a very long stretch of time' (# 10), when 'after the passage of a long time beyond' appears the Earth (# 11).

We may recall here the evolutionary time, as in Fig. 2, as follows:

Devolution 13.5 + billion years ago (bya) (# 10);
Evolution 13.5 - billion years ago (bya) (# 10);
Earth 4.55 billion years ago (bya) (# 11);
Anatomically modern humans 150 thousand years ago (**k**ya) (# 12).

Since Evolution comes to be mentioned in the same breath, namely, in the same paragraph just a line later, it appears that the Buddha is suggesting one period following the next almost upon its heels, so to speak. Thus we show the time of Evolution simply as 13.5 – bya. However it is in the next para that there comes to be mention of all being water and the Earth appearing, which in Westernscienceis shown to be 4.55 bya. Anatomically modern humans, as noted, are almost a blip in the time horizon, a mere 150,000 years ago.

[97] See next section for examples of such a maturation of an existing potential.

What all this leads to is that it is not before an evolutionary period of over 9 to 13 billion years that the 'Being of a greedy nature' (# 11) who tastes the Earth savour appears. What such a long time gap in turn suggests is that the original Ābhassara Beings have had many a life time, evolving from being 'spontaneous-born' to 'egg-born' to 'womb-born'. And so it is possible that over this long stretch of time, many a cellular change has taken place in the Ābhassara Beings. Thus it may be conjectured that in the two thirsts remaining ('to be' and 'to be not') may have begun to generate certain tendencies that would be species-friendly. And in this process, sense thirst could have come to co-evolve, if in nano but sure steps. This perhaps, then, explains 'a certain greedy being' – no, we won't mention names, shall we now!, in whom craving appeared (# 12). Beings having sexual intercourse can, then, be seen as the culmination of this process.

If this appears to take us into the fantasy domain, we may think of the *sotāpanna* 'streamwinner' and once-returner (*sakadāgāmin*). By definition back on Earth, possibly from Tusita heaven, fully limbed, and living in a family setting with conjugal relationships, a *sotāpanna* comes to be prone towards spiritual practice *eventually*, which then takes one to the next levels of Non-returner (*anāgāmin*) and / or Arahant. Only, while this entails a mere single lifetime, the scenario of an Ābhassara Being entails a few billion years, caught in the nexus of cyclical change!

8.2 Two Types of Ābhassara Beings

While all this may, then, appear to be a paradoxical case of the Brahmaloka wayfarers having a spiritual retrogression[98], we can say, with Canonical authority, that *it need not be*. We only have to consider that there are two types of humans who become Ābhassara Beings,

---

[98] While not put in these words, or explicitly so stated, the understanding in every study of AS, as far as the writer can tell, is that it is the same Ābhassara Being that is encountered in # 10 that also has sex in # 16.

this through the attainment to the 2nd *jhāna*: 'worldlings' (*puthujjana*) and 'Blessed One's disciples' (*bhagavato pana sāvako*), i.e., *ariya sāvakas.* Each type, for sure, upon passing away from the human world, comes to be "reborn in companionship with the devas of streaming radiance" i.e., in the Ābhassara Brahmaloka. But the end of life in the Brahmaloka at the end of the life-span brings contrasting results for the two types. A Disciple "attains final *Nibbāna* in that very same state of existence" (*tasmiṃyeva bhave parinibbāyati*). But in the case of a worldling, one goes to a lower realm[99] (A II 123), even though this may not be immediately (Ven. Bodhi, Tr., 2012, 1698, footnote 809). That is to say that *jhanic* states of the worldlings are by their very nature, temporary and reversible[100], unlike the path and fruit of the Ariyan stages which produce a permanent, irreversible change in the depth of the being.

What this suggests, then, is that the Ābhassara Beings showing up in the sky following the Devolutionary phase are of necessity and by definition not of the Buddha Disciple type, but of the *puthujjana* type in whose minds "lust invades" (A III 395).

It is thus that we can boldly proclaim that there is, then, no

---

[99] Interestingly, one is said to go "to hell, to the animal realm or to the sphere of afflicted spirits". Though a human rebirth is not mentioned in this context, there is no reason it should be ruled out.

[100] Alāra Kālāma and Uddaka Rāmaputra, the two teachers Samana Gotama, the future Buddha, goes to after leaving the household life, may serve as good historical examples. Practicing meditation under them, he attains to the level of 'nothingness' (*ākincaññāyatana*) under the first teacher and 'neither perception nor non-perception' (*nevasaaññānāññāyatana*) under the second, both higher than the 2nd *jhāna* (*viññānañcāyatana*). Himself reaching the peaks that each of them had come to experience, he leaves since the practice does not lead to the elimination of *dukkha*. This means that while each of the two teachers would have been reborn in the Brahmaloka, they would still be born again into human life eventually since they were not yet on the Ariyan path, namely, a life of *sīla* of the type as under the Buddha.

paradox indeed as headlined in our imaginary tabloid!

8.3 'Beings Reckoned Just as Beings' as New Strand of Sentience

While we could thus put an end to, once and for all, the gossip prompted by the tabloid headline, another look at the AS text may prompt an additional explanation, providing additional confirmation that there is indeed no paradox. Although the gradual evolution entailing the 13 + billion years comes be taken, by association, as relating to Ābhassara Beings, the Beings in which the dramatic, and drastic, changes are seen to take place, *may, in fact,* ***not*** *be* the Ābhassara Beings at all!

As the environmental conditions come to be more sentient being–friendly, an increase in the population could be conjectured, the emerging 'good times' of the availability of food, providing the conditions for more and more 'beings' (now with a lower case suggesting the reference is not to the spiritually higher Ābhassara Beings) to emerge to beef up the population. So we may envisage a brand *new* and a *distinct* strand of 'beings', ***Navaka sattā***, 'nouveaux beings' if we could so label them. These, like the Ābhassara Beings, can themselves said to be also *'spontaneously'* born, but in the *Evolutionary* phase as distinct from the Devolutionary phase in which the Ābhassara Beings came to be, gradually co-evolving with the increasingly friendly natural environment. In Westernscientificlanguage, it may be called a 'biological morphogenesis' (Sheldrake, 1990, 86), 'morphogenesis' meaning 'coming into existence of a form' (82) (more of it later), and in the present case, a biological form, *sattā* by definition entailing consciousness.

It is interesting to note that the Abhidhamma term for 'the material phenomena of sex' is *bhāvarupa*[101], literally, 'becoming form' (*bhāva* < *bhava* < *bhū*- 'to become' (PED)). The implication, of course, is that of the four types of life origination – spontaneous,

---

[101] See Ven. Bodhi (Gen. Ed.), 1993, 237.

moisture-born, egg-born and womb-born, the last may be considered the latest in the evolutionary ladder. So the new beings could well belong to this new evolutionary strand, beginning at this early stage with a spontaneous (*opapātika*) birth. Over time, to entertain a speculation, they may well be joined by 'moisture-born' (*saṃsedaja*) ones, evolving possibly into animals first, and then re-becoming as humans.

The process outlined above would be applicable, regardless of whether it is the Ābhassara Being strand or the *Navaka sattā* strand. Indeed, it could well be both.

But one may object that this suggests a 'beginning', when the Buddha seems to be saying otherwise. "Bhikkhus, no beginning of this samsara is to be seen. A first point is not discerned of beings roaming and wondering on hindered by ignorance" (*anamataggoyaṃ, bhikkhave, saṃsāro. pubbā koṭi* ***na paññāyati*** *avijjānīvaraṇānaṃ sattānaṃ...*) (S 2, 178) (bold added). But that does not necessarily mean that there is no origin. We have in AS the use of the same phrase *na paññāyanti* (not known) in relation to the Moon and the Sun, the Constellations, etc. (# 11). We have understood it as meaning not that they are not there but that they are covered by a dense atmosphere, and hence invisible (from the Earth below). By extension, then, we may say that it is not that the Buddha is saying that there is no beginning to life in a new Evolutionary phase, but that it simply can't be seen. As well, the 'beginning' in this Evolutionary phase may not be the 'beginning' of samsara of a given being in any case.

But does the text allows for such a plausibility of a *Navaka sattā*?

While the story in AS begins with Ābhassara Beings from a Devolutionary phase ending up in the Evolutionary phase, the next reference is to the time when it is 'all water' (# 11). Here, interestingly, it is said that ***'beings are just reckoned as beings'*** *(sattā sattā tv'eva sankhyaṃ gacchanti*). But why would the Buddha take the trouble to add this if by them are meant the *Ābhassara* Beings themselves? Wouldn't that constitute 'information noise'? That is hardly likely for the precise language user that the Buddha is. The introduction of this line by the Buddha can then be taken as some evidence that it is a distinct strain of beings that the Buddha is now talking about.

If the reference, then, to a 'certain being of greedy nature' (# 12) is to a *Navaka sattā*, there is again no paradox as in the tabloid headline – sense-thrist freed Ābhassara Beings having sex.

However, to strike a contrary strain, is it possible that in adding the line "beings reckoned just as beings" (# 11), the Buddha is merely seeking to indicate that there was in them no sexual differentiation[102]. This seems to be strengthened by the preceding line that there were no "females and males". And so, the addition may also be by way of 'foreshadowing', as in contemporary literary theory, but with the added element of contrast. In this interpretation, the line may be seen to serve as a contrast to the sexual beings that appear later. The interpretation is thus certainly plausible, again encouraging the understanding of the Beings as relating to the non-disciple Ābhassara Beings.

Our discussion, then, can be said to establish that there is indeed no paradox regarding the Beings that eventually engage in sex, taken as the non-Ariyan type Ābhassara Beings, having had a spiritual fall coming into the present state or our own intuited hypothesis of the brand new strain, *Navaka sattā*.

8.4 Why Introduce Ābhassara Beings?

If now the seeming quandary of sense-thirst-jettisoned Beings behaving like ordinary, unevolved, 'beings' has been hopefully resolved, we may still ask, "But why introduce Ābhassara Beings in the first place"? Why not begin with the average being?

The simple answer should be evident. None survived in the blaze of the seven suns!

If that is the first theoretical reason, we may also surmise that it is to allow the Buddha to introduce the very process of Evolution, hinting it to be cyclical. By first introducing the Devolutionary

[102] This again is as suggested by Ajahn Punnadhammo.

phase and then moving into the Evolutionary phases, the Buddha slashes any ideas of a theistic first beginning, as e.g., entailed in the Big Bang theory today, but in his own times, the idea of creation by Brahman in Vedism, as also implicit in the claims of Brahmins that Vāseṭṭha and Bhāradvāja encounter, as introduced at the beginning of the Discourse (# 3 of AS). It is thus to set the ball rolling of the evolutionary process that the Buddha can be said to have started with the Ābhassara Beings.

Ābhassara Beings also help introduce the idea of the presence of life, primordial as it may be, in preparation for introducing the later beings, of the same or a different strain as above, in the Evolutionary process. For, in addition to whatever else, a critical point in AS is to eventually show the presence, and the nature, of human life in the social context (see 'Brief Outline (Section 2). Had there been no reference to a form of life in the *persona* of Ābhassara Beings in the Devolutionary phase, a 'greedy being' in the Evolutionary phase would come across as being out of the blues, mythological and unnatural. Once the ball of the Evolutionary process had been set rolling, the Buddha could then be seen to introduce the heroes of the new phase, indeed the main characters for the rest of the drama.

So it is to cover all these bases, then, that the Buddha can be said to have begun with Ābhassara Beings.

8.5 Ride on a Straw Horse!

It is hoped, then, that our characterization has made a small beginning in filling the gaps of the broader outline provided by the Buddha in # 10 to 16. If the title of this Section, 'A Seeming Spiritual Paradox? *Kāma-taṇhā*-jettisoned Ābhassara Beings Engage in Sex!' may appear to be a straw horse, we hope that the horse will have, before being burned down, helped us gallop through an evolutionary maze of 13 + billion years.

9

Finding a Footing on Earth Revisited in Relation to Westernscience

The last section began with a look at how the Ābhassara Beings found a footing on Earth. But curiosity remains as to how these primordial Beings, be it Ābhassara Beings or *Navaka sattā*, eventually end up as human beings. So we turn to Westernscienceagain where we find some resonance in the idea of 'evolutionary creativity' and 'formative causation' advanced by Sheldrake[103]:

> The cosmic evolutionary process has a direction, an arrow of time[104]. This arrow ultimately depends on the expansive impulse inherent in the cosmos .... But because the growth of the universe has been accompanicd by the development within it of fields, particles, atoms, galaxies, stars, planets, molecules, crystals, and biological life, the arrow of time has a cumulative, developmental quality as well. ... According to the hypothesis of formative causation [see below], each new pattern of organization – of a molecule, say, or a galaxy, .. or a fern, or an instinct, involve the

[103] The following discussion, then, is basically based on his ideas.

[104] It is of interest to note Sheldrake's use of the term 'arrow', in the context of our own characterization of the Ābhassara Beings as 'hither-bound shining arrow'. The idea of 'coming into the present state', of course, equally applies to any other beings, such as the *Navaka sattā*, being born 'spontaneously' also resulting in a 'present state'.

appearance of a new kind of morphic field."
Sheldrake, 1990, 162-163.

By a 'morphic field'[105] is understood a 'pattern of force'[106] relating to a self-organizing system. A biological form, as is the *Navaka sattā*, or and Ābhassara Being, by definition constituted of a mind and body (*nāmarūpa*), is a *system* precisely because the two components are interactive, with each having no separate existence except in relation to the other. It is also self-organizing, as in the Buddha's Teaching of 'asoulity'[107] (*anattā*) – action without an actor. The *Navaka sattā* can then be said to constitute a novel morphic field making its appearance in the Evolutionary phase, following upon Ābhassara Beings, as if modeling after them in the natural evolutionary process.

Sheldrake explains this self-organizing process in terms of 'formative causation'[108]. But the Buddha's Theory of Conditioned Co-origination can be said to explain the concept more comprehensively,

---

[105] The concept of 'field' has been introduced by Faraday (Sheldrake, 66), and relates to all phenomena. Further, "fields, together with energy, have become the basis of physical reality". "All nature is now thought to consist of fields and energy" (Sheldrake 70).

[106] A 'pattern of forces' is "exemplified by the lines of force around a magnet" (Sheldrake, 67).
[107] Sugunasiri, 2011.

[108] The hypothesis of 'formative causation' was first proposed by Sheldrake in his 1981 study, *A New Science of Life* (1990, 88): "[S]elf-organizing systems at all levels of complexity, including molecules, crystals, cells, tissues, organisms and societies of organisms are organized by fields called 'morphic fields'. Morphogenetic fields are just one type of morphic fields, those concerned with the development and maintenance of the bodies of organisms." Although he sees 'formative causation' taking place in "abnormal organisms", in a process called 'evolutionary iteration', giving the example, "as when human babies are sometimes born with tails". But there is nothing to say that it cannot relate to a wider context.

since self-organizing is not a matter of just the coming together of conditions but the conditions *interacting* with each other, as well captured in the concept of 'co-' (*sam-*) in *samuppāda* of *paṭiccasamuppāda* (translated by this writer as 'Conditioned **Co**-origination' for that reason)[109].

"The cosmos is like a growing organism" (Sheldrake, 101). An 'intuitive attraction' of "the modern story (of evolution)" is "its affirmation of creativity in the universe" (101). This relates to not only "the universe itself in terms of atoms, galaxies, stars, etc."; it equally relates to "biological evolution" (100-101) as well. *Navaka sattā* again fits the description of 'creativity in the universe' since it is, by definition, new (*navaka*) and biological (*sattā*).

But this biological evolution "may not be a matter of material genes, but of **habits** inherited non-materially" (bold added) - "evolutionary plagiarism" as he calls it (113)! The inherited habits that "reappear spontaneously...", an example of 'morphic resonance', may be of ancestral species, even of those extinct for millions of years (112).

As a western scientist, Sheldrake's characterization relates to the "new born universe" (100), the Big Bang being the "primal orgasm" (101). This, of course, is the context of the Ābhassara Beings, but remembering that the Big Bang is, from the Buddhian perspective, the *end* of the Devolutionary phase (see above, Section 5). *Navaka sattā* appear in the Evolutionary phase, following billions of years, and in another phase of evolution. So we may say that the *Navaka sattā* may be seen as a 'case study' of what Sheldrake calls a 'spontaneous variation' (113), creatively emerging, taking ('plagiarizing') life elements from the previous Evolutionary phase preceding the current, and even preceding the preceding Devolutionary phase.

To continue to relate the above to the *Navaka sattā*., then, we may say that during the Devolutionary phase at the end of the earlier Evolutionary phase when the burning suns put an end to all human life, the two to three hundred billion cells of each human being[110]

---

[109] See also Section 14.1.2 for an elaboration.

[110] Although this could also include the other type of *sattā* 'sentient

escaped into the 'thin air' so to speak, and continued to exist. But this continuing to exist may not be simply in terms of a zillion individual cells, in some material form, but more than likely in some form of 'memory' in an 'informational field'.

But such 'memory', of course, would not be in any physical form (*pasādarūpa*) to begin with - hands dangling, legs kicks, tongues licking, minds ticking away thinking. It is rather that the different aspects of the mindbody will continue in the form of habits, or what we may call *nāmaness* (or 'nameness'), but also *rūpaness* (or 'formness') (*nāmatta* and *rūpatta*, to coin two terms), of some nano level, given that there could no 'name' (*nāma* 'consciousness') except in relation to 'form'. In this connection, it may well be to remember that an Ābhassara Being is characterized by the Buddha as being mind-based (# 10). A 'being' itself by definition, *Navaka sattā* can then be said to be mind-based as well. If that is its nameness, it also, of course, has a formness.

If the 'royal highnesses' of 'eyeness' and 'bodyness' are the ambassadors of formness, and 'mindness' the ambassador of nameness, there are also their hangars-on, or what the Buddha characterizes as *lakkhana* 'characteristics'. These are 'passionness' (*rāga*), and the triple 'thirstness' (*taṇhā*) – 'sense-, 'to be', 'to be not'. Since 'name', again, can't have an existence without 'form' (as of course, vice versa), these habits needing a physical home, they could still be understood as 'clusters' in the same Buddhian sense as 'aggregate' (*khandha*) as in the 'five aggregates' (*pañcakkhandha*). That is to say that they exist as form, sensation, perception, forces and consciousness[111], even though, of course, at the nanoest of the nanoest primordal level.

The mindbody constituents of the victims of the scorching sun can

being', namely, animals, we shall limit our reference to humans for the obvious reason that the beings in AS eventually end up as human beings of the homo sapiens type.

[111] In Pali, *rūpa vedanā saññā samkhāra viññāṇa.*

all be, then, said to continue to exist in some nano form somewhere in the universe, waiting their time out to show up and reclaim its territory in a next Evolutionary phase. Noting that "The conventional explanation of evolutionary creativity is in terms of random genetic mutation followed by natural selection", Sheldrake (115) opines that, "this is more a dogmatic assertion than an established scientific fact. Some kinds of mutations are purposive."[112] Of course, the 'thirst to be' can only be, by definition, purposive, the 'thirst to be not' in tow. And 'sense thirst', if also 'passion', the handmaids of the 'thirst to be' and the 'thirst to be not', in turn, would be purposive as well.

If this sounds like a backhanded way of introducing teleological intent of a 'soul' in action, we only have to remember that there are other characteristics of each of the 'nesses' that had marked them in their earlier life: non-continuity, i.e., change (*anicca*), suffering (*dukkha*) and asoulity (*anattā*). This then tells us that her highness the eyeness will not cast the same glance from one moment to another, but will have changed in its three stages – arising, staying put and breaking up[113]. So if there is telelogical intent, it comes to be cut down to size, if not rendered weak.

In this connection, we also happily read in Sheldrake (113),

> If mutant organisms which have picked up some of the developmental or behavioural habits of other species are favoured by natural selection, these features will become habitual by repetition, and will become a *normal* aspect of this new kind of organism (italics added).

---

[112] An example of such purposive behaviour is given: "When starving bacteria are in the presence of a sugar they are constitutionally unable to use, genetic mutations occur at frequencies far above chance levels to give the bacteria particular enzymes they need, just when they need them" (Sheldrake, 115).

[113] In Pali, *uppāda, ṭhiti, bhanga.*

Indeed, "Such unconscious borrowing may have played an important part in the evolutionary process" (113). So the *Navaka sattā* could be said to grow in numbers as the unconscious borrowing from earlier Evolutionary phases turn into habits, both borrowings and habits perpetuating themselves. Given the cyclical nature of the universe in the Buddha's understanding, then, it is that the 'nesses' come, as noted, from not just the Evolutionary phase just preceding the Devolutionary phase, but from even before, in any one of the earlier and earlier evolutionary cycles as well.

What we now have basically is the *Navaka sattā* itself being a party to its own evolution. Well, what else is new? This is as also, as noted, in embryonic growth. While a given life form begins with a single cell in the mother's womb, it multiplies through mitosis, in due course clustering towards eventually forming into full-fledged organs such as brain, nose, reproductive limbs, etc., participating in its own growth.

At a more mundane level, we may understand this personal involvement in one's own growth in relation to the classroom experience. A student first decides to walk to the class, takes a seat and listens to the Professor. Participation in learning (Pil) 1. She may also have had some prior reading, or attended a prior lecture on a related topic (Pil 2). She is already a psychologically willing recipient of new information (Pil 3). Now she listens as the Professor delivers the lecture (Pil 4) and may take down an occasional note (5). As the encoded information by the Professor is decoded by the student (6), the information interacts with whatever information, and knowledge, related to the topic in one's mind (7). Following the lecture, she returns to her pad, and goes through the notes or a relevant Chapter (8). At the end of the process, cells have come to grow in her mind that holds the information, her world now including the latest topic (9). The Buddha seems to confirm this personal participation in learning in the line, 'It is in this fathom-long body endowed with perception and mind that I proclaim the world...' (*api cāhaṃ āvuso imasmim yeva byāmamatte kaḷebare saññimhi samanake lokañca paññāpemi...*) (S.i.62.; A.ii.47f). If the student had not come to class, not listened to the lecture, not gone through the Chapter, etc., the information given by the Professor would not come to constitute part of her mindbody. It is only through her active personal involvement in learning does the learning become part of her.

Likewise then of the *Navaka sattā*, participating in its own growth at every turn.

Beginning their existence in the Evolutionary phase in the nanoest form of some primordial non-physical coming together of the triple thirsts, they eventually come to be sex beings deeply mired in sense thirst. While sense thirst is traditionally understood in terms of the thirst of the six senses, it may be understood from an evolutionary point of view as primarily relating to what may be called 'sex thirst'. *Kāma* in *kāma taṇhā* is from the root *kam-* (Skt *kram-*) 'to desire'. Out of the six sense doors (eye, ear, nose, tongue, body and mind) *kāma taṇhā*, can, then be taken primarily as relating to the 'body thirst' or thirst in the 'body door' (*kāyadvāra*), even though still allowing for the generic sense of sense-thirst as relating to all the senses. It may be noted in this connection that *rāga* 'passion' is a heightened manifestation of *kāma,* and that it is one of the three obstacles to be jettisoned, towards *Nibbāna.* This, then, affirms how *kāma taṇhā* could be seen as meaning the evolutionary mechanism of what we may call the 'generative imperative', to put it in Darwinian terms (or 'generative thirst' to put it in Buddhist terms), along with the other 'species continuity imperative' ('thirst to be' in Buddhist terms).

The life-span coming to an end over several life-times, at some point in evolution time, some of these *Navaka sattā* could have come to be born as animals, and then eventually come to be born as humans as in the Darwinian Theory[114]. What is of critical interest here

---

[114] As captured in Fig 2, this begins with the earliest chemical evidence of life (3.8 bya), and move through the earliest chemical evidence of Eukaryotes (2.7 bya), to four-limbed vertebrates on land (360 mya), to ancestors of humans and chimpanzees (5 mya) before anatomically modern humans come to be 150,000 years ago.

is that the Buddha allows for humans to evolve from animals. In the Saccasaṃyutta Sutta of the Samyutta Nikāya, e.g., we read, "So, too, bhikkhus, those beings are few who, when they pass away from the animal realm, are reborn among human beings"[115]. While to be 'reborn' is not the same as to 'evolve' as in the sense in Westernscience, an animal becoming a human can be said to qualify as an 'evolution' since it entails a change of sentient status, just as it is in evolution. Regardless of the terminology, the essential fact is that there comes to be an addition to the human population with one or more new beings, in due course, coming to be born human.

While those reborn as humans from the various domains – human, deva, hell, animal and ghost (S 56, 105- 131), may be few, as declared by the Buddha, once born as a human, there are going to be offspring, resulting in an increasing population. In addition to this first scarce source, there is a continuing secondary source when a few of the devas, animals, hell-beings and ghosts who come to be born as animals, in turn, come to be reborn as humans, few as it may be, again adding to the human population over the billions of years. The process of offspring multiplying would, of course, be continuous. All this, then, can be said to constitute to the population in which there comes to be individuals with 'sense thirst' as well as passion as in AS, both inherent to themselves or genetically inherited.

Given that the Earth appears over 9- billion years following the beginning of Evolutionary phase in which the *Navaka sattā* show up, and anatomically modern humans appear after the passage of another 4 plus billions (i.e., only 150,000 years ago), these humans may well be, then, the evolutionary product of the *new s*train of *'beings just reckoned as beings'*. Having come into being spontaneously, they can be said to have died in due course, and come to be born again

---

[115] The translation is from Ven. Bodhi (Tr.), 2000, 1887, the original being "*..evameva kho, bhikkhave, appakā te sattā ye tiracchānayoniyā cutā manussesu paccājāyanti; atha kho eteva bahutarā sattā ye tiracchānayoniyā cutā niraye paccājāyanti* ." (S 56.105).

and again and again, each time inching towards a mammalian life as explained in the Darwinian theory[116].

With a single characterization, namely, "beings reckoned just as beings", then, but with no fanfare, the Buddha, seems to introduce a distinct species, although it would take a perceptive listener to tune into it.

The Buddha has done it again!

There is undoubtedly much speculative thought in the above paragraphs. But while our characterization of evolution has been in the context of *Navaka sattā*, it could be seen, again, as being equally applicable to Ābhassara Beings that we encounter in the Devolutionary phase as well.

---

[116] While, of course, by the time of mammalian life, reproduction would be biological, as per the Darwinian model, in the earlier phases, it can be said to have made a switch, over time, from spontaneous birth to egg and/or womb birth.

10

A Concluding Overview

We have above sought to provide an alternative interpretation of segment, # 10 – 16 of the *Aggañña* Sutta in contradistinction to the view of many a western scholar that the Sutta, in its entirety, including the segment under discussion, is nothing but 'satire' and 'parody'. It is hoped that our discussion confirms that, in the particular segment, the Buddha could not have been more serious! Thus it is that the writer has sought to unravel the Buddha's intent, and the content, of the segment as being to provide an accurate picture of the cyclical unfolding of the universe.

We provide below, in summary, the specific critical parameters upon which the Buddha bases himself:

Identifying two evolutionary phases, the Devolutionary and the Evolutionary, using the specific term 'evolve'.

Using different wordings to distinguish a major evolutionary phase from the sub-phases, ie a 'standing' (*thāyī*) time frame, within an Evolutionary phase: 'after the passage of a long time beyond' vs. 'for a very long stretch of time'.

Evolution of Earth in thc ncw Evolutionary phase.

Precise characteristics of the Ābhassara Beings, each functional: mind-based, feeding on rapture, self-luminous, sky-traveling and glorious[117].

---

[117] While the discussion has shown the critical function of each of the first four characteristics, it has to be admitted that this writer

Three Types of Beings: Liberation-bound Ābhassara Beings, Samsara-based Ābhassara Beings and a New Strand of Beings.

The increasingly complex forms of nourishment: 'rapture' for the Ābhassara Beings; Earth-savour for the first post-Ābhassara Beings; coarse ground-*pappaṭaka* next; wider spreading wish-fulfilling creeper, *badālatā;* relatively complex rice for the matured human.

The bodies of the Beings getting increasingly coarser and variation in skin colour.

Mental chracteristics of sentience emerging in relation to an evolving body: craving, I-ness, lust.

Increasingly complex sociolinguistic manifestation, from a personal and private 'wondering' to impersonal communication in reference to a 'third party' and finally to 'you' in the second person.

It should be evident from the above summary of critical features built into a short seven paragraphs, how the principle of conditionality (as in Conditioned Co-origination) is at work here, and how every dimension of an evolving sentient being in the context of a changing universe comes to be accounted for.

If previous studies have been purely from the inside, namely, exclusively from a 'Buddhological' and traditional point of view, the writer is of the view that the breakthrough has resulted from going outside of the box, to Westernscience, a branch of which has made it its business to study the reality of the universe. Hopefully, this discussion has shown us how drawing upon Westernscience can help shed light on a Teaching of the Buddha that may baffle Buddhist scholars.

By way of a visual summary, we provide the following figure to capture, paragraph by paragraph, the points as laid out above in the segment, comparatively in relation to Westernscience:

---

has not been able to identify a particular functional role for this last characteristic, *subhaṭṭhāyino*, translated as 'glorious' but literally meaning 'remaining, continuing in glory' (PED). But does the Buddha mean something like 'Standing in good stead. Listener, this is for real'?

1	2	3	4	5
AGGAÑA SUTTA PARA	**AGGAÑA SUTTA PHASE**	**AGGAÑA SUTTA EVOLUTIONARY DETAIL**	**WESTERN SCIENCE EVOL. YEARS**	**WESTERN SCIENCE EVOL. DETAIL**
Part of # 10	Devolution "This world devolves"; "After the passage of a long time beyond"	Presence of Ābhassara Beings	13 + **Billion** years ago	Big Bang
Part of # 10; Part of #11	Evolution I "This world evolves"; "After the passage of a long time beyond"	Ābhassara Beings coming into 'the present state'; "All water"; No moon-sun; no female-male …	9 bya	Post-Big Bang
Part of #11 #12	Evolution II 'This world evolves again"	Appearance of savoury Earth (*rasapaṭhavi*); Eating of *rasapaṭhavi*; Appearance of moon and sun; Primordial language	4.55 bya	Formation of earth
#13 Part of #14	Standing-Evolution I "for a very long stretch of time"	Continue eating; Change of colour / coarseness; Continuing Language; Appearance / Eating of Ground-*pappaṭaka*;	575 **Million** years ago; 500 mya	Oldest animals Plants evolving
Part of #14	Standing-Evolution II "for a very long stretch of time"	Further change of colour / coarseness; Language; Appearance / Eating of *badālatā*	225 mya	Plant variegation; Vertebrates
#15 # 16	Standing-Evolution III "for a very long stretch of time"	Further Change of colour/coarseness; Language; Appearance of Rice & *linga*	150 **Thousand** years ago	Anatomically modern humans

Fig. 4 A Comparative Evolutionary Perspective as Between the Buddha and Westernscience

While the ***Devolutionary*** phase in AS (Col. 2, Row 1 of Fig. 4) accounts for part of the initial para # 10 in which Ābhassara Beings are introduced, the rest of the para captures their coming into the 'present state', ushering in the ***Evolutionary*** phase constituing the first *major* cyclical change. The physical characteristics of the universe at this stage – all water, no moon, no sun, etc., take up the first part of # 11, the change captured in the words, 'This world evolves'.

The rest of the para deals with the second *major* change when the Earth appears (replacing 'all water'), Ābhassara Beings now enjoying the savoury Earth. Though now within the Evolutionary phase, it is still a major change, as marked by the line 'This world evolves again'. Expanding upon the characteristics of the new Evolutionary phase, we have in # 12, the 'appearance of moon and sun', along with primordial language.

The next para, # 13, continues the characterization of the first 'standing evolution', meaning a sub-phase of Evolution, when the physical appearance – coarseness and colour, of Ābhassara Beings come to be impacted upon by the continued eating of the Earth savour. The duration of this time period is captured by the line 'for a very long stretch of time'.

Next is the appearance of ground-*pappaṭaka* taking the first part of para (# 14), the rest of the para introducing the impact of eating this new food in terms of continuing changes in coarseness and colour, but also next, the appearance of a new food source, *badālatā.* This again is captured by the line 'for a very long stretch of time'.

Becoming still coarser and change in colour continuing, there is also now more advanced language, para #15 showing another 'standing-still evolution(ary)' phase. Finally, in # 16, there is the growth of the third type of food, namely, rice, and the appearance of *linga.* Again all this is captured in the line, 'for a very long stretch of time'.

It may then be noted how each of the two major changes are captured with the words 'this world evolves (again)' and the sub-phases with the words 'for a very long stretch of time'. Paralleling in terms of time in Westernscience(Col. 4, 5), while the major changes – Big Bang to the formation of Earth, are countable in billions of years (up to Row 5), the sub-phases, from the 'oldest mammals' dating back to 575 million years (Row 6) to the 'Anatomically modern humans' dating back a mere 150,000 years (Row 8), are all countable not in billions but in millions of years.

The summary view of # 10-16 of AS as in the Chart, then, shows how well the breakdown into the two major divisions, and into the sub-phases of Evolution, is a perfect fit with the time breakdwon as calculated in Westernscience.

A perfect score, wouldn't you agree!

It is to be hoped, then, that there is enough fact and argument in our essay that show beyond a shadow of doubt that the view of the Buddha on the universe is not only ***not*** contradictory to the view one gets from Westernscience, but that it indeed *improves* upon it. While Westernscience is certainly far ahead in the discovery game in terms of detail, it seems to be stuck on the theistic concept of a first beginning, best captured by the 'Big Bang'. By contrast, the Buddha sees two distinct phases in the Big Bang theory itself – the 'bang' itself being the burning up of the earlier (Devolutionary) phase of the cycle and the cooling down the latter (Evolutionary) phase, pointing to a cyclical universe. Theoretical support, and internal consistency, for this can be said to come from his foundational teaching of Conditioned Co-origination. While there is indeed the 'steady state theory' of the universe in Westernscience that allows one to go beyond the more recognized linear model of the Big Bang, it has largely being rejected by the Westernscientificcommunity[118]. Thus we could say that we get a more comprehensive, realistic, non-mythical and non-theistic picture of the cosmic reality from the Buddha, in terms of a cyclical model, than from Westernscience.

If we may still wonder how the Buddha would have come to know the unfolding of the vast universe, it surely has to be through his mind's eye, sharpened through meditation towards a

[118] See Kafatos & Nadeau, 1990, 148-151 for the theory and a critique.

heightened one-pointedness (*ekaggatā*). But the universe is not the only physical reality that has opened up to his meditative eye, even without any physical evidence. He gives what seems to be an accurate geographic characterization of his very own land of the sub-continent of India, even though his travels presumably did not extend to the whole land area (see Law (1932, 1979) and Hart (2005) for treatments). As in the Mahāgovinda Sutta, the shape of India is given as being "broad on the north, narrow on the south" (*utarena āyataṃ dakkhinena sakatamukhaṃ*.., (D II 234)), literally, "like the mouth of a bullock cart", the back entrance of a roofed bullock cart being arched. This, of course, is the very shape of India. Minor as it may be by the standards of the universe, would this not then additionally speak to the Buddha's prolific supernormal mental skills?

PART II

11

Cutting through the Vedic Myth

Aggañña Sutta: Parody and Humorous Parable, or Cutting through the Vedic Myth?

Seeking to make the argument that the AS is nothing but a parody, Gombrich introduces us to the 'aetiological myth', the "only ancient text to offer any account of the origins of all these important things..", by 'important things' here meant the four *vaṇṇa* (#10) and the universe (#10-21). The reference is to what Macdonnell (1917, 207-211) calls the 'Hymn of Creation'. If up to # 9 of AS, the Buddha is "parodying Veda x.90" (195)[119], says Gombrich, in # 10-25, he "moves on to parodying Veda x 129" (207ff.) when "the four estates are separately discussed". In the Veda, notes Macdonnell (207) "... the origin of the world is explained as the evolution of the existent (*sat*) from the non-existent (*asat*)", "through the agency of a Creator (called by various names) as distinct from any of the other ordinary gods" (xxvi). Gombrich notes how, of course, the creation of *sat* from the *asat* "for the Buddha would be nonsense"[120].

---

[119] The specific reference is to the original source of the four *varṇa* from *Puruṣa* (Macdonnnel, 1 90:12, p. 201):

"His mouth was the Brahman,
his two arms were made the warrior,
his two thighs the Vaisya;
from his two feet the Śudra was born."

[120] We can only only agree with Gombrich. In the Kaccānagotta Sutta,

In a similar vein, agreeing in general with Gombrich, Collins, taking the total Sutta as "a story … offered with satirical and ironic wit in the manner of moral commentary", argues "that AS was intended by its earliest composer(s) and redactors to be a humorous parable: its serious intent was as moral commentary rather than as a 'myth of origins -- charter for society' or an account intended to be 'factually' or 'historically' accurate (1993, 314), a position in agreement with Dr. Rhys Davids who is of the view that "we may not accept the historical accuracy of this legend.", "a continual note of good humoured irony" (cited in Collins).

Despite such reservations, the scholars do adduce a seriousness to the Sutta. Gombrich, e.g., notes, "As a debunking job I think the sermon is serious: its main aim is to show that the caste system is nothing but a human invention". In addition to satirising Brahmanism, it is seen to be intended "to provide a non-satirical Buddhist charter for social arrangements". Collins observes that its "*raison d'etre* is to present a Buddhist-ascetic hierarchical model of society…".

In order to explore the validity of these claims and arguments, but first limiting ourselves to what Gombrich calls the 'aetiological myth' (AS # 10-16), we revisit below the Vedic Hymn of Creation (VH), referred to by him, in full, to get a fuller picture, quoting Macdonell (1951, 207-11) in its original quatrain form:

1. There was not the non-existent nor the existent then;
   There was not the air nor the heaven which is beyond.
   What did it contain? Where? In whose protection?
   Was there water, unfathomable, profound?

2. There was not death nor immortality then.
   There was not the beacon of night nor of day.
   That one breathed, windless, by its own power.
   Other than that there was not anything beyond.

---

e.g., noting that "This world …. depends upon a duality – upon the notion of existence and the notion of non-existence…" the Buddha rejects them both (S,12.15).

3. Darkness in the beginning was hidden by darkness.
Indistinguishable, it was all water.
That which, coming into being, was covered with the void,
That one arose through the power of heat.

4. Desire in the beginning came upon that,
(Desire) that was the first seed of mind.
Sages seeking in their heart with wisdom
Found out the bond of the existent with the non-existent.

5. Their cord was extended across.
Was there below or was there above?
There were impregnators, there were powers.
There was energy below, there was impulse above.

6. Who knows truly? Who shall here declare,
whence it has been produced, whence is this creation?
By the creation of this universe, the gods (come) afterwards:
Who then knows whence it has arisen.

7. Whence this creation has arisen,
Whether he founded it or did not.
He who in the highest heaven is its surveyor,
He only knows, or else he knows not[121].

Now to draw upon the Hymns, the first thing that comes to be evident is that AS indeed shares with VH some of the elements, but not others[122]. Despite the similarities, however, what we find in AS, as we

---

[121] While the original translation shows the lines as continuous, but alongside the Romanized verse on the left, we break it into lines to retain the quatrain style of the verse in the original Sanskrit.

[122] This undoubtedly speaks to the fact that the Buddha would have had the Hymn at the back of his mind, in discoursing the AS. This, of course, should hardly be surprising given his princely education.

shall see, is a *challenge* to the view emerging from VH.

First, then, to the *common elements*, 'H' in the following Figure meaning 'Hymn' and 'L' meaning 'Line':

NO.	VEDIC HYMN	*AGGAÑÑA SUTTA*
1	*"Was there water, unfathomable, profound?"* (H1 L4) *"Inistinguishable, this all was water."* (H3 L2).	"there was just (one vast mass of) water " (# 11).
2	*" There was not the beacon of night nor of day."* (H2 L2)	"... nor night and day.." (# 11).
3	*"Darkness in the beginning was hidden by darkness."* (H3 L1)	"all darkness, (just) blinding darkness." (# 11).
4	*"That one breathed, windless, by its own power".* (H2 L3)	"Âbhassara -Beings"
5	*"That which, coming into being, was covered with the void."* (H3 L3)	Âbhassara as "moving through space" (# 11).

Fig. 5 Some Common Elements in the Vedic Creation Hymn and the *Aggañña* Sutta

As for the overlapping elements in Fig. 3, as between AS (Col. 3) and VH (Col.2), we have 'water' (1), 'no night and day' (2), 'darkness' (3), 'That one' (4) and 'void' (5). But what is lacking in VH is much clarity. While 'water' figures in H1, it also figures in H3. Also, there is only a question, and nothing definitive: "*Was there water, unfathomable, profound?"*; *Inistinguishable, this all was water."* The absence of night and day occurs in H2, and darkness in H3. If 'That one' in H2 suggests a form of life, paralleling Ābhassara Beings in AS, there is also contradiction: 'breathing' is said to be in a 'windless' context! The elements in VH follow the order water, night, wind and void, the very reverse as in AS. There is also in VH a theistic origin in the term 'then' in the line 'There was not the non-existent nor the existent *then'* (H1L1). "That which, coming into being, was covered with the void" (5) (*tucyenābhvapihitaṃ yadāsit*) seems to be a wordy way of suggesting a Being in empty space.[123]

But if Fig. 5 shows how VH, in comparison to AS, is distinguishable for its lack of clarity and systematicity, numerous are the marks that put the two even more apart. This may be seen from Fig. 6 (next page).

We shall let the reader go through Fig. 6 and see for oneself the contrast between VH and AS in detail, drawing upon Col. 3[124]. What s/he would find in the VH is a haphazard, and incoherent, listing of features. Another is the indefiniteness, well reflected in the sort of rhetorical questions, and, of course, with no answers, as e.g., "Who knows truly?", "Who shall here declare whence it has been produced?" (VH 6), or "He only knows, or else he knows not" (VH7).

It is not just the number of disagreements that tells the tale, but the very conceptual differences. What an analysis of the VH shows is a mythical conception of the universe, in terms of a theistic ontology - the creation of *sat* from the *asat*, somethig that, as noted, "for the Buddha would be nonsense".

By contrast, what AS presents is a coherent, natural and conditioned, evolutionary development of a cyclical fashion that is

---

[123] Interestingly, just about the only line that can be said to have some conceptual clarity is 'That one arose through the power of heat' (H3 L4), the parallel in AS being the Ābhassara-Being, characterized by this writer as 'hither-bound *shining* arrow'.

[124] Figure 6, of course, is nothing more than a spread-sheet of data, having a place more in preparatory notes than in a finished article. But in this case, leaving the data in its raw form can probably allow insight into the issue of discrepancies, perhaps over and above what is offered by us. In this context, it may be worth nothing that indeed in literature, a writer of fiction , is well known to leave the end of a story open (Soviet writer Anton Chekov being a well-known example), letting the reader read into it whatever it is one imagines in the context of the total story.

	VEDIC HYMN	*AGGAÑÑA SUTTA, and/or* contrastive comments
1	*There was not the non-existent [asat] nor the existent then [sat]* (H1 L1).	Devolutionary phase preceding the Evolutionary, with no Beginning (# 10).
2	*There was not the air nor the heaven which is beyond..* (H1 L2)	Âbhassara characterized as "moving through air" (# 10) .
3	*What did it contain? Where? In whose protection*? (H1 L3)	Suggestion of theism, as contrasted with a natural process in AS.
4	*There was not death nor immortality then.* (H2 L1)	Death implicit in the Âbhassara Beings passing away from their Ābhassara -bodies, and coming hither (# 10).
5	*"That one breathed, windless..".* (H2 L3)	A contradiction, 'breathing' but 'windless'; Contradicted, with Âbhassara flying.
6	*Other than that, there was not anything beyond.* (H2 L4)	By contrast to a single Evolutionary cycle, a Devolutionary cycle preceding the Evolutionary cycle suggested (# 10).
7	*Desire in the beginning came upon that.* (H4 L1)	'Desire' comes to be in the Beings, at the point of tasting the 'savoury earth' (# 12), and not 'in the beginning'.
8	*(Desire) that was the first seed of mind.* (H4 L2)	Âbhassaras are characterized as already being 'mind-based' (# 10).
9	*Sages seeking in their heart with wisdom.. Found out the bond of the existent with the non-existent.* (H4 L3-4)	An untenable duality (see H1 L1).
10	*Their cord was extended across: Was there below or was there above? There were impregnators, there were powers. There was energy below, there was impulse above.* (H5 L1-4)	The theistic dualism continues.
11	*Who knows truly? Who shall here declare, whence it has been produced, whence is this creation?* (H6 L1-2).	Many unknowns ('who', 'whence') (L2,4). Reference to 'creation' (L3).
12	*By the creation of this universe, the gods (come) afterwards: Who then knows whence it has arisen* (H6 L3-4) .	Reference is just to 'Beings' (*sattā*).
13	*Whence this creation has arisen, Whether he founded it or did not. He who in the highest heaven is its surveyor, He only knows, or else he knows not* (H7 L1-4).	Reference to a Creator again, and many questions; Ambivalence.

Fig. 6 Some Contrastive Elements in the Vedic Creation Hymn and the *Aggañña* Sutta

also orderly and systematic[125]. And as we have sought to show above, it is also an accurate, scientific and historical picture of the process of the universe[126], to the extent that may be judged in relation to Westernscience.[127]

Going beyond the critique, it may also be noted with interest that

---

[125] It may be worth noting a parallel observation made by Ven. Nyanaponika Thera (1998, 8) in relation to the concept of mind and 'soul':

> "If we turn from the Abhidhamma to the highest contemporary achievements of non-Buddhist Indian thought in the field of mind and "soul", i.e., the early Upanishads and Sāmkhya, we would find that apart from single great intuitions, they teem with concepts derived from mythology, ritual, and abstract speculation. In comparison, the realistic, sober and scientific spirit of the Abhidhamma psychology (as well as its nucleus in found in the suttas) stands out very strongly."

[126] In Westernscience, one of the models proposed as an alternative to the "one shot" Big Bang theory of a single universe is the 'oscillating universe'. Though not as compatible as it may be in all its detail, and not accepted by all astronomers either (as, of course, is the Big Bang model), it seems to resonate with the view of the universe that emerges in AS.

Another model proposed is the 'steady state universe'. While today it has been ruled out, what is interesting is that in both models "the universe has no beginning" (see Lightman, 1991, 51ff. for a discussion).

[127] What this accurate understanding (as claimed by us) seems to provide, we conjecture, is an example of the Buddha's insights ushered in by the 'Cessation of Perception' (*nirodhasamāpatti*). This, of course, was the breakthrough made by the Samana Gotama, later the Buddha, upon leaving his two Teachers under whom he, like the Teachers, had reached the summits of 'Plain of Nothingness' (*ākiñcaññāyatana*) and 'the Plain of Neither-perception-non-nonperception' (*nevasaññānāsaññāyatana*) respectively. By definition, to experience Cessation of Perception may be said to wipe off the entire slate of received wisdom and knowledge of a life time, shaped by culture, language, history and geography, learning and experience, etc., and to go beyond, on to an empty and fresh template of the mind

while the VH comes to be in seven verses, the relevant section in AS comes to be in seven segments as well[128]. If this break up into sections is authentic to the tradition, it is as if the Buddha is trying to keep himself within the framework known to the two Brahmin youths, Vāseṭṭha and Bhāradvāja. This may also then explain why # 10-16 are terse, with many an understatement. However, it may have well suited the purpose of the Buddha as well, namely, to bring out the absolute bare minimum needed to characterize a given stage in the process of evolution without overwhlming his listeners (see below, under 'Intended Audience', II.12).

It may be intriguing to conjecture here if there is any significance, a sense of efficacy, to number seven. We may begin with the rather mundane observation of the seven days making up a week, but not insignificantly from the Buddhist point of view, reflecting a half time in relation to each of the waxing and the waning phases of the moon. More historically are the seven weeks the Buddha spends under the Bodhi tree following Enlightenment, and in Buddhist mythology, there are the seven peaked mountains (*sattakūṭapabbata*), seven seas (*sattasamudura*), etc.

We may also in this connection point to a concept called 'channel capacity' of the human brain[129]. So, limiting the related segment

---

upon, a *tabula rasa*, which reality begins to make its imprint all fresh and novel.

[128] This is as determined by Carpenter's PTS Edition as used by us. While the numbering in the Tipitaka Sinhala Translation (2006) differs from Carpenter's, what is interesting is that the relevant section in the Sinhala version, too, still comes to occupy seven sections, numbering from 5 to 11 (144 -150) (although there is a typographical error on p. 150 when the section following # 8 and 9 on p.149 comes to be again numbered as # 8 and 9, instead of 10 and 11.)

[129] See cognitive psychologist George A. Miller (1956), "The Magical Number Seven, Plus or Minus Two: Some Limits on Our Capacity for Processing Information". In it, the author shows "a number of remarkable coincidences between the channel capacity of a number of human cognitive and perceptual tasks. In each case, the effective channel capacity is equivalent to between 5 and 9 equally-weighted

(#10-16) to seven pegs may then be seen as an attempt on the part of the Buddha to keep himself within the boundaries as circumscribed by the Vedic Seers, constricted as they may have been by 'channel capacity', meeting them 'head on' as if it were[130].

---

error-less choices: on average, about 2.5 bits of information. Miller hypothesized that these may all be due to some common but unknown underlying mechanism."

[130] Before we leave the topic, regardless of the erroneous view of the universe contained in the Vedic Hymns, this writer believes that Vedic seers do deserve our respect, by way of gratitude (*kataññutā*) and expression of altruistic joy (*muditā*), for paving the way, as well as for the insights they themselves seem to have had. Just like in the case of the Samana Gotama's two teachers, the Vedic seers may even have peaked in their jhānic skills to see the characteristic features of the early universe. But, as in the case of the forefathers of Westernscience, beginning with Greek up to the time of Einstein, the Vedic Seers were working within the framework of the received wisdom, namely, belief in a Creator. Again as in the case of Westernscience, the Vedic seers can be said to have tried to fit what they came to see in their mental eye into this conceptual world with a Creator. If they didn't get them all right, that can be said to be indicative of lesser clarity of insight, governed as they were by culture and language, this as contrated with the Buddha who in *nirodha samāpatti,* succeeds in going beyond them. The Vedic Seers identify (as in Fig 5) the presence of water, air and heat. While these, of course, constitute three of the Four Great Elements, as also in Buddhism, they come to be mentioned not just as elements, but as part of the evolving universe. So is space, certainly also in their experience. In our day and age, we, in the West in particular, may think of these as nothing more than plain 'commonsense'. But 2500 years ago, the level of knowledge about the universe could hardly have been all that sophisticated. Hence we can only conclude that this is how it was seen by the Seers through their mind's eye in deep meditation. We may note, e.g., in this context, that identified in the Vedic Hymns is also the *absence* of night and day. This certainly couldn't have been on the basis of a mundane experience. We may then be tempted to see the identification of these items in the context of the universe unfolding, making them privy to some of the secrets of nature, as the outcome of their meditation, as

If as noted, it may also have been to be conscious of the channel capacity of his two seekers (again see II.12 for the fuller argument), the Buddha seems to want to make sure that the information regarding the universe was not only not beyond the memory capacity of the two of the Brahmin youth, but could also be shared by them with others, with similar, or even less (seven minus two) capacity. So we may envision a situation where the two seekers happen to encounter a group of Brahmins and announce that they are now the 'sons of the Sakyan'. And by way of showing the quality of the Sakyan in whose favour they had come to renounce their Brahmin lineage, relate, after much preparation undoubtedly, the Buddha's view of the universe, in seven terse 'paragraphs'.

The Buddha's explanation of the universe in a way that is neither theoretical nor extraneous, but as relating to the context of what had been said in # 1-9, can be said to have been necessitated by the context. To not introduce it here would have been to leave an open question on the minds of the two Brahmin seekers: 'The Blessed One has made us rethink the claims of our Brahmin brethren at the social level. But the Vedic view of the universe tells us a somewhat different story. It talks about a Creator. So could our brethren Brahmins not be after all correct in their claim to be born of that Creator?'

The Buddha introducing the explanation, at # 10, then, would now allow them to place the Brahminic claims in a cosmic context, beyond the micro social level. They would now see how the fallacy of the claims made by Brahmins at the social level as stemming from a lack of understanding of nature itself. Declaring the cosmic reality in # 10-16, then, is to confirm what the Buddha first says at the social level in # 1-9 and expanded upon in # 22-32.

The Buddha's explanation can also be said additionally to cut in two ways in relation to the teaching of death and rebirth in a samsaric cycle. First, the cosmic model, a Devolutionary phase giving way

---

the Buddha's accurate understanding itself was, though qualitatively higher.

to an Evolutionary phase, can be said to provide added legitimacy to the latter, namely rebirth. By the same token, the latter, a *sine qua non* of both the Buddha's Teachings and the Vedic Teachings[131], would add a parallel legitimacy to the former, meaning death..

The Buddha giving an alternative explantion to the same phenomenon (as in our case study in relation to the origins of the universe) is, of course, nothing new. His teaching of *anattā* 'asoulity' (or 'selfeless person' (Collins, 1982)) is an example, where the Brahminic concept of *ātman* comes to be turned on its head. Another would be the concept of *kamma* (Sanskrit *karma*).

So # 10 to 16 can then be said to directly address the issues relating to the Vedic universe. In the process, the Vedic myth comes to be cut through, and the reality as they have come to be (*yathābhūta*) established.

For these reasons, then, we may say that # 10-16 is a clear case of myth busting towards a refutation of the Vedic view. It appears to be a clear attempt by the Buddha to repudiate the traditional Vedic (thus Brahminic) view of the universe in no uncertain terms, just as done in relation to the Brahminic claims of superiority in # 1-9 and # 22-32 (see also II.14). And the relevance is not lost on the two listeners. Clearly well-schooled in the Vedic lore themselves, Vāseṭṭha and Bhāradvāja would know exactly what the Buddha was talking about, and be able to immediately relate to it. And the Buddha can be said to have found just the right audience, and niche, to share his discoveries of the nature of the universe, and the origins of (wo)man and society. It may be worth noting that it was the Buddha himself who broaches the subject, namely, the Brahminic claims, with the two Brahmin seekers, providing him with the context for coming out with the full story of Devolution and Evolution (see II.12, Intended Audience).

---

[131] What AS # 10-16 incidentally seems to confirm is that that, as noted, the education Siddhartha had as a Prince included a good grounding in the Vedas and the early Upanishads (which also explains why he was able to take on all comers, many of them Brahmins, in skillful debate). As Collins (312) notes, "Here, as in so many early texts, the Buddha is represented as knowing very well indeed the Brahmanism he rejects".

So, as far as we can see, then, there seems to be no sense of mocking in the Sutta, or satire or parody[132].

As noted, AS can be seen to have three segments: a middle segment relating to the process of Devolution and Evolution, juxtaposed between the repudiation of Brahminic claims of superiority. But the jump from segment one to two, and then back to three from two has been seen as "*ex abrupto*", to use a phrase used by Mrs. Rhys-Davids in relation to the Anupada Sutta: "We have first a stock formula of praise spoken not once only of Sāriputta. Then, *ex abrupto*, this tradition of his fortnight of systematized introspection. Then, *ex abrupto*, three more formulas of praise." (quoted in Ven. Nyanaponika, 1998, 115). While this writer sees no abruptness in AS, from segment 1 to segment 2 and back to segment, but a natural flow, sharing the view of Ven. Nyanaponika[133], what we see in the Anupada Sutta structurally is the same as in AS: a core piece embedded between a treatment of a common element, at the beginning and the end. To that extent, the structure of embedding can be seen to be intentional on the part of the Buddha in AS, the Anupada Sutta providing another example.

A Few More Points

But before we conclude the section, we need to respond to a few other points made by Gombrich and Collins. Regarding the term 'Beings' used by the Buddha to characterize the early form of existence (# 11), Gombrich (166) considers it to be a turning around of the Vedic terms 'sat' and 'asat', which, for the Buddha "would have been nonsense", "into a parodistic narrative". However, we would like to respond by saying that characterizing the form of life at this early period of time

---

[132] It may be relevant to note that the characterization in relation to the Seven Suns elsewhere (see I.5) has not been suggested to be satire.

[133] "… it seems to us quite natural that, between the words of praise at the beginnning and the end, there should be embedded an illustation to this eulogy of Sāriputta's wisdom.…".

just as 'Beings' is the only accurate way of talking about it without confusing the listener. All the Buddha is doing here is suggesting the presence of 'consciousness', i.e., life, strengthening it with other characteristics such as being 'mind-based'. There were no 'human beings' as yet, and no language either. So the Buddha seems to have adopted the most skillful language to capture the idea without letting the cart (namely the human being to appear later) before the horse (the early phase of evolution)[134].

In support of his contention, Gombrich (167) adds, ".. the verb *samvartatā* [(<*sam* + *vartatā*) (Vedic hymn 4)] may have been in the Buddha's mind and so account for the rather obscure expression [#10].. *ayam loko samvaṭṭati...*" However, the expression can be said to come out of the perceived obscurity into full plain semantic and conceptual view, with sharp clarity, when taken to have the meaning 'devolving', taking it to mean 'turn' (< *Sanskrit vrt-* > *vartate, as in vartamāna)*[135], seen from the evolutionary perspective as presented in this study.

Again, noting that "If this myth is to be taken serious, the failure to explain why the same behaviour should affect some but not others would be a logical flaw" (Gombrich, 168), it is dismissed with the words, "But such criticism is hardly appropriate to a parody". The

---

[134] In this connection (of a generic 'Being', *sattā*), it is of interest to note how the term 'animal' (*sattā* it would be in the Buddha's world) comes to be used in Westernsciencegenerically, in a contemporary description relating to evolution:

"The oldest recognizable multicellular organisms are red algae dating back 1.2 billion years. Our own multicellular lineage, the animals, don't leave fossils until about 575 million years ago. "Animal" is a generous description for the creatures that left these marks." (Zimmer, 2001, 67).

[135] Ven. Bodhi translates ***vaṭṭa*** from *vartate* as.... *'existence' sam- / vi-*(Ven. Bodhi, Ed 1999, 295). But the term *bhava* also comes to be translated as *existence* by him (p. 122). So we may ignore that translation.

behaviour referred to is the tasting of the savoury Earth by Beings, resulting in different beings coming to look different from each other in skin colour and body coarseness.

First it is hardly illogical that two sentient beings eating the same food can be affected differentially. To take an example from contemporay life, eating a couple of slices of pineapples ('solid food'[136]), some may begin to sneeze and show signs of allergy, while others may eat half the pineapple with no health hazards. Again, a 'peanut allergy' caution on labels in a supermarket speaks to the danger of it to some, children in particular (with cases of resulting death), while for the general population, there seem to be no such danger. To give yet another example, some may return from a holiday in the tropics with a tan ('contact food') while others may show burns. Such differences, then, are simply a matter of variation in the cellular and metabolic structure of the individual mindbodies. After all, Gombrich and Collins, not to mention this writer, respond to the very same material, namely the AS text, and Abhidhammically '(visual) contact food', 'volition food' and/ or 'consciousness food'), very differently, although, of course, with overlap and agreement in places. So, different Beings having different reactions to eating the same food is by no means to be illogical. It is simply a case of recognizing indivdual variations; to put it in a contemporry dictum, 'Different blokes, different strokes'!

Collins (357) notes that "The profusion of imprecise time-words - *hoti kho so... samayo yam. kadāci karahaci, dighassa addhuno accayena, yebhuyyena* 'usually', 'as a rule', might suggest that there is a studied vagueness about the cosmogony here". This, too, we see as hardly tenable in that there is, as noted, much understatement, the Buddha skipping billions and millions of years[137] in order to not only

---

[136] This is one of the four food types identified by the Buddha. See the rest of the para for the other three.

[137] See in this connection the words of Charles Darwin which seems to resonate well: "If the theory be true," he wrote of evolution by ntural selection, "it is indisputable that before the lowest Cambrian stratum was deposited, **long periods elapsed**.... and that during **these**

to not overwhelm, but also to be precise and terse. The counting of time being in terms of billions of years, being more precise would make no difference to the point being made. *After exactly how long* would be irrelevant to the continuity of the evolutionary story, while the *fact* of *vevaṇṇatā* (as in Gombrich above) is relevant to explaining the emergence of diversity, very much related to the issue of the four 'estates', i.e., the social classes.

Finally, Gombrich makes a nice link between the "Buddha parodying Veda x.90.12" and "parodying Veda" (x. 129). While this writer is not unwilling to consider the assertion in relation to the former, dealing with the four vannas, as parody, nothing in our research, and discussion, allows us to consider the assertion in relation to the latter, relating to the universe, too, as parody.

By contrast, on the basis of this writer's analysis, he agrees wholeheartedly with Collins (334) when he says that "The story of origins, then, far from being an extraneous and disconnected insertion, as has been alleged, is intimately tied to the focus of the text as a whole." And he adds a helpful a critical point about the apparently sudden transition from # 9 to # 10: "The immediate transition from # 9 to # 10 is effected by the replacement of the Vedas by the Dhamma (the Word of the Buddha) and of Brahma by the Buddha, who 'has the best body', and 'is the best' (*brahma-kāyo, brahma-bhūto*)". (More of it later, in II.14)

If this still doesn't argue the case for serious intention and delivery of # 10-16, we may take another look at # 10-16 from another angle. In showing that the Brahmins were wrong in their haughty claims, the principle the Buddha seems to have followed is to replace myth with fact – Brahmin women giving, birth, etc. It is nothing but reasonable, then, that that is exactly what the Buddha is doing when it comes to the Vedic Creation Myth (another Brahminic claim), too. That is to say, replace myth with fact. So if the seven Vedic Hymns

---

vast periods, the world swarmed with living creatures…" (cite d in Zimmer (2001, 64-65)) (bold added). We may note not only the use of "imprecise time words", but repetition as in the Buddha.

constitue myth, the seven paragraphs in AS can only be seen as fact, by way of a parallelism.

This would also be to teach *dukkha*, at least *vipariṇāma dukkha* 'change as dukkha', by way of identifying the change process (*anicca*) entailed in evolution. The way out of suffering entails the parallelism: if showing that the Brahmins were wrong at a mundane level is part of showing the way out of suffering, so would showing that the Brahmins are wrong in their understanding of the reality of universe. What it tells the two Brahmin youth in no uncertain terms would be that the concept of a Creator, entailed in the myth is dead wrong! It would at the same time be to corroborate the idea of evolutionary change at a cosmic level, parallel to what was seen at the micro level in terms of the emergence of the four *vaṇṇas*. It may even be worth wondering if the Buddha limiting his outline of the evolutionary change to four phases (see Fig. 1) has anything to do with the fact of the *vaṇṇas* being four. Further, the cosmic model of a cyclical evolution of nature would be to bye the bye provide additional confirmation of the samsaric cycle at the micro, human level[138].

Once again, then, we contend that the only reason the Buddha presents an explanation of the workings of the universe is that it is the truth, it is reality, and knowing reality, namely Dhamma (*aggañña*) (passim), is the best![139] It is also to say that if in # 1-9 and and # 22-32 satire has been used as a means to an end, the same cannot be said

---

[138] Should we envision the Buddha walking in one direction presenting each 'para' of the 'presentation', and then turning back to indicate the introduction of a new point? This suggests a pacing back and forth of thirty two times, given the number of paras (as in Carpenter) constituting the AS. If we were to allow each directional walk a duration of about 1 to 3 minutes, the Buddha can be said to have incidentally, or perhaps even intentionally, got a good workout after sitting in meditation (!), if also allowing him ample time to get his communication across effectively.

[139] See II.14 for an elaboration.

of # 10-16 (21). It is no satire. It speaks to hard facts, and nothing but the truth!

Finally, is it anything less than a non-recognition of the Buddha's cognitive and interpretive skills to take a breakthrough relating to the workings of the uinverse as plain satire? We know that the finger pointing to the moon is not the moon itself. So satire there may be in AS, if also to add colour to the drama, as any good communicator is wont to do. But it is merely as a technique, the medium, not to be confused with the message.

So once again we contend that # 10-16 (- 21) is serious and not satirical or parodical.

Despite what this writer considers to be overwhelming evidence that the Buddha was indeed dead serious in # 10-16 (21), let us grant for a moment, without being disrespectful, and in a similar somewhat satirical and lighthearted vein, the wishes of Gombrich and Collins, that indeed AS (#10-16 in particular) is parody and satire. So we first ask the simple but perhaps naïve question, "But why would the Buddha engage in such light-hearted and facetious banter?", the way satire and parody can be characterized. The Buddha says that he teaches only two things – *dukkha* and the way out of *dukkha*. So if the segment is lighthearted banter, where is the teaching of *dukkha* and the way out? So unless it meets this criterion, the Buddha can be said to have nothing to do with it. Parodying may be fun and entertaining, but liberative?

Also, would the Buddha not be indulging in 'gossip' (*sampappalāpā)*, if the intent were satire and parody and nothing substantial and meaningful? It is as if he has nothing better to do! In the Pāṭika Sutta, he asks Sunakkhatta, "would the Tathāgata make any statement that was ambiguous?" (*Api nu Sunakkhatta Tathagato taṃ vācaṃ bhāseyya yā sā vācā dvaya-gaminī ti*) (D. xxiv. 1.18).

Case closed!?

12

Intended Audience

Gombrich correctly points out that "If we try to discover the original meaning of the Buddha's sermons, we need to know what cultural knowledge and presuppositions he shared with his audience." (Gombrich, 1992, 160-161). Precisely! While Gombrich doesn't say anything beyond this regarding the Buddha's audience, Collins is so convinced that the Buddha was addressing the monks that he replaces 'Vāseṭṭha' throughout with 'Monks' in his translation of AS, (beginning in # 3 "Monks, you were (both) born brahmins" and thereafter). Argues Collins (349):

> "The text has 'Vāseṭṭhaṃ' in the accusative singular here [i.e., in # 3)]; and the Buddha's words (here and throughout) use the vocative singular Vāseṭṭha; but the pronouns and verbs are in the plural (some mss. have the vocative plural Vāseṭṭhā'). As RFG 164--5 suggests, since the Buddha in # 9 says to his audience 'you... are from various castes ...', from that point on he must be taken to be addressing these two individuals as part of a wider audience. I translate the vocatives simply and neutrally as 'monks'."

In this section, we shall explore the issue of just to whom the discourse is addressed by the Buddha, first in relation to AS itself, i.e., internal evidence, and then in relation to other Suttas in which the Buddha talks on the topic of the 'Primeval' (external evidence).

12.1 Internal Evidence

12.1.1 *Tumhe*

The issue of whom it is addressed to by the Buddha comes to turn on the two words *tumhe* 'plural you' (in # 3 and # 9) and Vāseṭṭha (throughout), and on the line 'you... are from various castes ...' in # 9.

We may begin with line 1 in # 3 which reads, 'Then the Blessed One addressed *Vāseṭṭha*' (*atha kho bhagavā Vāseṭṭhaṃ āmantesi),* it is addressed to a single person, i.e., *Vāseṭṭha*' and *Vāseṭṭha* alone. The next line reades, "You're indeed, Vāseṭṭha, Brahmin-born, of Brahmin high caste and have gone forth from a Brahmin home to homelessness" (*Tumhe khvattha, Vāseṭṭha, brāhmaṇa-jaccā brāhmaṇa kulinā brāhmaṇa-kulā agārasmā anagāriyaṃ pabbajitā*). Even though again only *Vāseṭṭha* is identified by name, as is throughout, the plural *tumhe* here clearly refers to the two listeners identified, namely, Vāseṭṭha and Bhāradvāja, as the context demands. So what we get from the two opening lines is that while the addressee is one, the reference may be to one or two.

The next use of *tumhe* is in # 9: "You're indeed, Vāseṭṭha, varied-born, of a variety of names, of a variety of clans and have gone forth from varied homes to homelessness". What we note here is a pattern similar to # 3, as we can see when the qualifiers of the two lines are shown below each other:

# 3	*brāhmaṇa-jaccā*	*brāhmaṇa-kulinā*	-	*brāhmaṇa-kulā*
# 9	*nānā-jaccā*	*nānā-nāmā*	*nānā-gottā*	*nānā-kulā*

Fig. 7 Parallels Between Lines in # 3 and # 9 using *tumhe*

The only difference between the two occurrences is the replacement of *brāhmaṇa kulīnā* with *nānā-nāmā* and *nānā-gottā,* the latter two associated as e.g., in *nāmagottaṃ najīratī.* While again it is addressed to a single person, Vāseṭṭha, the reference is to a group. This may indeed allow the possibility that the Buddha is addressing, as Collins contends, the monks.

However, the reference to a variety - in terms birth, name, clan and family, could be seen as a manner of speaking, drawing from the general to the local, and vice versa. Just as when *Vāseṭṭha* was addressed in line 2 of # 3 but meaning both, the last example could still be be taken to mean 'The two of you, like the many others from a variety of families who have *gone from home to homelessness*' (*anagāriyaṃ pabbajitā*). It needs to be noted that both Vāseṭṭha and Bhāradvāja are still *seekers*, i.e., not ordained. The reference here therefore is not to the ordained Sangha, but to those who are *yet to be ordained*, but having *gone forth.* At the next stage, they may or may not become ordained under the Buddha, although most likely all of them would (and have). Even though *pabbajitā* as above can literally mean 'ordained', it seems to be used only as an expression to mean 'homelessness'; the phrase occurs, in # 3, too, when Vāseṭṭha and Bhāradvāja are not yet ordained. So what we see in # 9 is a linguistic and literary parallelism, hardly allowing it to suggest that the Buddha is addressing the monks[140].

---

[140] To make it clearer in a lighter and a satirical vein, let us take the hypothetical case of the Buddha sending an email, addressed to a single Professor, but cc'ed to a second. It reads, "You're from different parts of the world, and have earned your academic credentials from different Universities and varied Departments. But you have switched (=gone forth) from your 'home' Discipline (say Neurology, Psychology, Philosophy, Physics, Sociology, etc.) to the 'homelessness' of my Teachings (which you now call Buddhism)…. Don't your colleagues wonder and ask you why?". The assumption here, of course, is that there are now many a Professor in the West who have moved from a strict 'pure' Discipline they had come to specialize in, now to study the Buddha's Teachings from their disciplinary perspective but wider. Or to take a rather mundane example, we may envision a teacher in a multicultural school talking to a student leader, with a buddy from the same ethnocultural community in tow. S/he says, "You're from various countries with a rich variety of cultures, and you've left home and come here. So how about helping us to bring you all together for a

That by *'tumhe'* in # 9 is meant only the two Brahmins is again clear from the next sentence: "When asked who you are" (*ke tumheti puṭṭhā..*), you may reply (*paṭijānātha*) with the words, "We're the sons of the Sakyan" (*sakyaputtiyāmhāti*). Here clearly the Buddha is talking to the two Brahmin-seekers, and not to the wider Sangha. 'This is something that others who have gone from home to homelessness can and will say as well', the Buddha seems to be implying. 'So you can say so, too'.

We may then say that in both # 3 and # 9, *'tumhe'* can be said to be used by the Buddha, ever respectful of the listener, in the sense of the 'plural majesticus' (PED, under *tuvaṃ* and *tvaṃ*)[141], along the same lines as the honorific 'we' when referring to oneself. Further in using *tumhe,* the Buddha seems to want to assure Bhāradvāja that he is also included each time he is addressing Vāseṭṭha.

Continuing with linguistic evidence, we note in # 2 that Vāseṭṭha's first words are, "Come, friend Bhāradvāja, let's go to him", (*āyāma āvuso),* addressing his colleague by name, not "Come, friends" in the plural, with a possible reference to the Sangha amongst whom they were at the time. Likewise, "Alright, friend" (*evaṃ āvusoti)*, agrees Bhāradvāja. Again not plural. Besides, how likely, or appropriate, would it have been for two laymen to suggest to monks to go see the Buddha!

12.1.2 Other internal evidence

We may note that, prior to pacing back and forth, the Buddha was in meditation. We may then reasonably assume that the Buddha would

---

multicultural festival under our school flag?" This, of course, is a way of easing into a point, to begin a conversation relating to all. The two students are being addressed since they also under the the immigrant rubric. But that hardly suggests that the teacher is talking to all the students.

So, just as the plural 'you' in these two examples, the plural '*tumhe*' in # 9, and # 3, then, can be said to clearly refer to Vāseṭṭha and Bhāradvāja, and not to the monks.

[141] This would e.g., be like 'vous' in lieu of 'tu' in French.

see in his divine eye that Vāseṭṭha and Bhāradvāja were not just eager to listen to him, but that they were also ready, not just intellectually abut also psychologically, given that they had left Brahmnism and were desiring ordination (*bhikkhubhāvaṃ ākankhamānā*) (# 1). He would also have seen that they had Nibbanic potential, which, of course, comes to be confirmed when in the end the two seekers do become Arahants. It is therefore critical that no other monks would join them. The Buddha is, of course, not unknown to create situations to facilitate anyone who has the potential for liberation to encounter him, Angulimāla being a classic case study[142].

It is to be noted that it is the Buddha himself who initiates the topic and that it relates to the two youth being reviled by other Brahmins. It would therefore have been critical that no other monks would be around. Or at least the topic would be of no relevance to the Sangha inasmuch as they may have been familiar with it from hearsay if not from a Teahcing from the Buddha himself or his senior disciples. So this, then, was an intended as a private audience with the Blessed One for the two seekers.

It may also be worth remembering in this context that what the two Brahmins were hoping for was a 'Dhamma talk'. Surely, is pointing out to them that Brahmins are not special (# 23-26) but verily like others a great 'Dhamma-talk', something the young seekers themselves could not have been privy to? Indeed in looking to become Buddha's disciples, they had already rejected the Brahminic claims. So the real Dhamma-talk, meaning also what is new, especially for two versed in the Vedas (see below) would be the understanding about the nature of the universe that is different from what they themselves must have been exposed in Vedism.

And, having had many a Brahmin disciple, surely the Buddha's question, "Do the Brahmins revile you?", was nothing but rhetorical!

[142] Not heeding to the pleadings of the people, the Buddha proceeds towards the forest where Angulimāla is keeping an eye for his next victim. In the end, of course, Angulimāla ends up being an Arahant (see Gombrich, 1996, 135-164, for an excellent detailed treatment).

The question thus may have been a specific act of compassion on the part of the Buddha to help the duo, tormented by Brahmins as surely they were on their own admission, to get something off their chest. But more likely, it may have been to get them to revisit the issue, of being reviled by Brahmins. That would be the opener for the Buddha to weave his way into the subject of the nature of the universe as a legitimate backdrop to the rather mundane issue, namely the claims of Brahmins (mundane in comparison to the complex issue of the nature of the universe).

So what the Buddha wanted to talk to them about was a topic of the greatest depth. The maestro communicator, and the teacher that he was, he would ease them into the conversation by asking about something that they would be quite conversant with. "„.. surely they must revile and abuse you…." Could there be a better conversation gambit, a better opening of learning doors? Guiding them through # 2 -9, the Buddha can be said to prepare the ground by pointing out how and why the claim of superiority of the Brahmins – that they are born of the Brahma's mouth, can't stand its ground: "Brahmin women, (the wives) of Brahmins, are seen to menstruate, become pregnant, give birth, and give suck.". Again, all this would be of no relevance to the monks in general.

By contrast, Vāseṭṭha and Bhāradvāja would be the perfect audience for the Buddha Themselves Brahmins, the two were aspiring to become Bhikkhus. Having a clarification of the issue of the false claims of the Brahmins would make them feel even better that they were on the right track in their decision to seek ordination under the Buddha.

Secondly, # 10 to 16 directly addresses the issues relating to the Vedic universe, cutting through the Vedic myth. Could there have been a better audience than *Vāseṭṭha* and *Bhāradvāja?* While the two 'graduate' students, though still *sekhas*, would have found the Buddha's explanation most illuminating, despite the many things left unsaid by him relating to the evolutionary process, would it have meant anything to the 'undergraduate' monks[143], also *sekha*? Indeed might not the Discourse have caused confusion in the latter, and even engendered scepticism among the lesser faithful among the Sangha?

So it seems highly likely that the Buddha deciding to come out, and walk, possibly at an angle that would be visible to the two, would have been an intentional instructional ploy of the highest consideration on the part of the Buddha intended for the two youth alone. Here the Buddha was with two critical clients, to speak in contemporary business talk, who was looking to enter into a 'partnership' with the Buddha – a spiritual partnership. Would the Buddha not have known that, through his ability to read others minds? Should it be surprising, then, that he would not have wanted to have the monks included?

Suttas are known to be long in detail, often repetitively; thus there is hardly a reason why AS would not say that the rest of the Sangha had joined the two youth, if indeed they had.

At a practical level now, it may be relevant to note that the Buddha is not seated, but pacing back and forth. Given that he is pacing in the shade in the afternoon, we have to assume that he is walking North-South, with the mansion to his left (i.e., West). Since he is seen by Vāseṭṭha and Bhāradvāja, it may be assumed that the monks, among whom they were, are to the East, but away from the Buddha[144], since, as the text says, the two of them 'approached' him,

---

[143] Here, e.g., is how "a number of bhikkhus who dwelt on the ground floor of the *Migāra Mātā* mansion" on one occasion when the Blessed One was dwelling in it comes to be described. They "were restless, puffed up, personally vain, rough-tongued, rambling in their talk, muddle-minded, without clear comprehension, unconcentrated, scatter-brained, loose in their faculties" (S V51) (Ven. Bodhi, Tr., 1731). Even though the context here is not AS, it gives us some indication as to the possible quality of at least some disciples who may frequent the premises. And there is nothing to say that on the occasion of AS, there would not have been at least one or more such rumbustious disciples in the group, something the Buddha would well have come to know through his mind-reading skill (*paracittavijānañāṇa).*

[144] Or perhaps they are on the ground floor of the Migāra Mātā mansion, the Buddha's meditation taking place at the upper level.

having also talked about the Buddha, something not likely to happen in his immediate presence.

Perhaps a critical point to note is that Vāseṭṭha and Bhāradvāja join the Buddha in his pacing. They approach him as he paces, pay their respects, and follow him in pacing back and forth (*anucankamisṃsu*). What more evidence do we need to say that it was the two youth that the Buddha was talking to?

Pursuing the point, we may assume that either the two of them are on either side of the Buddha, one on each side or both on the same side, or behind him. In terms of communication, it is more likely that they are on either side.

If, however, as suggested by Collins, his audience is the Sangha, then we would have to imagine that the Buddha is either flanked by them, or, more oddly, that the Sangha are walking backwards to hear him better! And at the end of each directional walk, run back as if in military fashion, to form a line again facing the Buddha! If on the other hand, he is flanked, then we would have to imagine a long line on the East (to his right, as he walks north), or on the West (to his left) pacing south. Given that the Buddha is walking in the shade, being flanked on both sides, however, may likely put him off the shade, depending on, of course, how many are in the Sangha group and the height of the mansion (determining the shade). We are reminded here of a relevant comment made by Gombrich (1996, 142) on the Angulimāla story "Who was Angulimāla?". He aptly notes that "No one considers how vast and bulky a necklace [dangling from his neck] of a thousand fingers would be". In a similar vein, we may wonder how clumsy it would be for a Sangha retinue to join the Buddha in his pacing up and down, flanking him or to the front / back.

Another question remains - as to just exactly when the claimed monks would have joined him. Would it not be rude to join the Buddha after he has begun talking to the two? For it was the duo that had approached him first.

So what we can envision is the Buddha pacing North-South,

with Bhāradvāja and Vāseṭṭha, yes, in that order, but both to his right/left. Even though the two of them speak not a word but simply begin to fall into step with the Buddha, the Buddha addresses Vāseṭṭha, suggesting that he knew (presumably through his ability to see the minds of others) who the initiator had been in coming to see him. There is nothing to say that he also did not see in Vāseṭṭha both more of a readiness as well as a higher ability to grasp the Dhamma at a deep level. It may have been to ensure that he would be kept focused untrammeled that the Buddha keeps repeating the name of Vāseṭṭha. And, ever the smart communicator, the Buddha would have ensured that Bhāradvāja was closer to him than Vāseṭṭha. That way, he would have wanted to make sure that the former doesn't feel left our as he addresses the latter, past him.

Collins' discovery of the Vinaya as the source of many of the references itself may be indicative of the intended listeners. Surely the Sangha would have been knowledgeable of the rules! And so it may have been as instructional material for the two newcomers that the Buddha would have specifically drawn upon the Vinaya.

We may also ask why, if indeed the Buddha had wanted to address the monks, he didn't go to them directly from meditation when they were clearly not far? The practical reason may be seen as not wanting to have yet another sitting session! But equally, or more likely, was it not because he didn't think that they as a group were ready to understand the deeper part (another possible meaning of *agga*?), namely, relating to the universe? As hinted, we may think of a class of freshman in a post-graduate class of two students. Wasn't the pacing back and forth in full view of where the Sangha were, then, a clear invitation to Vāseṭṭha and Bhāradvāja to join him, and a signal for the others to please stay away?

The Buddha repeatedly addressing Vāseṭṭha by name indeed appears to again indicate, if our interpretation holds, an intimate talk between the two, with Bhāradvāja an assenting and privileged beneficiary.

From our look at the Vedic Myth (Fig. 5 and 6), and how the Buddha shatters it unequivocally, it should be more than clear that the Buddha's intended audience were the two Brahmin youths and not the Sangha in general. This indeed is implicit in Gombrich's point we started out with, that "we need to to know what cultural knowledge and presuppositions he shared with his audience" if indeed we were to try to discover the Buddha's original message. With whom else, in the context of AS, would he have shared the knowledge and the presuppositions relating to the Vedic Creation Myth other than the Brahmin duo who is characterized as being adept in the Vedas (see below)? There is no evidence of any of the senior disciples of the Buddha being in the gathering among whom Vāseṭṭha and Bhāradvāja were at the time the Buddha begins pacing. And so it seems clear that the only ones who shared the 'cultural knowledge and presuppositions' about Vedism with the Buddha were the two young Brahmins.

If thus far we have talked of the issue from the point of view of the Buddha, we may now look at the issue from the perspective of the two Brahmin youth. It may be of relevance to note again that Vāseṭṭha and Bhāradvāja might not have come with a blank slate on the topic. Not only are the two of them Brahmins, but they come learned in the Vedas. So, learned in the Vedas, what is the view of the universe they might have been privy to? This is why it was imperative that the Buddha shatter the myth they would have had in their mind.

12.2 Some External Evidence

There is also some evidence external to AS that seems to point to the two Brahmin youth as being the intended audience, and indeed to be the most qualified to be so. This emerges from a comparison of the three Suttas in which the characterization of the Primeval is part, namely the Pāṭika, Brahmajāla and Aggañña (D. 24, 1, 27 respectively). As will be seen from the Chart below, the Buddha can be said to release information about the Primeval and impart knowledge in a well managed, graduated sequence, as determined by the suitability of the audience, and the context. But taken together, what emerges in the end, as will be seen, is a total picture relating to both natural and human evolution.

A SUTTA / STAGE	B DATA RELEASED	C CONTEXT	D AUDIENCE & AUDIENCE QUALITY
1 Opening gambit *(PĀṬIKA).*	Just the topic.	In response to a complaint.	Sunakkhatta: "Foolish man".
2 Formal introduction of topic *(PĀṬIKA).*	"I have Knowledge of the Primeval. And more."	Responding to a question.	Bhaggava, 'a wanderer', of "different views, inclinations and influences".
3 Expansion *(PĀṬIKA).*	Devolution / Evolution initial segment.	Responding to a question.	Bhaggava, 'a wanderer', of "different views, inclinations and influences".
4 Expansion *(BRAHMAJĀLA).*	Devolution / Evolution initial segment.	Challenging Brahmins & ascetics.	Buddha's disciples.
5 Full picture *(AGGAÑÑA).*	Devolution / Evolution in Detail; Evolution of Human society.	Challenging Brahminic claims of superiority.	*Vāseṭṭha and Bhāradvāja* - Knowledgeble ordination seekers.

Fig. 8 Graduated Sequence of Information Release by the Buddha of his Knowledge of the Primeval

As can be seen from Fig. 6, it appears that the Buddha releases his Knowledge of the Primeval[145] (as I shall translate *aggañña* in this context) in a graduated sequence, from an 'Opening gambit' (1A; 1B), to full release (5A; 5B), and in three disparate Suttas – beginning with the Pāṭika, through Brahmajāla and culminating in

[145] K and P are in caps here to highlight the two critical dimensions of the topic.

the Aggañña[146]. What data is released (Col. B) seems related to the context (Col. C) and audience quality (Col. D) - matched to the level of receptivity and preparedness, both psychological and intellectual, of the receiver / decoder of the message.

Thus at step 1B in the Pāṭika (1A), the topic, Knowledge of the Primeval, is merely introduced when the Buddha questions Sunakkhatta, "Did I ever say to you, 'Come under my discipleship, Sunakkhatta, and I will make known Knowledge of the Primeval'?"[147].

At 2B, the Buddha claims to have the Knowledge of the Primeval (# 2.14), following an extended response to a question by Bhaggava-gotta (Bhaggava for short): "Has indeed Sunakkhatta left the Buddha, as told by Sunakkhatta himself (# 1.3)?" Saying that Sunakkhatta indeed had left, the Buddha goes on to give three contexts in which Sunakkhatta figures (# 1.7 – 2.13), but of no particular relevance to us here. And then he introduces the topic by saying, "Bhaggava, I have Knowledge of the Primeval as well" (*aggaññcahaṃ Bhaggava pajānāmi*) (# 2.14). But significantly (see later why), he next hints, "... and even more" (*tato ca uttariĩaraṃ*).

In the same process, however (3B), the Buddha lays out in brief the Devolutionary phase (literally 'world' (*loko*)). First, in this world are, as in AS, Devolving-Ābhassara-Beings[148] (*Pāṭika* # 2.15). This is followed by an Evolutionary phase, as when '*an empty brahmavimāna*'[149] appears (*vivaṭṭamāna loke suññaṃ*

---

[146] Does the sequencing of the release of information suggest the possible chronology of delivery of the three Discourses.?

[147] Here it smay be noted, however, that the question that prompts the response is initiatated by Sunakkhatta, and to that extent it may not be valid to credit the Buddha with step 1. But here we are only taking an external look at the process of information sharing. And the issue of who should be credited for initiating may have no bearing on the point being made.

[148] See this writer's translation (I.3) for the interpretation of this.

[149] Although the original Pali shows the word '*brahmavimāna*' with a capital B, and the translation by Walshe likewise, 'Palace of Brahma', our use of the lower case reflects a different interpretation (see later).

brahmavimānaṃ pātubhavati).

Then a 'certain Being' (note the singular), at the end of its life-span and merit-span, quits the Ābhassara body and comes to be born in this 'empty *brahmavimāna*' *(aññataro satto āyukkhayā vā puññakhayā vā ābhassara kāyā cavitvā suññam brahmavimānaṃ upapajjati*...).

But, now to give the context, soon the Being longs for company, a wish that comes to be fulfilled, when other Beings (note the plural) appear in that same empty *brahmavimāna*. Now the one who appears first thinks of itself as Brahma, Mahā Brahma, with those who follow agreeing that they are indeed 'progenited' (to coin a verb from a noun, seeking your understanding) from, i.e., created by, Brahma (*brahmuṇā nimmitā*) (# 2.16), the so self-identified. Now yet another Being, at the end of its life- and merit-span, comes to be born in the *empty brahmavimāna*. Over time, the Being leaves the household life. Cultivating the mind, it sees its immediate past life, but none further back. So he decides, referring to the first Being, "That Brahma... he is permanent, stable, eternal, not subject to change, the same for ever and ever. But we who were created by that Brahma, we are impermanent, unstable, short-lived, fated to fall away, and we have come to this present state." (*Yo kho so bhavaṃ Brahmā .... so nicco dhuvo sassato avipariṇāma-dhammo sassati-samantath'va ṭhassati. ... Ye pana mayam ahumhā tena bhotā mayaṃ Brahmuṇā nimmitā te mayam aniccā adhuvā appāyukā cavanadhammā itthattaṃ āgatā ti)* (# 2.17).

Here the Buddha points out, "That, Reverend Sirs, is how it comes about that you teach that all things began with the creation by a god, or Brahma" (Walshe, 381).

Moving along, at 4B of the Chart, the Buddha, in the Brahmajāla (2.2-2.5), provides the identical details as re the Devolution and Evolution process, but towards a related though different purpose: "This is the first case whereby some ascetics and Brahmins are partly Eternalists and partly Non-Eternalists" (# 2.6). Here he is challenging the first of many spiritual views making the rounds at the time.

Finally, at 5B in Fig. 6 relating to AS, the Buddha, while talking about the phases of Devolution and Evolution, unfolds brand new material (# 10-16) not found in the *Pāṭika* or the *Brahmajāla*. This, of course, is the detailed process of natural evolution, as in our interpretation, leading to the process of human evolution.

So then, we first note how the Buddha unveils the information systematically. First, in the Pāṭika, is just mention of the name, next a claim to having the Knowledge of the Primeval, immediately teasing, as it were, that he knows more, and then the first few details relating to the Devolutionary / Evolutionary phases. This last is repeated in the Brahmajāla, the evolutionary process laid out in full in AS. This, then, is the first piece of comparative evidence of the Buddha's intentionality.

The 'small print', so to speak, in the three Suttas provide additional evidence of such intentionality.

First we may note the introduction of the 'empty brahmavimāṇa' (*suñña brahmavimāṇa*) in the Pāṭika. It has been translated by Walshe, in keeping with the traditional interpretation, as 'an empty palace of Brahma' (Walshe, 75). But 'palace' is suggestive of a physical building, although, of course, it could be taken allegorically, or symbolically as well. This writer, however, prefers to take it, as in PED (630), in the more literal sense of 'covering a certain space'. It is said to be 'empty', suggesting a simple 'void' or sky. But it could be understood as a particular 'level' (from the perspective of Earth) of the sky, empty of gravitation.

No part of space, of course, is 'empty' in a physical sense at any level. So it may be understood relatively. Gravity is what keeps an aircraft pulled to Earth, requiring energy fed by fuel to cut through it. And, as we know from space travel, once past the zone of gravity, a shuttle require no fuel to course through millions of miles, once set in a trajectory[150] on a free-course. In our context, too, as in AS,

[150] It may be compared to a bullet which requires a trigger to release it,

Beings are said to be 'traveling through the sky' (*antalikkhacarā*). So being gravity-free would be the ideal condition for such travel, and the reference to *suñña* 'empty' can then be said to be an intentional description on the part of the Buddha.

While the term Brahma in *suñña brahmavimāṇa* has been taken by Walshe, following tradition, in the sense of a personage, the literature also allows us to understand it in another sense, i.e., as a quality that is 'noble' or 'ideal'. (PED) [151].

So *suñña brahmavimāṇa* may then be understood as 'an ideal empty space', being a certain ideal level in the sky, a transitional stop, a 'half-way house' so to speak, where the Beings migrating from a Devolutionary phase to an Evolutionary one could hang their hat, preparatory to a later landing on Earth, the locus of AS and the eventual home of Beings that leave the Ābhassara bodies. A critical need for sentient existence is water[152], as we also know from the AS description of it being 'all water' (AS # 11). Hence, this level of empty space could be understood to be with relatively easy access to land where alone would there be water towards further evolution. So we may take *suñña brahmavimāṇa* to mean 'a gravity-free level in the sky in proximity to water'[153].

---

but once out of the barrel of the gun, requiring no such 'push'.

[151] Here are some examples, as given in PED (492-493):

- *brahma uposatha* 'highest religious observance' (with meditation on the Buddha and practice of the uposatha abstinence);
- *brahmacakka* 'excellent wheel' i.e., the doctrine of the Buddha;
- *brahmadaṇḍa* 'highest penalty';
- *brahmadeyya* 'excellent gift';
- *brahmapatta* 'arrived at the highest state, above the devas;
- *brahmapatti* 'highest good';
- *brahmayāna* 'way of the highest good';
- *brahmavihāra* 'sublime state of mind.

[152] It may be noted that 70% of our bodies are made up of water.

[153] This ideal empty space may be way up high in the sky, such as the ionosphere, "A region of charged particles in a planet's upper atmosphere; the part of the Earth's atmosphere beginning at an altitude of about 25 miles and extending outward 250 miles or more."

Our interpretation here, let it be noted, is not to squabble with a translation, but to be in line with our interpretation of the AS in scientific terms.

But what is the significance of the Buddha introducing the concept of an empty *brahmavimāṇa level,* and avoiding any description relating to Earth? In AS, Beings coming 'to the present state' leaving their Ābhassara bodies, come to be associated (following a long period of changes in nature – darkness to light, seasons, months, etc.), with Earth, changed from 'all water'.

But to go that route in the *Pāṭika* or the *Brahmajāla* would be to create 'noise' – an unnecessary detail that will detract from the purpose the Buddha has in mind. A Being born in this empty *brahmavimāṇa* is said to take to the homeless life, suggestive of life on Earth, clearly after the lapse of another long period of time (even though not so said in the Sutta). However, the Buddha does not step on to that Earth in this Sutta, still staying with the empty space.

Why? Stepping down to Earth would require an explanation of all other associated features of nature – all water, no sun and moon, vegetation, humans, etc. that are outlined in detail in AS. Such details would be irrelevant to the context (Col C of Fig. 6) of how the first arrival (as in the *Pāṭika* 1.1-1.3) comes to be considered the Mahā Brahma. The purpose of the *Pāṭika* Sutta is to dethrone the various views about the beginning of things held by various Samanas and Brahmanas, and it is in this context that an empty space comes to be introduced.

The purpose in the *Brahmajāla* (4 in Fig. 6) is to challenge the views of Samanas and Brahmanas who are "partly Eternalists and partly Non-Eternalists" (*ekacca sassatikā ekacca asassatikā,*

---

http://space.about.com/od/glossaries/g/ionosphere.htm>. It "plays an important part in atmospheric electricity and forms the inner edge of the magnetosphere." Further, "It has practical importance because, among other functions, it influences radio propagation to distant places on the Earth" <http://www.ask.com/wiki/Ionosphere>.

ekaccaṃ sassataṃ ekaccaṃ asassataṃ) (# 2.1). Again, even though the Samana Brahmanas are clearly Earth-bound, the issue relates to the origins - the cosmos as eternal or otherwise. Again, a description of how Earth and human society comes to be formed would constitute noise. It is thus that, here, too, Earth comes to be not introduced.

Yet, the Beings leaving their Ābhassara bodies have already come to have an implicit footing on Earth – the one who leaves home to homelessness in the *Pāṭika* and Samanas and Brahmanas who hold views in the Brahmajāla. So, it is to formally introduce what is merely implicit in the earlier two Suttas that the Buddha can be said to introduce the Earth in AS. However, it may be noted in this connection that "at that time, there was just (one vast mass of) water" (# 10). This means that the Ābhassara Beings are still up in the sky. So it is thus that the Buddha draws upon a certain empty space in the earlier Suttas, as appropriate to the context.

However, this home, *suñña brahmavimāna,* finds no mention in AS, again because in that context, it is an irrelevant detail for the completion of the picture of the *Earth* he seeks to present. What is central to the Buddha's purpose in AS is mocking the Brahmin claim of superiority. The primary stage upon which this drama unfolds is the Earth, and so the Buddha provides the details relating to Earth, keeping out the empty brahmavimāna, although, of course, its presence is implicit, just as Earth is in the other two Suttas. It is from this empty space that beings eventually land on Earth, naturally, over time, Beings being initially characterized as 'moving in the sky'.

In summary then, we have now seen how the 'small print' in the Suttas amply speaks to how each description well matches the contextual intentionality of the Buddha when irrelevant details, snipped out, come to be conspicuous by their absence.

Finally we come to Col. D of Fig. 6 - Audience & Audience Quality. We may discuss this in relation to the receptivity and the preparedness of the 'decoders' of the Buddha's message.

We know that Sunakkhatta (D1) has been called a "Foolish man" by the Buddha. So we see the Buddha not going beyond repeating the topic after Sunakkhatta, knowing well that any detail would be beyond the comprehension of the foolish man.

But, talking to Bhaggava (D2), the Buddha discloses a bit more. To re-enact the scene in rather mundane and contemporary terms, we might imagine the Buddha saying, "You know what, Bhaggava. What's so surprising is that a foolish man wants to know how the world began, unaware, or not wanting to face, the reality of the darts of *dukkha* received as a continuing gift of folly! It's not that I don't know. I indeed do have the Knowledge of the Primeval. But Sunakkhatta is such a fool as you know[154] that whatever I say will go over his head. It just wouldn't have a meant a thing to him."

Also, it is not as if the Buddha does not try to appease a disappointed Sunakkhatta. He performs not one but three miracles, even pushing a claim, "Has a miracle being performed or not?" (1.10)[155].

[154] Bhaggava knows that Sunakkhatta has been called a foolish man by the Buddha, not just once but thrice, hearing it from the Buddha himself. When Sunakkhatta agrees that the Buddha had never promised him to show miracles, or make known his Knowledge of the Primeval, as a condition for coming under his rule / tutelage, the Buddha doesn't mince his words, calling a spade a spade: "Such being the case, you foolish man, ..." (# 1.3, 1.4, 1.5).

[155] Two of the miracles constitute of two predictions made by the Buddha coming true: (1) that the naked ascetic Korakkhattiya, walking on all four and taking food with his mouth, but considered a 'true Arahant' by Sunakkhatta, will die of food poisoning in seven days (# 1.7ff); (2) a prediction that the naked ascetic Kandaramsuka who "has enjoyed the greatest gains and fame of all in the Vajjian capital" (# 1.11), for undertaking seven rules, chastity among them, and again considered an Arahant by Sunakkhatta, will "before long be living clothed and married" (#1.13). A third miracle relates to a yet another naked ascetic Pāṭikaputta, who claims to be the Buddha's equal in wisdom and capacity to perform miracles. "If the ascetic Gotama will come half-way [physically] to meet me, I will do likewise." (# 1.15). Sunakkhatta reports this to the Buddha who then says, "Sunakkhatta, that naked ascetic Pāṭikaputta is not capable of meeting me face to face unless he takes back his words, abandons that thought, and gives up that view..." (# 1.16). The Buddha then, as if tacitly meeting

By contrast, in Bhaggava the Buddha finds a potential partiality towards the Dhamma. We may remember that it is the Buddha that goes to him that morning, possibly seeing it in his mind's eye his capacity to understand the Dhamma. We find evidence for this when at the end of the Discourse, Bhaggava, who has been made privy as to the details regarding the false accusations, says "I think the Blessed One is able to teach me to attain ..." (# 2.21). The Buddha says that it would be difficult for him: "It is hard for you, Bhaggava, holding different views, being of different inclinations and subject to different influences...". But Bhaggave insists, "I will place my trust in the Blessed One". And it may be said, then, that it was as an encouragement to Pāṭikaputta to cultivate a trust in him that the Buddha first makes the claim of knowing "even more", and then unveils the preliminary stages of evolution, confirming to Bhaggava as it were that he indeed did have Knowledge of the Primeval (# 15-2.17).

In the *Brahmajāla* (D4), it is the monks (*bhikkhave*), already his disciples, that the Buddha is addressing, when he directly comes to the topic of his Knowledge of the Primeval, in the context of some views held by Samanas and Brahmanas (# 2.1). And we may note the Buddha laying out the same details to them as to Bhaggava. The monks, who already come with not only trust in the Buddha but also with some understanding of the Dhamma, can be expected to benefit perhaps a bit more than Bhaggava (of 'different views'). Yet, they, too, are still the average ordained, the Buddha thus going no further.

And it is to Vāseṭṭha and Bhāradvāja (5D), then, that the total disclosure is made. If being adept in the Vedas make them intellectually more prepared, seeking ordination would put them into

---

Pāṭikaputta's condition, retires to the park of Pāṭikaputta itself for his mid-day rest, letting Bhaggava know of it and saying, "You may tell him whatever you want". Despite the attempt by several to get Pāṭikaputta to make good on his word, now that the Buddha had indeed come half-way, he finds it impossible to get up from his seat! "What's the matter with you, friend Pāṭikaputta? Is your bottom stuck to the seat, or is the seat stuck to your bottom?" asks one (#1.21).

a psychological readiness. By comparison, they would undoubtedly be far more prepared than either Bhaggava or the Bhikkhus, neither with any or much background in the Vedas, which as noted, provides the backdrop to # 10-16 of AS outlining the evolutionary process.

As we can see, then, our analysis provides external evidence to show how and that AS was directed specifically at the two adepts Vāseṭṭha and Bhāradvāja, making another argument incidentally supportive of viewing AS as being serious.

Addressing Sāriputta, the Buddha says, "Sāriputta, I can teach the Dhamma briefly. I can teach the Dhamma in detail. I can teach the Dhamma both briefly and in detail. It is those who can understand that are rare." (A I.134). Saying that "It is the time for this", Sāriputta assures the Buddha that "There will be be those who can understand the Dhamma." It is as if the Buddha has found in Vāseṭṭha and Bhāradvāja those rare ones who would understand what he has to offer.

We find some confirmation of our position indeed in the words of Collins himself (318). Pointing to "the references to Brahmanical ideas and texts for whose presence Gombrich argues", and to "those to the Vinaya I adduce here", he suggests that "AS was composed in and for an educated milieu familiar with both styles of thought …. and appreciate its serious intention". He further notes how "they would thus be a good audience both for the references to Vedic hymns and for the 'etymologies' in AS".

This writer, then, affirms again Vāseṭṭha and Bhāradvāja to be the exclusive, and intended, audience of the Buddha in AS[156], and the appropriacy of the context for the Buddha to present his discovery of nature, which are, in the words of Collins, "not the ware of the ordinary".

Releasing the information gradually may, then, be seen as the Buddha's strategy to ensure that when the full picture hits the

---

[156] It may be of relevance to note that the Buddha addresses Vāseṭṭha and Bhāradvāja in the Tevijja Sutta (D 13), too, in relation to 'the way of Brahma'.

stands, so to speak, i.e., comes to the ears of the Sangha, it will not all go over their heads, or be in simple disbelief. What is said in a Discourse by the Buddha can undoubtedly be expected to make the rounds among the Sangha community. If the name-dropping, namely the claim to have Knowledge of the Primeval, draws their initial attention, the announcement of knowing even beyond can be said to tweak their interest further, at least those within the Sangha that are more intelligent, curious and spiritually advanced. If the description of the early phases of the Devolution and Evolution cycle feeds their hunger to some extent, they may have been only too happy to finally get the whole story!

12.3 A Final Look

To revisit the scene of AS for a final look, we may envision the two seekers returning to the fold of the Sangha community where they had been prior to going to meet the Buddha, and being asked by them as to what Dhamma talk they had had from the Buddha. Still fresh in their minds, and exuberant at their novel understanding, they would repeat what the Buddha had shared with them.

We may also envision the two youth running into a Brahmin community at another time, and repeating their act, undoubtedly to the chagrin of the Brahmins, and perhaps reaping more scorn upon themselves.

In that sense, then, the two of them can be said to have become, as not unlikely expected by the Buddha, *de facto* Dhamma messengers who had accepted the Buddha's invitation 'to hear, bear and carry the Dhamma (*sunātha dhāretha carātha dhamme*), though not specifically invited.

Confirming the Buddha's intentionality and picking the right audience to deliver the message, this also establishes again that AS is no parody or satire but very serious business!

For reasons such as the above, then, we would have no choice but to consider Collins' replacement of Vāseṭṭha with monks an unwarranted license.The symbolism of the loftiness associated with the mansion, and Vāseṭṭha later becoming an Arahant, also add to the conclusion that imagining an audience of monks would be an unreasonable reading into the text.

So we may conclude with the words, by turning around a contemporary maxim, the gem is in the detail[157]! Gems now discovered, we can say we have a clear picture of Vāseṭṭha and Bhāradvāja as the intended audience, establishing once again the serious and realistic-historical nature of # 10-16 of AS.

---

[157] Of course, the saying is 'the devil is in the detail'.

13

Unfolding the Primeval as Buddha's Intent

What indeed is the Buddha's intent in AS?

As noted, AS has been seen as satire, moral commentary, model of society and an etiology - serious but of no historical accuracy, etc. Since some of these matters have been responded to in the above sections, it is not the writer's intent here to pursue them again, unless they bear on a view or argument being made. The attempt rather is, as for Gombrich (1992, p. 160), only to "discover the original meaning…" As with Collins (314), "the issue then becomes one of what, if anything, we can say about the original sense and motivation of AS."

Happily we feel that we can indeed see, with a large measure of confidence, what the original sense and motivation of AS was. But before we come to it, it is clear that unfolding the Primeval, as in our study, in terms of Devolution and Evolution, is one of them, if, as we shall see, only as a backdrop.

13.1 Unfolding the Primeval as Buddha's Intent

The writer has sought to show above that the Buddha is dead serious in sharing with us his discovery of the evolution of the universe in terms of a Devolutionary-Evolutionary cycle (# 10-16), and, though not dealt with in any detail here, of the evolution of human society

(17-22). So the writer first contends that laying out the evolutionary parameters of the universe and human society is indeed an intent of the Buddha's in the AS.

In fact, we could say that there has been a foreshadowing of this intent in the Pāṭika and the Brahmajāla Suttas (see II.12). The "Charlatan" (to use Walshe's term) Sunakkhatta, in the Pāṭika, called a foolish man (*moghapurisa*) by the Buddha, complains, "The Blessed one has not made known to me [His] Knowledge of the Primeval" (# 1.5) (*Na hi pana me bhante bhagavā aggaññaṃ paññāpetīti*). The Buddha placates him by simply pointing out that in the first place he was never given a promise of making known his Knowledge of the Primeval as a condition for coming under his discipleship.

However, the Buddha picks up the topic again (in the same Discourse), after going on his alms round and retreating to a nearby park for a mid-day rest, this in a slightly different scene but with Sunakkhatta still very much involved. Here, the Buddha continues to address the Licchavi Bhaggava (the Sutta beginning with the Buddha visiting him) and says in no uncertain terms, "Bhaggava, I have (literally, 'know') Knowledge of the Primeval. Not just that, but even beyond …' (…*uttarītaram pajānāmi*) (# 2.14).

Continuing (# 2.15-17) he begins with the same opener as in AS # 10, up to the point of the *Ābhassara* Being leaving the *Ābhassara* body and coming into the 'present state'. And then, giving some details *not found in the AS*, he goes on to explain how the first Ābhassara Being longs for other Beings: "Oh, if only some other Beings would come here!". Then other Ā*bhassara* Beings, their life-span and merit-span exhausted, end up in the present state, too.

While, as noted, the Buddha then takes a different route in each of the Pāṭika and the Brahmajāla Suttas, in the AS he lays out his Knowledge of the Primeval in full, meaning enough to show the cyclical nature, Devolution followed by Evolution.

Why, then, did the Buddha decide to lay it out all in AS, having hinted at it in the other two Discourses?

In AS, *agga* of *aggañña* seems to be used intentionally by the Buddha as a *double entendre*, to capture the sense of both 'primeval' as well as, as we shall see, 'best'. A closer look at # 10-21, as above, will show us that the sharing of his Knowledge of the Primeval was intended for a specific purpose.

By the time the second segment begins (# 10), the point the Buddha wants to make, namely, dismissing the Brahminic claims (with the references to Brahmin women giving birth, etc.), actually comes to be already made. So there is hardly a reason to include this far-fetched characterization of origins (# 10 to 20) to make that point.

But let us now assume a potential scenario when Vāseṭṭha and Bhāradvāja encounter a group of Brahmins, and asked who they were, say exactly what the Buddha had suggested they say: "We're the sons of the Sakya". In an ensuing give and take, the Brahmins come to understand the context of their words. Now a brash Brahmin youth among them decides to go on the offensive, and say, (to put it in contemporary language) "But, you know, my friends, we're not total dummies. When we say we're Brahma-become (*brahmabhuto*) or we're born of the mouth of Brahma, we were only being circumspect in polite company. We'll even admit to going a bit overboard..., really, for the benefit of the ignorant masses. Of course, we are born of Brahma's vagina (*brahmayonija*), our Creator now manifesting his, er, her femaleness. And the term 'mouth' was, again a mere polite, euphemism. In any case, what really matters is not one or the other orifice. The bottom line is that we're Brahma-become, i.e., the 'chosen people'"!

Given that Vāseṭṭha and Bhāradvāja are still seekers, i.e., hedging their bets but not yet thrown in the dice, would the talk by the brash Brahmin youth throw a curve on to their faith in the Buddha? At a minimum, the brash Brahmin youth would have effectively met the Buddha's counter-argument head on that Brahmin women 'menstruate, get pregnant, give birth and give suck' (AS # 4), etc., agreeing to a birth through the vaginal canal.

If the Buddha's argument were to be thus countered successfully, then the Brahminic claim of superiority would still stand. However, there is still one claim not spoken to by our imaginary brash Brahmin youth. For one to be 'Brahma-become', never mind the orifice, there has to be a Brahma in the first place. So this, then, is the crux of the matter. The Buddha wants to leave the Brahmins no wiggle room, or any outs, to let them regain lost ground. And the best way to plug it would be to not just deny birth through the mouth of Brahma but to destroy the myth about Brahma itself! The purpose of # 10-16 can then be said to do precisely that – to pull out the very roots of the tree of the myth (Brahma), not just the manifestation of the branches and fruits (Brahma-become). If how the first Ābhassara Being comes to be seen as Brahma by the later arrivals serves as an explanatory preparation, the universe in the form of a Devolutionary and Evolutionary cycle would, then, establish beyond a shadow of doubt that there is no Brahma out there, and that it is a pure fiction of the imagination of the Ābhassara Beings, and, of course, Brahmins! That would render it an issue of the colour of the hair of the offspring of a barren woman. That is to say that since the basic premise of a barren woman having offspring is baseless, any answer to the question would be faulty. Likewise, the claim of being 'Brahma-become' would fall flat on its face if indeed Brahma can be shown to be non-existent!

It can then be said that the Buddha was seeking to elevate his argument regarding the absurdity of the claim that Brahmins were born of Brahma's mouth. Segment two of AS (# 10-16) would take away any residual doubt that Vāseṭṭha and Bhāradvāja may continue to entertain, or be potentially strengthened by an imaginary brash youth, the Vedic Creation Myth still in their heads. Thus it is that the Buddha decides to expose the Creation Myth itself. That he was successful in erasing any doubts in the minds of the two youth can be seen when later they enter the Order, and eventually experience Arhanthood.

However, if AS segment # 10-16 can thus be said to have been to speak in the language of a sophisticated (this in Brahmin thought) Vāseṭṭha and Bhāradvāja, it can also said to serve another purpose. And that would be to provide a supportive scaffolding for the case to be made relating to the evolution of human society in # 17-21. While for the average disciple of the Buddha, this latter and # 1-9 earlier would be convincing enough, for the sharper-minded seeker of 'liberation through wisdom' (*paññāvimutti*), there may still remain the larger issue. Explaining the process of Devolution and Evolution and the mechanism of conditionality can then be said to provide a parallel, and a preceding, process to the mechanism of the evolution of human society, rendering it more plausible.

In presenting the cyclical principle that governs the universe, the Buddha can be said to seek as well to establish the absence of a first cause. And it may be said that it is to show this reality, be it at the level of nature (#10-16) or human society (# 17-21), that segment two (# 10-16) can be said to have been included. So while as in # 1-9, the issue of the claims of Brahmin superiority may be seen as a mere social issue, easily disprovable logically and empirically, to provide a descriptive explanation would be to ground the untenability of the claim on a solid theoretical footing. The argument, of course, can be said to cut both ways – the fallacy of Brahminic superiority reinforcing the fallacy of a Creator God, and vice versa.

The Buddha talking about it in this sophisticated manner would also to be in the same league as with the rest of his explanations of phenomena, namely, to be comprehensive. In explaining 'visual consciousness', e.g., Westernsciencetalks about the physical components within the body – retina, optic nerve, etc., with a bye-the-bye reference to a stimulus. But the Buddha's analysis includes 'stimulus' as one of four conditions. If there were to be no stimulus impinging on a sense door, there would be no consciousness. Hence stimulus (an object, colour, shape, etc.), external as it is, comes to be an explanatory component of consciousness. The presence of a stimulus, however, would not result in consciousness unless there were two other conditions; taking the example of visual consciousness, 'light' and 'attention'[158]. This is no more than saying that while this page on the screen could not have been seen on a dark screen, it would not enter your consciousness unless you were to look at it, paying attention, and read it. In the same vein, to speak of the conditioned process of the evolution of human society without

[158] See Ven. Bodhi (Ed.), 151-152).

speaking of the conditioned process of the universe itself would be to be less than comprehensive.

So there are then at least four reasons why the Buddha would have delved into the issue of Devolution and Evolution:

1. to meet the needs of the two speicific seekers;
2. to serve as a support base for understanding the evolution of human society, and
3. as a backdrop to disproving the Brahminic claims of superiority by elevating the argument to a higher level, and
4. for the theoretical reason of being comprehensive.

There is yet another that might have prompted the Buddha to lay it out all - compassion[159]. As noted in II.12, the incremental unfolding of the characterization relating to Knowledge of the Primeval through the three Suttas is a clear indication of the Buddha's serious interest of sharing his Knowledge of the world with the world. If surely a 'foolish man' like Sunakkhata was looking for Knowledge of the Primeval, wouldn't there be others among the rest of the 'deranged' (*ummattakā*)[160] of the world who would want to have their minds arranged around the Primeval, displayed on their mind's screen for all to see? It may also not be off the mark to think that even if everything he had to offer would go over the heads of the contemporary many, the Buddha would surely have been projecting to a future time when knowledge of reality of nature, universe, etc., will come to be unfolded, *kadāci karahaci*! So he would have foreseen that some day somewhere somebodies would come to see for themselves the understanding he has. Would it then not be a vindication, as if he needed any, of his conviction that we are

159 We may be reminded here how a certain Brahma Sahampati would talk a reluctant Buddha into sharing with the world what he had just discovered under the Bodhi Tree.

160 'The masses, the entire lot, are deranged" (*sabbe puthujjanā ummattakā*).

writing about it today?

If the above provides external evidence for establishing that AS is no etiology,... etc., a closer textual analysis provides internal, and additional, evidence to show the Buddha's serious intent. And this, as noted above, is his use of language with the precision of a linguistic surgeon.

As noted, there are two phrases that come to be repetitively used in the description as in # 10-16, summarized in # 18. First is *kadaci karahaci dīghassa addhuno accayena* 'after the lapse of a long period of time beyond' and the other, *ciraṃ dīghaṃ addhānam* 'for a very long stretch of time'. Another sentence that appears just once is *ayam loko puṇa vivaṭṭati.* 'This world evolves again." Let us then see how these lines come to be used.

We find *kadāci karahaci dīghassa addhuno accayena* used in the following contexts:

1. Initially, when the world devolves (# 10);
2. When the world next evolves (# 10);
3. When water comes to be overrun by savoury Earth (11);
4. Summarily reviewing the evolutionary process, as outlined in detail in # 10-16, beginning with the appearance of the Earth, in a single paragraph (# 18).

It appears, then, that the phrase comes to be used to characterize the *longer* time periods, presumably countable in billions of years, but with conditions for human (and presumably animal) life still absent. The single occurrence of [*ayam loko*] *puṇa vivaṭṭo hoti* comes to be at the end of this description of the longer time spans when the conditions for life begin to appear: moon and sun, night and day, months and fortnight, year and seasons (# 12 end).

Here, then, are the contexts in which *ciraṃ dīghaṃ addhānam* 'for a very long stretch of time' occurs:

1. Ābhassara Beings staying put, mind-based, self-luminous, etc. during the Devolutionary period (#10).

2. Ābhassara Beings staying put, having come into the 'present state', during the Evolutionary period (#10)
3. Feasting on the savoury Earth, resulting in the Beings becoming coarser, arrogant with self-conceit emerging, and the savoury Earth disappearing (# 13, twice).
4. Feeding on *pappaṭaka* / *ahicchattaka* – the first food to grow on Earth, Beings becoming coarser, arrogant and with self-conceit, and the *pappaṭaka* disappearing; giving way to creepers, and arrogance (# 14, twice).
5. Enjoying creepers, Beings becoming coarser, arrogant and self-conceited, and the creepers disappearing (# 15, twice).
6. Disappearing Creepers giving way to rice, Beings enjoying it, bodies becoming coarser, i.e., more variegated, differentiated, female and male sex organs appearing (# 16, twice).
7. In summation: moving through air, etc; enjoying the savoury Earth; enjoying *pappaṭaka* ; enjoying creepers; enjoying rice (# 18, 5 times).

It may be noted that the phrase comes to be repeated twice, in relation to each of the four critical vegetational changes identified (3, 4, 5 and 6). While repetition may be considered an aspect of oral transmission, it is conceivable here that it is to emphasize that the changes were taking place *within* a single Devolutionary (# 10) or Evolutionary (# 10 and later) phase, as contrasted with the longer changing phases entailing billions of years[161].

[161] The present phase begun 13.5 billion years ago, the shorter period within a Devolution and Evolution phase may be then countable in terms of a three to four billion years, on an average, considering four such sub-stages identified by the Buddha. But, of course, that has to be modified in view of the fact that homo sapiens sapiens, that's us humans, can be dated only as far back as 150,000 years, far less than a single million, never mind a billion. It is, of course, both possible and impossible that the calculation would run similar in the numerous Devolution and Evolution revolutions. It would be similar because

The phrase occurring in the summary paragraph # 18 would be automatic since it recaps the process in summary form, again hinting that the processes are within a a single evolutionary phase, *ciraṃ dīghaṃ addhānam* five times, matching the individually outlined five times earlier, now collectively (# 13-16).

If the above summarizing shows the organized critical essayist in the Buddha, it also affirms the evolutionary sequence in no uncertain terms. So we can see then that the two repetitive phrases are being used quite intentionally, and with a view to a clear discrimination between the primary phases and the sub-phases.

We may envisage the Buddha seeking to establish in the minds of Vāseṭṭha and Bhāradvāja the realilty of the evolutionary process, both inter- and intra- so to speak, countering the Vedic myth (see II.11).

Our discussion confirms again that the Buddha was indeed trying to provide an accurate, and 'historical' account of the process of evolution. While the Pāṭika and Brahmajāla Suttas provide the opening ambits, AS can be said to provide the context which makes the characterization of the primeval relevant, in terms of both topic and audience. It is thus that the Buddha can be said to have grabbed the opportunity to make a 'power point presentation' on the screen of the mind of his two listeners, highlighting only the critical stages and sub-stages.

It may be of parenthetical interest, perhaps far-fetched even (or is it?), that even the context of the Buddha walking back and forth in the shade and open air (AS # 1) seems to be symbolic of the phases of the universe. We may then visualize the Buddha walking in the shade for a segment of the Sutta, then going beyond in order to signal

---

nature can be expected to 'behave' in identical manner from one cycle to another. It would be dissimlar in that the 27 billion years constituting a single cycle of Devolution and Evolution, as per the current calculations, will allow a zillion changes and permutations, each of which may impact upon the process differentially. But all this, of course, is speculation.

the beginning of the next segment / line, and then walking back into the shade for the next sub-phase, thus helping to sink in the idea of first the phases and next the sub-phases of change in the universe, as in relation to day and night, now symbolized by shade and non-shade.

A final piece of structural and linguistic evidence seems to lock in the argument that the Buddha's intent indeed was to speak of the primeval. The term *agga* comes to be used in AS in both segment two (# 10-16) as well as the other two segments. But while we shall come to its meaning of 'best' in the rest later (see II.14), in # 10-16 it seems to be used in the definite sense of 'primeval'. It occurs three times (# 13, 15, 16), always immediately following *porāṇa*. This seems to be, then, the way that *agga* 'primeval' in the context of the section dealing with the story of Devolution and Evolution comes to be distinctly associated with an ancient past. Indeed, the addition of *porāṇa* here may be understood as an intensifier, allowing us to take *porāṇaṃ aggaṃ* to mean 'ancient and primeval'.

To this writer, then, it is clear that segment two (# 10-16) was to intentionally set the picture of Brahmin claims (and their falsity) within the context (or, against the backdrop) of a larger canvass of the reality of nature. But it also appears that, given that he was not wont to saying things that were of pure abstract importance[162], he had waited for the right opportunity to lay it out all. And negating the claims of Brahmins seems to fall within this criterion, since it is to suggest the wider issue of the equality of all human beings. The issue also can be said to have provided the right context.

---

[162] We are reminded of the Buddha holding some leaves in his hands, and declaring that what he has in hand is what he has taught, but what constitutes his knowledge is the forest. This suggests that what he has said in AS was only what was called for in teaching the two things he says he teaches – sufferng and the way out of suffering.

14

'Dhamma is Best' as Buddha's Real Intent

The writer has spared no pains to argue that the Buddha's intent was indeed to share his Knowledge of the Primeval. However, for all the hoopla, namely the attempts at showing that what the Buddha says about the universe is an accurate, and scientific, picture, it is also this writer's contention, as foolhardy as it may sound, that it is *not* the Buddha's *primary* intent.

As part of quashing the Brahminic claim early in the Sutta, the Buddha adds that anyone of the four classes can become an Arahant (# 7). Here he adds a significant phrase, that this is all "in accordance with the Dhamma and not in non-accordance" (*dhammen'eva no adhammena*). As noted, two lines then follow:

"Dhamma for people is the best
In this life as well as indeed the next"[163].

(*Dhammo hi Vāseṭṭha seṭṭho jane tasmiṃ diṭṭhe c'eva dhamme abhisamparāyañca)*.

This I consider to be the first hint at indicating the **primary intent** of AS: to show that "Dhamma is the best" (*dhammo hi*

[163] Taking a cue from Walshe, the writer has tried his poetic hand here, although in the text, it is a continuing prose.

Vāseṭṭha seṭṭho). We may also incidentally note that the addressee is, as elsewhere, identified by name, providing the context of an intelligent audience (2.2).

Now let me hasten to add that this identification of the Buddha's intent, however, is not orginal with me. In fact, it is Collins (331) who insights this. He accepts "Gombrich's (92a: 169--70) analysis of *aggañña* as an adjective formed by the ending *-ñña* added to *agga* in the sense of 'first'; *aggañña* thus means, in his rendering, 'primeval' or 'original'". But Collins also sees, contextually, "…a deliberate play on words here with *agga* in the sense of 'best', found in # 7 and # 31 (see # 7.2)." What is original with this writer, then, is the contention that getting the message across that 'Dhamma is the best" indeed is the first and foremost intent of the Buddha in AS. Thus we agree with Collins' suggestion regarding AS that "its serious intent was as moral commentary rather than as a 'myth of origins' or a 'charter for society'…".

14.1.1 Repetition as Argument for Dhamma

One bit of evidence is that the refrain 'Dhamma for people is the best, in this life as well as indeed the next' is repeated six times (# 7, 8, 21, 23, 25, 26), twice, as if to introduce, before getting into the detailed and abstract characterization of the Primeval, and four times, as if to emphasize, after. The phrase "In this life and as well as indeed the next" relates the reality as being part of the life-cycle, and thus "in accordance with the Dhamma and not non-accordance".

The term *Dhamma,* of course, may be taken to mean 'The (Buddha's) Teachings', as e.g., in *Buddhadhamma.* But in all of the six occurences of the refrain, it is used in the sense of and in relation to a higher morality.

Let us then see if the contexts themselves of the refrains shed any more light:

7 and # 31: Becoming an Arahant;
8: King Pasenadi, who receive Homage from the people,

himself paying Homage to the Tathāgata;
21: Mahāsammata is so called because "He gladdens others with Dhamma";
23: In relation the origin of the class of Brahmins;
25: Explaing the origins of Suddas, being called so because they hunt, thus reminding of the Dhamma by contrast, and
26: People of all four castes going from Home to Homelessness, "dissatisfied with his own Dhamma".

The occurences seem to then suggest an intention on the part of the Buddha to emphasize the *efficacy* of the Dhamma, as Teachings and/or as a code of conduct. But Dhamma, then, could well mean 'nature' or 'reality' as well, as in *dhammen'eva no adhammena.* The Buddha seems to be saying, to put in colloquial language, to make it come alive and give it a presence, "It is reality, of nature, man, and not cooked up". Dhamma could also be understood, in this context, as 'truth'. Laying out *agga* in the sense of 'primeval' in # 10-16, then, can be seen as providing for the perfect context for laying out the other sense of, 'best', and of course, *vice versa*. What we see here, incidentally, again is a hand of communicative efficiency.

It may be instructive to note here that in the two lines in # 7, as also repeated in # 31, it is the term *seṭṭho* (as in *Dhammo hi Vāseṭṭha seṭṭho*) that is used, and not *aggo*. However, it is surely no accident that the term *aggo* comes to be used in the line just above, talking about Arahanthood, in the same sense of 'supreme': *yo hoti ... arahaṃ ...* , *so tesam aggaṃ akkhāyati* 'Anyone [of the four castes] who becomes ... an Arahant, he is proclaimed supreme...'. What we then see is *aggo* and *seṭṭho* used synonymously in the sense of 'best', and in relation to a higher morality, in this case being an Arahant, in both # 7 and # 31. What the Buddha seems to be seeking to convey here here, by association, is that *aggo* is to be understood in this context in the sense of 'best' and relating to Dhamma as Teaching, and not in the sense of 'Primeval' as in Segment two (# 10-16), and in the context of nature.

This then is a critical element that supports the contention that the Buddha's real intent in AS to proclaim that the Dhamma is best.

And most interestingly, however, Dhamma relates to 'knowing' reality as well, and this of the origins of Brahmins (# 23). I quote the section in full (using Walshe's except for the last line):

> *However, some of those [B]eings, not being able to meditate in leaf-huts, settled around towns and villages and compiled books. People saw them doing this and not meditating. "Now these do not meditate" is the meaning of Ajjhāyaka, which is the third regular title [after Mahāsammata and Jhāyaka] to be introduced. At that time, it was regarded as a low designation, but now it is the higher. This, then, Vāseṭṭha, is the origin of the class of Brahmins in accordance with the ancient titles that were introduced for them. Their origin was from among these very same [B]eings, like themseves, no different, and in accordance with the Dhamma, not otherwise.*
>
> *Dhamma for people is the best*
> *In this life and as well indeed the next".*

Clearly here "Dhamma for people is the best" can be re-written, "Knowing the truth (or the reality about truth) is the best", the reference being to the origins of Brahmins as meditators. It isn't accidental either that the particular occurence comes at the end of the second segment, which has just ended showing the origins of both the universe (in the current phase) and human society.

While, then, 'Dhamma' is used in several senses, the primary sense seems to be that it is conducive to liberation. This is captured in the pre-final section (# 30) where the Buddha declares that a Khattiya [Brahmana / Vessa / Sudda], "restrained in body, speech and mind, cultivates the seven 'factors partial to Enlightenment' (*bodhipākkhiya dhamma*), [and] attains Nibbana in this very life".

14.1.2 Fall of man as Argument for Dhamma

In # 12 of AS, we read that "other Beings", in imitation of the first

"Being of a greedy nature", taste the Earth-essence when "craving came upon them." And as they continued to enjoy the food, "their self-luminosity came to disappear. As their self-luminosity disappeared, the moon and the sun made its appearance."

In the next section (# 13), "enjoying the Earth-essence", Beings become coarser and coarser in their bodies, with differences in (skin) colour showing. Some of them coming to be good-looking begin to despise those who were ugly when "...class-conscious to a fault and conditioned by their colour-pride, the *savoury*-Earth came to disappear..."

In both cases, change in sentient beings conditions a change in nature. If in the first it is for the good, in the second, it is for the worse, since the very source of nourishment comes to be lost.

But surely it is not that the Buddha believes that today the greedy Beings eat to their fill, and tomorrow they become coarse, and the next day, lo and behold, there is the sun shining, bright and clear! Or that the good-looking Beings despise the ugly today and savoury Earth disappears tomorrow. It is rather that the changes in Beings are in a Conditioned Co-origination relationship, over billions of years, and both the appearance of the sun and Beings becoming coarse and complex result from a gazillion quanta of change. Indeed it is said that the changes take place "To the extent they continued for a very long stretch of time".

It is significant to note that the Buddha's term which has been translated as 'Conditioned Co-origination' is *paticca* ***sam****uppāda* and not *paticca uppāda* (or more correctly, *paticcuppāda*), the qualifier *sam-* in *samuppāda* strongly indicating the 'necessary' *co-relationality* of change, using 'necessary' in its technical sense of 'minimum' though not necessarily sufficient. What is entailed may be seen as a 'spiral reciprocity', visually as follows:

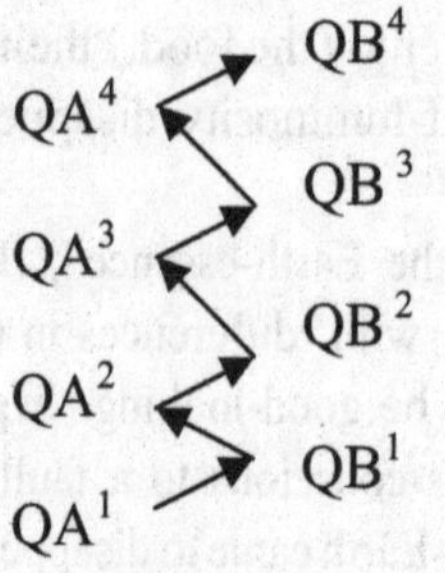

Fig. 9 Indicative Reciprocal Micro-conditioning Process as between Loss of Luminosity in Sentient Beings and Appearance of the Sun

Q = Quanta
A = Condition A (e.g., loss of luminosity in human bodies)
B = Condition B (e.g., sky luminosity)

The process entailed in Fig. 9 can be explained in terms of a micro-conditioning - making a subtle change in the conditioned which in turn conditions a subtle change in the original condition. A single example of coarser food resulting in the micro-cellular death in a human body, the energy thus lost in terms of entropy joining the universe, and attracted towards an element that would eventually come to be the sun. Over billions of years, then, the human body is found to be with no luminosity, while the sun comes to be in full luminosity.

The implicit understanding we get from a reading of AS, is that each change is conditioned by the 'fall' of man, implying again that 'Dhamma is best!'. This is the message that the Buddha seems to want to get across in the entirety of the passage # 18 summarizing the four sub-stages of evolution laid bare in # 10- 16. The first lines begin with the self-reflection,

> 'And then those being came together lamenting: "Bad and unwholesome ways have come to be rife among [us] Beings" (*pāpakā vata bho dhammā sattesu pātubhūta*).

They then recall how at first they had come to be "mind-based, feeding on delight, self-luminous…", but how when they began to eat up from the savoury Earth, their self-luminosity disappeared, when the moon and the sun, etc., come to appear. Reviewing each of the stages of evolution, the pitch is made how each fresh change (except the last, namely, the appearance of sex organs and thereafter), comes to be as a result of 'bad and unwholesome ways' (... *pāpakānaññeva akusalānaṃ dhammānaṃ pātubhava..*).

Where this writer finds the idea of Dhamma is best most cogently appearing is in relation to the choice of *Mahāsammata* 'the Great Elect', on the basis of being relatively better (*-taro*) than the rest, in four areas, the first three being 'handsome, good-looking and charismatic' (*abhirūpa- dassanīya- pāsādika-*). What is of interest is the link in the Abhihamma between *kusala citta* ('wholesome') and the *sobhana citta* ('beautiful') (Ven. Bodhi (Gen Ed), 1999, 45). The apparently causal connection seems to be captured more directly in the last of the four qualities: 'Great Sage' (*mahesakkha- < mahā + īsa + ākhyaṃ,* with an alternative rendering, *mahà + isi* (from Sanskrit *Ṛsi)* (PED), both Collins ('with greatest authority') and Walshe ('capable') capturing two dimensions of the more traditional meaning. (See also Gombrich, 1996, 161, for a discussion of the term.).

Of course, it may be ironic that the 'good'[164], namely, the very changes that mark the evolutionary process, comes to 'result' from bad. However, the Buddha's point seems to be not that the changes in and of themselves are by any means bad, given that they are a natural process conducive to sentient life. But it is to highlight how badness has made Beings lose the qualities they had come by. The implication seems to be, stretching the point here, that badness results in bad change, which is not contributive to liberation.

14.1.3 Approval by Brahmins as Argument for Dhamma

Finally, it is interesting that AS closes with the Buddha's words,

---

[164] This, of course, is from a human point of view, for we would not be here without the moon and the sun, Earth, etc.

> For those who rely on clan, the *khattiya* is the best among people. In similar vein is one with knowledge and good conduct the best among devas and people."

But it is first put in the mouth of Sanaṃkumāra with much significance[165]. First, Sanaṃkumāra literally means 'Forever youthful' (S I.6 (Brahmana Samyutta) (Ven. Bodhi, Tr. 2000, 440). Here is a suggeston, by implication, then, that whatever is said by him, and approved by the Buddha, will never die and will be an eternal truth! Second, Sanaṃkumāra is but another name for Mahābrahma (see D 18 (Janavasabha Sutta)), immediately assiging the statement authoritative status. For the Brahmin youths Vāseṭṭha and Bhāradvāja, it would be nothing but of immediate resonance. Third, a 'Brahmin' is, in its classical sense of meditators, the type the Buddha respects when he claims himself to be a Brahmin. Thus the name brings spiritual authority. So when the Buddha repeats the line in agreement with Sanaṃkumāra, all of these can be said to be brought to bear upon the thinking of the two youth.

Indeed a 'clever strategem' (*upāya kosalla* (D III.220)) in communication alright!

So here we have the Buddha coming out straight to bat for (having) knowledge as the best, even though the term used here is *seṭṭho* and not *aggaṃ*. Thus, knowledge of the Primeval regarding the universe can be said to be shared with Vāseṭṭha and Bhāradvāja since knowledge of reality, providing the base implicitly for 'being of good conduct' (*caraṇasampanno*), is conducive to liberation. And the two youths alone, with their knowledge of the Vedas, would be able to benefit from it immediately, which explains why the Buddha is addressing, as claimed by us, only the two of them and not the Sangha.

---

[165] It is surely a further mocking of Brahmins to have these words come from a Brahmin! See next.

This then tells us how the sharing Knowledge of the Primeval comes to be relevant in the total context of AS since it is Dhamma, namely reality, knowing this in itself being 'best' for the people, 'in this life as well as indeed the next'. This can, then, be taken to be another hint that while # 10-16 is not insignificant in terms of knowing the truth (as argued for above), it is subservient to knowing the truth as a value and a higher morality, this incidentally showing the independence of each, as pointed out earlier (2.3). The truth shall conquer indeed!

That Dhamma is indeed the best finds support from what may be considered an unexpected source. Throughout this study, Ābhassara Beings have been interpreted primarily in relation to Westernscience. But if I were to now fall back upon again its translation by Walshe and Collins as 'Ābhassara Brahma', giving in to tradition, we find an immediate link to the idea of Dhamma being the best, interestingly, not just in this life but the next, too.

In AS, we first encounter Ābhassara Beings during the Devolutionary phase. This means that these are mindbodies that seem to have survived the destruction of the heat of the seven suns ushering in the end of the Devolutionary phase. As in the literature, the destruction is said to turn to ashes all beings up to the level of the Ābhassara Brahma world, the highest abode in the Second Jhana Plane of the Fine Material Sphere Plane (*rūpāvacarabhūmi*) (Ven. Bodhi (Gen Ed], 1999, 192). So who then are these beings that end up in Ābhassara Brahma world in the first place upon 'the breakup of the body after death' (*kāyassa bhedā paraṃ maraṇā*)?

As in the Abhidhamma characterization, it is those who meditate, and reach the level of second *jhāna* that comes to be reborn in the Ābhassara Brahma Abode. Thus it is living by the Dhamma that provides protection from the burning suns. It is significant that the Buddha does not fail to add the characteristic 'feeding on rapture' (*pītibhakkā*) to the very first, and continuing, Ābhassara Being(s), noting that it is the term *pīti* that he uses here and not other terms such as *pāmojja* 'delight' or *sukha* 'happiness', etc., also falling within the same semantic range. *Pīti*, of course, is a quality of mind experienced in the second *jhāna* (D xxii.21,313), 'supercalm in knowledgeability' as translated by this writer[166], and it is in the Ābhassara Realm that the one who experiences the second *jhāna* comes to be born into (see Ven. Bodhi (Gen.Ed.), 186-187 for a Chart).

It may also be remembered that the Seventh Sun that sets ablaze at the end of a Devolutionary Phase burns up everything, but stops at the Ābhassara boundary. So it would be reasonable to think, then, that the original home of the Coming-hither-shining-arrow is the Ābhassara Realm. It is thus that it can be said that 'Dhamma is best' both in this life as well as the next, since the Dhamma helps elevate one to the spiritual level of the Second *jhāna* in this life, ensures rapture in the next life, indeed ensure survival thereafter, giving an opening to earn yet another human life allowing the cultivation of the higher levels of *jhāna*.

To add one final supportive point that Dhamma is indeed the best is when the Buddha points that Arahants 'Worthy Ones' are from all the four classes, and that indeed they are the 'best' (# 7 of AS). This, then, is clearly indicative of the Buddha's intent.

14.2 The Hierarchy of Intent

Ch. 13 in this study opened with the words, "Happily we feel that we can indeed see, with a large measure of confidence, what the original sense and motivation of AS was." We have now identified not one but two motivations. While the less obvious one is the unfolding of the Primeval, as in Ch. 13, in terms of Devolution and Evolution, the easier decipherable but more hidden is how knowledge of the Dhamma surpasses them all, as in this Chapter.

Hierarchically speaking, then, **Dhamma being the best runs**

---

[166] In the *Satipaṭṭhāna* sutta, 'mindfulness' (*sati*) requires the support of not only being deligent (*ātāpi*), i.e., having continued attention but also be 'clearly knowing' (*sampajañña*), i.e., being 'knowledgeable' (see Ven. Analayo, 2003, 52).

away with the tropy in terms of the intent of the Buddha in AS, the description of the reality of the universe winning the Silver.

However, we may also see several other runners-up, namely, sub-texts. They are:

1. Everything, natural or human, is the outcome of evolution.
2. Change, therefore, is reality (*anicca*).
3. Change results in *dukkha*, as e.g., when self-luminosity disappears upon tasting the Earth and craving arises[167].
4. Conditionality (as in *paticcasamuppāda)* is thus reality, too.
5. 'Asoulity' (*anattā*) is the reality.
6. There is no beginning point to the evolutinary process, which cuts at the very roots of the myth of a Creator.
7. Taking to a life of self-discipline coming to be encouraged (as in all the Teachings).
8. Confirming that the Buddha teaches only two things: suffering and the way out of suffering.
9. Underscoring the point that the Buddha's exposition of the universal flow is as a backdrop to his exposition of the human flow, so to speak.

---

[167] 'Separation from the loved is dukkha' (*piyehi vippayogo dukkho*). While this is generally understood to be in relation to loved sentient beings (family, pets, etc.), it can also refer to a 'loved condition' such as food, even darkness for Beings who have got used to it, for it calls for a re-adjustment.

15

Closure

15.1 *Aggañña Sutta:* A Clumsy Patchwork?

Despite Gombrich's characterization of AS "an extended satire", he agrees that "... the sermon is serious", even though this seriousness relates to showing "that the caste system is nothing but a human invention". Pointing out that "other texts present versions of # 10-21 with apparently straightforward seriousness", Collins (1993:323) also grants that there is serious intent in AS. The characterization[168] of AS in terms of seriousness by them both, then, is what can be said to have kept this writer going.

These, then, are the thoughts, that brought this writer to this exploration. It will then be seen that the writer comes to this study not as an expert but as a seeker, and a creative thinker looking to benefit from cross-disciplinary study. An it is in this process that the writer has come to think of AS not as a 'Clumsy Patchwork' but as a well thought out complex Teaching[169].

As a concluding reflection, then we could unreservedly say that

[168] The term 'characterization' is used here, and elsewhere, instead of 'story' in order to highlight our take on AS as being serious, 'story' giving a sense of being light-hearted and concocted.

[169] It is interesting that Mrs. Rhys-Davids uses the same term 'patchwork' in relation to the Anupada Sutta (M 111): "The sutta ... is a patchwork of editorial compiling" (quoted in Ven. Nyanaponika, 1998, 115).

AS is no 'clumsy patchwork', as Collins opines initially (if only to ditch it), but a clever, and dynamic piece, its diverse dimensions indicative of it.

First is the apparent simplicity, which as noted, stems from the fact that each of the three segments, or at least segments one (# 1-10) and three (# 17-32) on the one hand and segment two (# 10-16) on the other, can stand by itself.

Behind a deceptive simplicity, however, is a complex composition in terms of its organization. The first segment presents a simple argument, irrefutable by its simple logic of the incompatibility between the Brahminic claims of being born of Brahman, indeed of his mouth, and the reality of Brahmins being born of Brahmin women. This comes to be strengthened in segment three, as in a closure in a good essay. Segment two may be seen as the 'meat' of the argument (with apologies for the palpably unsuitable metaphor), but reserved for the erudite and the clever, namely Vāseṭṭha and Bhāradvāja playing the role, which means, of course, that it is dispensable without doing harm to the structure of the discourse.

Taking segment two in particular, and the *modus operandi* of delving into the origins with no forewarning (although the first segment can be seen as a preparing the ground for what was to come) can also be seen to make the Buddha the 'Maestro of the Understatement'. For packed into the seven paragraphs is a 'history' of the universe and a process spanning, by Westernsciencecalculations, over 13 + billion years! The segment may then be seen, for its brevity, as a classic case study of the leaves in the hand of the Buddha, as compared to the forest he declared constituting the extent of his knowledge of reality. However, for those who have the eyes to see it, the middle segment could be considered the fringe ornamentation of the crestgem of the crown, namely the message that 'Dhamma is best'.

We have above shown # 10-16 as a 'Cosmic Narrative'. But, as we have seen, AS contains yet another narrative, relating to the Dhamma as Best. So combining the two, and taking it as a whole, we may see AS a '**Knowledge Narrative**', to include both Knowledge of the Primeval as well as Knowledge of the Best, *agga-* in *Aggañña* meaning both 'primeval' and 'best'.

To conclude this segment, Collins (313) makes the cogent point that "We should approach the text as we have it respectfully, looking not to make hasty and superficial judgements about its disunity, but to seek out principles of structure and sequence which can give us a sense of why this particular crystallization of meanings took the form it did." He adds, " I think such principles can be found". The monastic Life and Ideals, as in the Vinaya, he comes to discover in the AS certainly provides some such principles. He also finds "coherence in the structure of the sutta as a whole", in terms of what he sees as the keywords of the text (Part IV). I hope that our analysis, too, speaks to a higher dynamic, dynamism and a complexity in the totality of AS, but most importantly, that it gives us some insight into the 'principles of structure' as well as the structure itself.

15.2 A Clumsy Patchwork of Research?

While you will have seen this writer's great indebtedness to scholars Walshe, Collins and Gombrich in this study, it was without the benefit of any of them that he began his exploration. Of late in particular, he has been struck, primarily through some of his own recent research, by the benefits of falling back on Westernscience in understanding some of the more esoteric teachings of the Buddha. It was while he was in this frame of mind that he came to read that two Western Scientists, Prof. Richard Gordon and Prof. Alexei had come to 'discover', contrary to the received wisdom, that there was life *before* the Earth came to exist (<http://www.digitaljournal.com/article /348515 #ixzz 2R9WpPINk>). That it was based not on Physics but on a mathematical calculation based on a computer model did not seem to bother him, both Disciplines equally distant to him.

But this was when it hit him that perhaps he should take a closer look at the Buddha's concepts of *saṃvaṭṭa* and *vivaṭṭa*, translated here as 'Devolution' and 'Evolution', in relation to Westernscience. Going through the *Aggañña-Sutta* in its Pali original, a particular repetitive phrase stood out for him: *kadāci karahaci dīghassa addhuno accayena.* When at its very first occurrence (# 10, Line 1) it came to be followed by the words *ayaṃ loko saṃvaṭṭati* and at the second occurrence in the same paragraph, by *ayaṃ loko vivaṭṭati* (L 4), his interest was tweaked. While he was yet to explore the usage in detail, they immediately satisfied his granted bias that the Buddha was indeed talking about the natural cycle of cosmic change. A closer reading of the seven paragraphs (# 10-16) would later show him how indeed the line happens to mark critical stages in the evolutionary process.

Something else struck him as well. And this was how the critical stages entailing the 'fall of man', more accurately 'Beings', were associated with evolutionary change. While, e.g., there was no sun or moon at the initial stage (# 11), they came to appear as the Beings began to taste the 'savoury Earth' (*rasa paṭhavi* (# 12)), i.e., with greed or thirst (*taṇhā*) emerging. That is to say that there was an element of morality (*sīla*) in it all.

Convinced that the Buddha was on to something important here, he now began to re-read the text in Pali, in more detail, and more thoroughly, trying to figure out what this was all about. This is when he reached out to his bookshelf and began to look through the translations by Rhys-Davids (PTS) and Walshe (Wisdom).

This phase of the research ended up in a short paper of about 8 pages, in which he sought to point out that the Buddha's view was that there was life before Earth. This, of course, was on the basis that Earth is said to appear after the Ābhassara Beings 'come to this state', leaving their Ābhassara bodies. The Pali term translated as Beings, of course, is *sattā,* the Buddha's term for sentient beings. In the article, this writer had come to interpret 'Ābhassara' non-traditionally, as 'hither-bound-shining-arrow', using concepts in Westernscienceas he had come to understand them.

The piece run by a Physicist colleague for fact-checking, the writer was happy to be told that while it was no scientific piece, the science was fine! Shown to a Buddhologist, his attention was drawn to Collins, and so now he was reading Collins with enthusiasm, also because it helped him with an additional translation source. Finding in Collins references to Gombrich (1988), and enough disagreements, it was that this wriiter was next reading Gombrich.

This background has been outlined to say how our own study may qualify more as a 'clumsy patchwork' of research, the way, in fact, Collins (301) sees AS. It is also to reveal that this writer clearly came to this study with a hypothesis – that the AS was about the cosmic process, or as he would come to refine its, as Devolution and Evolution. But, in sensing that the Buddha was on to something in relation to cosmology, the writer came to be happy that he was encouraged by the contrary views expressed in both Collins and Gombrich.

15.3 Beauty Lies in the Eye of the Beholder

Seeing AS in terms of parody and satire, by Gombrich and Collins if also others, can be seen as an example of the challenge faced by a translator when confronted with a difficult, and/or unfamiliar topic. Not quite knowing what to make of the references to *saṃvaṭṭa* and *vivaṭṭa* (Devolution and Evolution as has been translated here), the scholars seem to have looked for a way to say that while the Buddha is surely not wrong, we can only make sense of it only along literary concepts and categories.

Besides, the received wisdom of the culture of their inheritance, namely Western, is that the Big Bang is the beginning of the universe[170]. Buddhologists they may be, but born and living in a Western civilization, it is understandable, if the writer is permitted a role of the psychoanalyst, that they would be most comfortable to be identified as being of a scientific bent. So thinking of the universe in terms of an ongoing Devolution and Evolution cycle might perhaps have been hard to digest[171]. This is even if the characterization were

[170] See Kafatos & Nadeau, 1990, 152-158 for a critique of the Big Bang Theory.

[171] As another example of 'attachment to views' (*diṭṭhi taṇhā*), meaning

to be more in tandem with what they well know to be the Buddha's Teachings of the cyclical nature of *saṃsāra* in relation to human life, and Conditioned Co-origination (remembering the reciprocity)[172] in terms of theory, both of which suggest not an 'origin' but a conditionality which allows no 'first cause'. To see the Discourse as parody, allegory or satire then seems to have been the best way out of the conundrum, getting, as it were, to both keep the cake and eat it as well.

The differential interpretation of AS by the western scholars on the one hand, and by this student of Buddhism on the other, seems to find an explanation in the Buddha's words, 'It is in this fathom-long body endowed with perception and mind that I proclaim the world..." (*api cāhaṃ āvuso imasmim yeva byāmamatte kaḷebare saññhimhi samanake lokañca paññāpemià*) (A.ii.45 49). When confronted with a textual but also a contextual issue, the only thing a translator can do is to impose upon it one's own perspective, the worldview one brings to it. The Buddha not seen as a scientist, and perhaps never even given thought to the possibility of a scientific view to be contained in the Suttas, and thus reading them along traditonal Buddhological lines, the thought may never have entered the minds of the scholars to give it a shot from a scientific perspective. By contrast, this student, coming with perhaps a naïve bias of seeing the Buddha as a scientist (see Sugunasiri, 2009) would find a scientific gold mine in the Discourse. So the interpretations can clearly be said to be, as pointed out by the Buddha, based in one's perception. Indeed can it not be then said that beauty lies in the eye of the beholder?

Let it be kindly noted that the comments above are not made with disrespect, malice or one-upmanship, but merely as a methodological point[173], if only to point out how difficult the task of translation can be,

---

a stubborn refusal to go against the received culture and thought, among western Buddhist scholars, would be the refusal to accept the concept of 'Rebirth' (see e.g., Bachelor, 1977; see Sugunasiri, 2009, for a critique), no matter how many times the Buddha speaks of it.

[172] Please note 'co-evolution' in Westernscience (Zimmer, 189 ff.).

[173] Indeed a classic example of divergence of understanding between

as he should know himself as a translator (Sugunasiri, 1960; 1964)[174].

15.4 Going Interdisciplinary at One's Own Peril!

This study clearly reflects this writer's interdisciplinary[175] bias, not wanting to be bound by the narrower confines of Disciplinary lines. Within Buddhist studies itself, it is the customary practice for scholars to strictly keep to the Suttas or to the Abhidhamma, of course for commendable scholarly reasons. While this study is primarily based in the Suttas, it has, for better or worse, drawn upon the Abhidhamma as well where it contributes to the point, to the likely chagrin of puritan scholars, allowing them a fool rushing to where angels fear to tread!

As if crossing intra-Buddhist boundaries were not bad enough, the writer also crosses the boundaries of 'Religion' and 'Science', making Buddhologists and Scientists both to flee from the scene, again possibly afraid of contamination by the 'impurities' of each.

---

scholars, but with no malice, relates to the Anupada Sutta (M 111). While, as noted, Mrs. Rhys Davids "throws doubts of the Anupada Sutta ... as a genuine discourse of the Buddha", Ven. Nyanaponikaera Thera asserts, "we do not agree at all" (Ven. Nyanaponika. 1998, 115). Further, "It is regretted that such a gifted scholar .. marred the value of her later work by hasty and prejudiced judgments" (116-117). We make no further comment.

[174] The writer's translations into Sinhala are Bertrand Russel, *Commonsense and Nuclear Warfare* (1960) and A B Keith, *Classical Sanskrit Literature* (1964).

[175] To give an example of the benefit of crossing such boundaries in this study itself, the AS notes that "no femininity or masculinity" is to be seen in the Ābhassara Beings in the early phase of Evolution (# 11). But as humans evolve, there come to appear sexual organs (#16). In explaining this, the writer draw upon the Abhihamma analysis that shows how femininity and masculinity (*bhāvarūpa*) are inherent to sentience as 'alternatives' or 'changeables' (*vikārarūpa*) (see Bodhi, Gen. Ed., 1999, 239; 262-263).

But the writer comes with the conviction that it would be remiss not to consider it his responsibility to make his interdisciplinary case as best as he can, for the very reason of the experiences he has had in crossing boundaries. While, then, one goes interdisciplinary at one's own peril, the research and academic benefits far outweigh any personal discomforts. And it is to be hoped that this study itself stands as a putative case study, showing how an interdisciplinary approach can, in suitable contexts, far outweigh the benefits of traditional exclusive research methods.

While the writer then invites scholars to cast the most critical of eyes on his research, he would equally invite them, most respectfully, to go past the leaves, and look for the trees to discover the sound health of the forest.

15.5 Concluding Remarks

Our attempt in this study can be said to be to establish that the Buddha couldn't have been more serious in presenting in AS # 10-16 a picture of the cosmic process, in two phases, the latter including human and societal evolution. If the message is the medium, to turn on its head Marshall McLuhan's famous dictum 'The medium is the message', happy, too, will the writer be for the study to be seen for its message – an attempt of an inquiring mind seeking to make interdisciplinary synaptic connections.

If this could be called a breakthrough, it is readily granted that there may be many a hole. It will be then be the task for a budding team of astrophysicists, astrobiologists, molecular biologists, paleontologists, psychologists and anthropologists, to name only a few of the members of the team, to fill the gaping gaps in the next hundreds, if not thousands of years, just as this writer is seeking to try his hands after 2500 years after the Buddha.

A methodological concern for some scholars of this study may be that it crosses boundaries, first as between Sutta and Abhdihamma, and then across to Westernscience. A weakness of this study is that the author has not sought to bring the full force of the literature to corroborate every claim or argument made in the discussion. While that would be indeed a task beyond the capacity of the writer, it would be of little additional benefit to this study which merely seeks to make an initial exploration of the link between the Buddhian insights and Westernscience. Leaving further exploration to future scholars, this author is satisfied to rely on his instinct, intuition and creative thought, founded in knowledge, and hopefully a measure of wisdom, gathered over several decades in the cross-disciplinary and intra-disciplinary academy. Once an idea has been shaped in his mind, and the evidence found, in his mind or textually, to the extent needed, the author has adopted it, with a mind to cross-validation with other *related* issues within the context, but only minimally.

Given that the Pali commentarial tradition makes no mention of the Vinaya in the context of AS, Collins, providing material from the Vinaya as a backdrop to some of the material in the Discourse, says that "For some readers, perhaps, this in itself might be enough to render what I say an over-speculative and purely modern reading." (323). This writer's interpretation, going completely out of the traditional realm of Buddhist studies, is certain to run the risk of likewise being considered, 'over-speculative' and 'a purely modern reading', if also naive. However, it would be to our disadvantage not to see relevance in the words of Fayerabend, a radical theorist, that "Progress in Science occurs… when scientists think "counterintuitively", and make radical departures from practiced norms of thought" (cited in Kafatos & Nadeau, 1990, 7). Would it, should it, be any different when it comes to the study of Religion? It may also be relevant to note the Buddha claiming to go against the current (*paṭisotagāminī*).

Happily, too, Collins goes on to say that "with a text as context-sensitive as I believe AS to be, perhaps we might accord ourselves greater interpretive autonomy". So it is that this writer hopes that the interpretive autonomy that has smiled upon him will not bring two many frowns in, and from either or both the Buddhist Academy and the Sangha scholars. It is his expectation, as well, that there will be an occasional if reluctant pencil smile on the faces of some reading this study, until such time that it comes under the critical scrutiny of Buddhist scholars with a background in Westernscience. In the meantime, it is hoped that this writer will be allowed the luxury of enjoying the happiness he has come to have in this exploration, finding comfort in Einstein's remark, "Science without religion is lame, religion without science is blind" (cited in Pais,1982 (page facing vii)).

BIBLIOGRAPHY

Analayo, 2003, *Satipaṭṭhāna: the Direct Path to Realization*, Kandy, Buddhist Publication Society.

Anguttara Nikāya, Pali Text Society.

Apfel, Necia H., 1985, *It's All Elementary: From Atoms to the Quantum World of Quarks, Leptons and Gluons*, New York: Lothrop, Lee & Shepard Books.

Bachelor, Stephen, 1977, *Buddhism Without Beliefs*, Wisdom.

Bodhi, Bhikkhu (Gen. Ed.), (1993) 1999, *A Comprehensive Manual of Abhidhamma* – The *abhidhammaṭṭhasangaha*: Pali Text, Translation and Explanatory Guide, Kandy, Sri Lanka: Buddhist Publication Society.

Bodhi, Bhikkhu (Tr.), 2000, T*he Connected Discourse of the Buddha – A Translation of the Samyutta Nikāya*, Wisdom.

Bodhi, Bhikkhu (Tr.), 2012, *The Numerical Discourse of the Buddha – A Translation of the Anguttara Nikāya*, Wisdom.

Buddhadatta Mahathera, A P, 1979, *English-Pali Dictionary*, Pali Text Society.

Buddhaghosa, *Visuddhimagga*, 1975 (Edited by Rhys Davids, C A F) Pali Text Society.

Capra, Fritjof, 19, The Tao of Physics, 1975, 1983, Shambala.

Carpenter, J Estlin, 1992, *The Digha Nikāya*, Vol. III, Pali Text Society.

Chauhan, Y. S., N. Venkataratnam And A. R. Sheldrake, 1987, "Factors affecting growth and yield of short-duration pigeonpea and its potential for multiple harvests", *J. agric. Sci., Camb.* (1987), 109, 519-529 519.

Collins, Steven, 1982, *Selfelss Persons*, Cambridge University Press.

Collins, 1993, "The Discourse on What is Primary (*Aggañña-sutta*), An annotated Translation", *Journal of Indian Philosophy* 21, 301-393.

Davids, Rhys & David Stede, 1979, *Pali-English Dictionary* (PED), Pali Text Society.

Dhammapada, Pali Text Society.
Digha Nikāya, Pali Text Society.

Frank, Gunder, 1966, "The Development of Underdevelopment", *Monthly Review,* September.

Gombrich, Richard F., 1992, "The Buddha's Book of Genesis?", Indo-Iranian Journal 35, 159-178.

Gombrich, Richard F., 1996, *How Buddhsim Began: The Conditinoed Genesis of the Early Teachings*, Munshiram Manoharlal.

Gray, Henry (1905), 1994, *Gray's Anatomy*, London: Senata

Hart, Major R. Raven, 2005, *Where the Buddha Trod*, Pannipitiya, Sri Lanka, Stamford Lake (Pvt) Limited.

Harvey, Peter, 2000, An Introduction to Buddhist Ethics, Cambridge University Press.

http://animals.nationalgeographic.com/animals/invertebrates/sea-anemone/.

http://answers.yahoo.com/question/index?qid=20080715061808AACF6No.

http://appsychnotes.weebly.com/biology-of-the-brain.html.

http://dictionary.reference.com/browse/Stratosphere.

http://en.wikipedia.org/wiki/Animal_communication#Animal_communication_and_linguistics.

http://en.wikipedia.org/wiki/Hadean.

http://en.wikipedia.org/wiki/Sun#After_core_hydrogen_exhaustion.

http://en.wikipedia.org/wiki/Volvox.

http://map.gsfc.nasa.gov/universe/uni_age.html.

http://oar.icrisat.org/1698/.

http://quantummechanics.ucsd.edu/ph130a/130_notes/node469.html

http://science.jrank.org/pages/301/Amoeba.html.

http://space.about.com/od/glossaries/g/ionosphere.html.

http://www.agridept.gov.lk/index.php/en/crop-recommendations/890.

http://www.answers.com/topic/libido#ixzz2lxcjnzRJ.

http://www.answers.com/topic/phallus#ixzz2lxboE1tP.

http://www.answers.com/topic/psychosexual-development-2#ixzz2lxb4uTdd.

http://www.ask.com/wiki/Ionosphere

http://www.newworldencyc lopedia.org/entry/Eukaryote.

http://www.newworldencyclopedia.org/entry/Eukaryote.

http://www.science.uwaterloo.ca/~cchieh/cact/applychem/ entropy.html.

http://www.vepachedu.org/linga.htm.

http://www.wellsphere.com/healthy-cooking-article/ragi-finger-millet-and-its-health-benefits/352804.

Issacs, Alan, 1963, *Introducing Science*, Penguin.

Kafatos, Menas and Robert Nadeau, 1990, *The Conscious Universe: Part and Whole in Modern Physical Theory*, Springer-Verlag.

Keith, A. Berriedale 1923, *Classical Sanskrit Literature,* London: Oxford University Press.

Kirtisinghe, Buddhadasa P. (Ed.), Buddhism and Science, 1984, Delhi: Motilal Banarsidass.

Khuddaka Nikāya, Pali Text Society.

Law, B C, (1932) 1979, *Geography of Early Buddhism,* New Delhi:, Munshiram Manoharlal Publishers.

Lightman, Alan, 1991, *Ancient Light: Our Changing View of the Universe*, Mass.: Harvard University Press.

Majjhima Nikāya, Pali Text Society.

McLeod, Ken, 2014, "How is the Medium Changing the Message?", *Insight* Journal Newsletter, Barre Centre for Buddhist Studies, Barre, Mass., USA

Nanamoli, Bhikkhu & Bhikkhu Bodhi, 1995, *The Middle Length Discourses of the Buddha: a Translation of the Majjhima Nikāya*, Wisdom.

Nyanaponika Thera, 1949; 1998, *Abhidhamma Studies,: Buddhist Explorations of Consciousness and time,* Wisdom.

Olomucki, Martin, (French original , 1925), 1993, *The Chemistry of Life*, McGraw-Hill.

Pais, Abraham, 1982, *'Subtle is the Lord': The Science and the Life of Albert Einstein,* Oxford University Press.

Ponnamperuma, Cyril, 1972, *The Origins of Life*, London: Thames & Hudson.

Samyutta Nikāya, Pali Text Society.

Sapir, Edward, 1921, *Language*, New Year : Harcourt, Brace &B World.

Sheldrake, Rupert, 1984, "Pigeonpea physiology", in P R Goldsworthy (ed.), *The Physiology of Tropical Crops,* Oxford: Blackwell.

Sheldrake, Rupert, 1990, *The Rebirth of Nature: The Greening of cience and God*, London: Century.

Sugunasiri, Suwanda H J., 1978, *Humanistic Nationism: a Language- and Ideology-based Model of Development for Post-Colonial Nations*, 1978 (unpublished Doctoral Thesis, University of Toronto, available online at <https://tspace.library.utoronto.ca/browse?type=author&value=Sugunasiri%2C+Suwanda+H.J.&sort_by=2&order=ASC&rpp=20&etal=0

Sugunasiri, Suwanda H J., 1995, "Whole Body, Not Heart, as the Seat of Consciousness – the Buddha's View", *East West Philosophy*, Vol. 45, Number 3, 409-430.

Sugunasiri, Suwanda H J., 2009, "'Against Belief': Mindfulness Meditation as Empirical Method, *Canadian Journal of Buddhist Studies*, Number Five, 59-96.

Sugunasiri, Suwanda H J, 2010, *Untouchable Woman's Odyssey*, Nalanda Publishing Canada.

Sugunasiri, Suwanda H J., 2011, 'Asoulity' as Translation of Anatta: Absence, not Negation", *Canadian Journal of Buddhist Studies*, Number Seven, 101-134.

Sugunasiri, Suwanda H J., 2012, *Arahant Mahinda - Redactor of the Buddhapūjāva*, Toronto, Canada: Nalanda Publishing Canada; also online, <http://www.scirus.com/srsapp/search?q=sugunasiri&submit=Go&rep=tspc>.

Sugunasiri, Suwanda H J., 2013, "Life there was … before Earth – Scientists agree with the Buddha" <www.buddhistcouncil.ca>.

Sugunasiri, Suwanda H J., 2013 b, "Devolution and Evolution in the Aggañña Sutta", *Canadian Journal of Buddhist Studies*, number 9, 17-104.

Sugunasiri, Suwanda H J., forthcoming, "Triune Mind, Triune Brain".

Tipitaka, Sinhala translation, 2006, *Buddha Jayanti Tripitaka Grantha Mālā*, Sri Lanka: Dharma Chakra Child Foundation.

Vinaya Pitaka, Pali Text Society.

Walshe, Maurice (Tr.), *The Long Discourses*, 1987, 1995, Wisdom.

Webster's Dictionary.

Zimmer, Carl, 2001, *Evolution: the triumph of an idea,* Harper-Collins.

ABBREVIATIONS

A	*Anguttara Nikāya*
AS	*Aggañña Sutta*
Bya	Billion years ago
D	*Dīgha Nikāya*
K	*Khuddaka Nikàya*
Kya	Thousand years ago
M	*Majjihma Nikāya*
Mya	Million years ago
PED	*Pāli-English Dictionary*
PTS	Pali Text Society
S	*Samyutta Nikāya*
Sn	*Sutta Nipāta*
V	*Vinaya Pitaka*
VM	Vedic Myth

INDEX

A

Ābhassara 3, 11, 17, 23, 24, 25, 26, 26, 40, 44, 49, 51, 52, 52, 53, 54, 55, 56, 59, 62, 64, 64, 66, 75, 78, 80, 92, 92, 95, 96, 97, 98, 99, 101, 102, 103, 104, 105, 106, 107, 108, 109, 110, 111, 112, 113, 114, 119, 121, 122, 122, 123, 124, 132, 133, 134, 158, 159, 161, 162, 163, 170, 172, 175, 176, 187, 188, 194, 197

Aetiological myth 129, 130

After the passage of a long time beyond 17, 21, 29, 49, 104, 121, 123

Agga 1, 5, 6, 7, 9, 33, 34, 43, 44, 45, 47, 49, 51, 53, 55, 57, 59, 61, 63, 65, 67, 69, 71, 73, 121, 123, 123, 123, 127, 129, 132, 134, 134, 144, 155, 156, 157, 157, 158, 170, 178, 180, 181, 191, 192, 193

Aggañña sutta 11, 13, 15, 17, 19

Analayo, Ven. Bhikkhu 188

Anatomically modern humans 11, 13, 15, 17, 19, 66, 67, 80, 104, 117, 118, 125

Anattā 112, 115, 139, 189

Angulimāla 151, 154

Anicca 49, 115, 114, 159, 189

Aqueous life 56, 57, 60, 62

Animal life 28, 67, 68, 175

Animals 36, 37, 57, 60, 62, 65, 66, 68, 68, 76, 77, 78, 89, 108, 114, 117, 118, 123, 141

Apfel, Necia H. 51

Arahant 8, 105, 151, 164, 168, 179, 180, 181

Arrow 51, 53, 111, 133, 188, 194

Asexual 40, 44, 55, 58, 59, 61, 91, 99
Asoulity 112, 115, 139, 189
Atmosphere 24, 50, 63, 108, 161
Attention 84, 85, 167, 173, 188, 194
Audience 4, 88, 127, 136, 139, 147, 149, 151, 152, 153, 154, 155, 156, 157, 158, 159, 161, 163, 165, 166, 166, 167, 168, 177, 180
B

Bachelor, Stephen 196
Badālatā 14, 15, 19, 36, 63, 69, 70, 72, 75, 79, 80, 91, 122, 123, 124
Bee 57, 65
Bhaggava 157, 158, 164, 164, 165, 165, 166, 170
Bhāradvāja 5, 7, 9, 88, 89, 110, 136, 139, 148, 149, 149, 150, 150, 151, 152, 153, 154, 155, 156, 157, 165, 166, 168, 171, 172, 177, 186, 186, 192
Big Bang 45, 46, 47, 66, 67, 110, 113, 123, 125, 125, 135, 135, 195, 195
Billion 34, 45, 46, 47, 48, 48, 49, 56, 63, 67, 67, 68, 104, 105, 107, 110, 113, 118, 123, 141, 176, 177, 192
Biological evolution 75, 113
Bodhi, Ven. Bhikkhu 2, 9, 22, 23, 27, 40, 45, 46, 47, 51, 52, 54, 61, 82, 83, 85, 96, 106, 107, 118, 136, 141, 153, 173, 174, 185, 186, 187, 188, 197
Brahma 6, 7, 23, 47, 54, 88, 92, 95, 96, 97, 98, 102, 143, 143, 158, 159, 160, 161, 162, 166, 171, 171, 172, 172, 172, 174, 187
Brahmaloka 23, 54, 105, 106
Brahmana 182, 186
Brahma Realm 96, 97, 98
Brahmavimāna 158, 159, 163
Brahmin 5, 6, 7, 9, 136, 138, 139, 143, 144, 148, 150, 151, 152, 155, 156, 156, 163, 167, 171, 172, 173, 178, 186, 192
Brahmin women 6, 143, 152, 171, 192,
Buddhadatta, Ven. A P 25, 32, 82
Buddhian 113, 114, 199

C

Cambrian Era 63, 67, 75
Carpenter, J Estlin 2, 97, 144
Caste 5, 6, 32, 130, 148, 191
Channel capacity 136, 137, 138
Chronological Paradox 40
Cluster 86, 96, 98
Collins, Steven 1, 2, 4, 9, 10, 21, 21, 22, 23, 25, 26, 27, 28, 29, 32, 34, 35, 57, 95, 130, 139, 140, 142, 143, 145, 147, 149, 154, 155, 166, 167, 169, 180, 185, 187, 191, 192, 193, 194, 195, 199
Colour 17, 18, 19, 20, 27, 28, 31, 32, 57, 58, 82, 90, 91, 101, 122, 123, 124, 142, 145, 172, 173, 183
Communication 35, 49, 62, 69, 72, 73, 92, 122, 144, 154, 186
Conditioned Co-origination 26, 33, 96, 122, 125, 183, 196
Consciousness 23, 26, 36, 44, 52, 53, 54, 55, 64, 64, 65, 69, 84, 85, 89, 96, 107, 114, 141, 142, 173
Consciousness-food 64
Cosmic process 2, 45, 67, 195, 198
Cosmology 45, 54, 195
Craving 18, 31, 37, 45, 79, 101, 105, 122, 183, 189
Creepers 19, 35, 37, 57, 62, 63, 79, 176
Cyclical 2, 10, 23, 45, 48, 105, 109, 116, 121, 124, 125, 133, 144, 170, 173, 196

D

Darkness 17, 24, 56, 131, 132, 162, 189
Darwin, Charles 53, 57, 142
Davids, Rhys 34, 35, 130, 140, 191, 194, 197
Davids, Rhys Mrs. 34, 35, 130, 140, 191, 194, 197
Deva 118
Devolution 1, 2, 7, 22, 50, 55, 104, 123, 139, 140, 157, 159, 160, 167, 169, 170, 173, 174, 176, 177, 178, 188, 193, 195
Devolutionary phase 24, 26, 45, 46, 47, 49, 50, 52, 53, 56, 65, 66, 67, 68, 98, 104, 106, 107, 108, 110, 113, 113, 116, 119, 124, 125, 134, 138, 158, 161, 187, 188

Devolve 21, 22, 23
Devolving 17, 22, 49, 103, 104, 141, 158
Dhamma 2, 4, 5, 6, 7, 8, 9, 10, 12, 14, 16, 18, 20, 22, 23, 24, 26, 28, 30, 32, 34, 36, 38, 40, 42, 44, 46, 48, 50, 52, 54, 56, 58, 60, 62, 64, 66, 68, 70, 72, 74, 76, 78, 80, 82, 84, 86, 88, 90, 92, 94, 96, 98, 100, 102, 104, 106, 108, 110, 112, 114, 116, 118, 120, 122, 124, 126, 127, 128, 130, 132, 134, 136, 138, 140, 142, 143, 144, 146, 148, 150, 151, 152, 154, 155, 156, 158, 160, 162, 164, 165, 166, 166, 167, 168, 170, 172, 174, 176, 178, 179, 180, 181, 181, 182, 183, 184, 185, 186, 187, 188, 189, 190, 192, 192, 194, 196, 198, 200,
Dhamma is best 4, 127, 179, 181, 182, 183, 184, 185, 187, 188, 189, 192
Dhammapada 23
Discover 147, 156, 169, 193, 193, 198
DNA 26, 58, 103

E

Earth 3, 17, 18, 20, 24, 27, 29, 30, 33, 36, 38, 44, 45, 47, 47, 48, 49, 50, 51, 51, 54, 55, 56, 57, 58, 59, 61, 62, 62, 63, 64, 65, 66, 67, 68, 69, 70, 70, 70, 71, 72, 75, 75, 77, 78, 79, 80, 81, 85, 90, 91, 91, 92, 95, 97, 98, 99, 101, 104, 105, 108, 111, 113, 115, 117, 118, 119, 121, 122, 123, 124, 125, 134, 142, 160, 161, 162, 163, 175, 176, 183, 185, 189, 193, 194,
Earth-savour 18, 91, 101, 122
Egg-born 44, 61, 99, 103, 105, 108,
Einstein, Albert 51, 137
Embryonic 63, 71, 86, 89, 98, 116
Enlightenment 8, 136, 182
Eukaryotes 66, 68, 70, 71, 76, 77, 117

Evolution 2, 4, 6, 7, 8, 10, 12, 14, 16, 18, 20, 22, 24, 26, 28, 29, 30, 32, 33, 34, 35, 36, 38, 40, 42, 43, 44, 46, 48, 50, 52, 53, 54, 55, 56, 58, 60, 61, 62, 64, 65, 66, 67, 68, 68, 70, 71, 72, 73, 74, 75, 76, 77, 78, 80, 81, 82, 84, 86, 88, 90, 91, 92, 94, 96, 98, 100, 102, 104, 106, 107, 108, 109, 110, 112, 113, 114, 116, 117, 118, 119, 120, 121, 122, 123, 124, 125, 126, 128, 129, 130, 132, 134, 136, 138, 139, 140, 141, 142, 144, 146, 148, 150, 152, 154, 156, 157, 158, 159, 160, 161, 162, 164, 165, 166, 167, 168, 169, 170, 172, 173, 174, 176, 177, 178, 180, 182, 184, 185, 186, 188, 189, 190, 192, 193, 194, 195, 196, 197, 198, 200

Evolution of human society 196, 172, 173, 174

Evolutionary change 90, 144, 194

Evolutionary creativity 111, 115

Evolutionary phase 3, 25, 30, 33, 44, 45, 47, 48, 49, 50, 52, 54, 55, 64, 65, 66, 67, 68, 70, 72, 91, 102, 104, 107, 108, 110, 112, 113, 115, 116, 117, 118, 121, 124, 125, 139, 158, 177

Evolutionary process 23, 62, 75, 98, 110, 111, 112, 116, 152, 160, 166, 175, 177, 185, 194

Evolve 18, 21, 66, 70, 80, 81, 98, 103, 105, 118, 121, 197

Evolving 17, 22, 25, 27, 52, 56, 66, 68, 73, 78, 81, 89, 90, 92, 98, 103, 105, 108, 122, 123, 137

F

Feeding on rapture 17, 17, 53, 54, 121, 187

Female 20, 25, 33, 40, 59, 60, 61, 65, 82, 83, 84, 86, 87, 88, 90, 102, 123, 176

Fingers 3, 29, 31, 36, 61, 62, 67, 75, 78, 80, 81, 91, 154

Fire 56, 88, 98

First Ābhassara Being 170, 172

Five aggregates 86, 114

Food 3, 18, 19, 20, 31, 33, 36, 37, 44, 54, 61, 62, 64, 65, 68, 69, 70, 71, 72, 73, 74, 75, 76, 78, 79, 80, 81, 82, 90, 91, 107, 124, 142, 164, 176, 183, 184, 189

For a very long stretch of time 17, 18, 19, 20, 82, 90, 104, 121, 123, 124, 175, 183

Frame 121, 193
Framework 22, 136, 137
Frank, Gunder 103
Freud 84
Freudian 84, 85, 86, 90

G

Gombrich Richard
Gordon Richard
Gray Henry
Great elements 51, 137
Greedy 17, 28, 64, 78, 81, 90, 101, 105, 109, 110, 183
Greek 76, 137

H

Hands 18, 29, 36, 61, 62, 75, 78, 80, 81, 91, 114, 178, 198
Human 3, 4, 26, 32, 38, 43, 57, 60, 61, 65, 67, 68, 72, 73, 77, 78, 81, 84, 85, 87, 92, 96, 96, 97, 98, 99, 102, 103, 106, 110, 111, 112, 113, 114, 118, 118, 122, 130, 136, 136, 141, 144, 157, 160, 163, 169, 170, 172, 173, 174, 175, 178, 182, 184, 185, 188, 189, 189, 191, 196, 198
Human being 4, 77, 81, 84, 87, 98, 103, 141
Human evolution 157, 160
Human life 3, 57, 73, 81, 96, 97, 98, 102, 103, 106, 110, 113, 188, 196
Humans 7, 54, 60, 65, 66, 67, 68, 70, 74, 75, 76, 77, 80, 81, 90, 96, 99, 103, 104, 105, 108, 114, 117, 118, 123, 125, 162, 176
Humorous parable 129, 130

I

Ignorance 32, 33, 41, 73, 101, 108,
Independence 77, 187
I-ness 32, 41, 101, 122
Intent 4, 6, 22, 29, 29, 87, 115, 121, 127, 130, 145, 169, 170, 171, 173, 175, 177, 178, 179, 180, 181, 182, 183, 185, 187, 188, 189, 191

J

Jhāna 54, 96, 97, 106, 187, 188

K

Kafatos, Menas 51, 52, 53, 59, 125, 195, 199
Keith, A B 197
Kurakkan 79

L

Land animals 57, 62
Land life 87, 60, 61, 99
Land plants 66, 75
Language 28, 33, 46, 60, 68, 69, 70, 71, 72, 73, 74, 82, 87, 88, 92, 108, 123, 124, 135, 137, 141, 171, 172, 175, 181
Language entrepreneur 60
Language user 108
Liberation 97, 98, 99, 102, 122, 151, 173, 182, 185, 186
Life 3, 6, 8, 9, 25, 26, 27, 28, 36, 41, 44, 45, 46, 47, 48, 49, 52, 53, 55, 56, 57, 58, 58, 59, 60, 61, 62, 63, 64, 65, 66, 67, 68, 69, 73, 75, 77, 78, 80, 81, 89, 91, 92, 96, 97, 98, 99, 102, 103, 103, 104, 105, 106, 107, 108, 110, 110, 111, 112, 113, 115, 116, 117, 117, 119, 132, 135, 140, 141, 142, 159, 162, 175, 179, 180, 182, 185, 187, 188, 189, 193, 194, 196

Life-span 92, 106, 11
Linga 3, 20, 25, 33, 40, 61, 81, 82, 83, 85, 86, 87, 88, 89, 93, 102, 123, 124
Lingapasādarūpa 85
Lingua 3, 81, 93

M

Mahā Brahma 159, 162
Mahāmangala Sutta 25, 88
Male 20, 25, 26, 33, 40, 58, 59, 61, 82, 84, 86, 87, 88, 90, 102, 123, 176
Mammalian 60, 119
Mammals 66, 68, 70, 72, 75, 103, 125
Matter 30, 39, 49, 52, 52, 53, 59, 64, 82, 84, 85, 90, 95, 96, 102, 113, 142, 165, 172, 196
Mind-based 17, 23, 29, 32, 52, 53, 54, 55, 96, 114, 121, 134, 141, 175, 184
Mindbody 37, 64, 84, 96, 103, 114, 117
Moisture-born 61, 99, 108
Monks 21, 147, 149, 150, 151, 152, 153, 154, 155, 165, 167, 168
Moon 17, 18, 24, 45, 56, 65, 81, 108, 123, 124, 136, 145, 162, 175, 183, 185, 194
Morphic field 112
Morphic resonance 113
Morphogenesis 107
Mother 25, 26, 88
Moving through space 17, 24, 132
Muditā 137

N

Nadeau, Robert 51, 52, 53, 59, 125, 195, 199
Nāma 12, 14, 16, 52, 83, 96, 114, 148
Nāmarūpa 23, 52, 96, 96, 112
Navaka Sattā 4, 92, 107, 108, 109, 111, 112, 113, 114, 116, 117, 118, 119
Noble Eightfold Path 28
Non-disciple Ābhassara Beings 109
Nourishment 31, 54, 64, 122, 183,
Nyanaponika, Ven. Thera 135, 140, 191, 197

O

Olomucki, Martin 26, 52, 55
Organic compounds 77
Organic life 59, 69
Organic matter 64
Organic soup 78
Organic synthesis 63

P

Pappaṭaka 18, 19, 35, 36, 62, 63, 67, 69, 70, 71, 72, 75, 78, 79, 80, 91, 122, 123, 124, 176
Paradox 3, 40, 93, 101, 103, 105, 107, 109, 110
Parody 121, 129, 141, 143, 145, 167, 195, 196
Passage of a long time beyond 17, 21, 29, 49, 104, 121, 123
Passion 20, 41, 41, 61, 64, 82, 85, 86, 89, 102, 115, 117, 118
Paṭiccasamuppāda 113
Photon 52, 55, 95, 96, 103
Physical 29, 31, 33, 49, 62, 65, 67, 72, 78, 83, 84, 85, 86, 86, 88, 89, 89, 90, 96, 97, 112, 114, 117, 124, 126, 160, 160, 173
Plant 35, 36, 37, 58, 62, 63, 65, 67, 68, 69, 71, 72, 75, 77

Placental conception 60
Pliocene era 67
Ponnamperuma Cyril
Post-Ābhassara-Aqueous-Being 56
Pre-Cambrian Era 63, 75
Pre-Devolutionary 44, 45
Primeval 4, 6, 63, 127, 147, 156, 157, 158, 160, 164, 165, 165, 167, 169, 170, 171, 173, 174, 175, 177, 178, 179, 180, 181, 186, 187, 188, 192, 193
Primordial 4, 6, 63, 127, 147, 156, 157, 158, 160, 164, 165, 167, 169, 170, 171, 173, 174, 175, 177, 178, 179, 180, 181, 186, 187, 188, 192, 193,
Primordial Being 4, 98
Prokaryotes 76, 77,
Pseudopods 76,
Punnadhammo, Ajahn 24, 28, 48, 76, 77, 79, 89, 90, 109
Punnaji, Bhante 6

R

Rapture 17, 53, 54, 96, 121, 122, 187, 188
Rebecoming 41
Rebirth 106, 138, 139, 196
Rice 19, 37, 38, 39, 40, 63, 67, 69, 70, 72, 75, 79, 82, 91, 122, 123, 124, 176
Rūpa 27, 54, 114
Rūpaness 114
Russel, Bertrand 197

S

Samana Gotama 106, 135
Sanaṃkumāra 9, 186
Sāriputta, Arahant 7, 140, 166, 166, 166
Satire 121, 140, 144, 145, 167, 169, 191, 195, 196,
Savoury-Earth 17, 18, 29, 101, 183,
Self-discipline 189

Self-luminous 17, 51, 53, 121, 175, 184
Senses 27, 27, 36, 57, 86, 96, 117, 117, 182
Sentient beings 26, 32, 36, 41, 54, 62, 74, 101, 142, 183, 184, 189, 194
Sentient life 3, 25, 27, 65, 185
Seven paragraphs 122, 144, 192, 194
Sex 3, 31, 33, 40, 41, 82, 83, 84, 85, 86, 87, 87, 88, 89, 89, 90, 91, 96, 101, 105, 107, 109, 109, 110, 117, 117, 176, 185,
Sex organ 31, 40, 84, 85, 86, 87, 88
Sexual 20, 20, 44, 58, 59, 61, 64, 67, 69, 73, 82, 82, 84, 84, 85, 86, 89, 91, 99, 102, 105, 109, 197
Sexuality 83, 84, 85, 86, 87, 88, 89,
Sharov, Alexei 49
Sheldrake, Rupert 39, 107, 112, 113, 115
Siddhartha 139
Sīla 106, 194
Sinhala 25, 34, 35, 79, 136, 136, 197
Sky 49, 50, 51, 52, 54, , 55, 56, 66, 95, 99, 106, 121, 160, 160, 161, 163, 184,
Smell 17, 19, 19, 27, 28, 57, 62, 91
Space 3, 17, 24, 44, 49, 50, 51, 55, 56, 65, 85, 95, 132, 133, 137, 160, 161, 162, 163,
Spatial life 49
Spiral reciprocity 183
Spirituality 54
Spiritual Paradox 3, 101, 103, 105, 107, 109, 110
Spontaneous 44, 55, 59, 61, 98, 99, 105, 107, 108, 113, 119
Spontaneous beings 61
Spontaneous generation 61, 98, 99
Stratosphere 50
Structure 4, 27, 32, 37, 46, 52, 57, 71, 72, 86, 93, 140, 142, 192, 193,
Sun 17, 18, 22, 24, 38, 45, 46, 47, 48, 49, 55, 56, 56, 56, 56, 63, 65, 80, 81, 108, 114, 123, 124, 162, 175, 183, 184, 185, 188, 194,

T

Taste 17, 18, 19, 27, 33, 57, 61, 62, 64, 69, 70, 71, 74, 78, 80, 84, 91, 183, 194
Tathāgata 7, 145, 181
Thirst 28, 29, 32, 37, 41, 78, 97, 98, 102, 103, 104, 105, 109, 115, 117, 118, 194
This world evolves 17, 68, 104, 123, 124, 175
Thousand 24, 48, 67, 104, 123, 154
Training Principle 6
Translation 1, 2, 3, 5, 6, 10, 11, 13, 15, 17, 19, 21, 22, 23, 25, 26, 27, 27, 29, 30, 31, 33, 34, 34, 35, 37, 39, 41, 43, 45, 46, 47, 98, 99, 118, 131, 136, 141, 147, 158, 158, 162, 187, 195, 196

U

Universe 1, 2, 3, 7, 10, 22, 23, 27, 34, 44, 45, 46, 46, 51, 52, 53, 55, 65, 67, 67, 74, 80, 111, 113, 115, 116, 121, 122, 124, 125, 125, 126, 129, 131, 133, 134, 135, 137, 138, 139, 143, 144, 151, 152, 155, 156, 169, 170, 172, 173, 174, 177, 178, 179, 182, 184, 186, 189, 192, 195
Upatthambakapaccaya 84

V

Vāseṭṭha 5, 6, 7, 8, 9, 17, 18, 19, 20, 21, 30, 34, 35, 81, 82, 88, 89, 90, 91, 101, 110, 136, 139, 147, 148, 149, 149, 149, 150, 151, 152, 153, 154, 155, 155, 156, 157, 165, 166, 166, 167, 168, 171, 172, 177, 179, 180, 181, 182, 186, 192
Veda 129, 143
Vedic Myth 4, 127, 129, 131, 133, 135, 137, 139, 141, 143, 145, 152, 155, 177
Vegetation 35, 37, 46, 56, 162
Very long stretch of time 17, 18, 19, 20, 23, 69, 70, 71, 72, 82, 90, 104, 121, 123, 124, 175, 183
Volvox 58, 59, 61, 62, 65

W

Walking back and forth 177
Walshe, Maurice 1, 9, 21, 22, 23, 25, 27, 28, 33, 34, 35, 95, 158, 159, 160, 161, 179, 185, 187, 193, 194
Water 17, 22, 24, 27, 29, 33, 35, 39, 40, 44, 51, 55, 56, 58, 60, 61, 65, 66, 67, 68, 85, 98, 99, 99, 104, 108, 123, 124, 130, 131, 132, 137, 161, 162, 163, 175
Water-born 44, 60, 61, 99,
When somehow or other at times 17, 81
Woman 61, 83, 172
Womb-born 6, 44, 103, 105, 108

Z

Zimmer, Carl 56, 57, 58, 63, 65, 67, 68, 141, 143, 196

AUTHOR BIO

Venerable Bhikkhu Mihita (former **Suwanda H J Sugunasiri)**, is a US Fulbright Scholar, and a Canadian Buddhist scholar. With multidisciplinary academic credentials (BA, MA, MA, MEd, PhD) from the Universities of London, Michigan, Pennsylvania and Toronto, he calls himself a **CRINTFREETH** 'Creative Interdisciplinary Free Thinker' (see his Interdisciplinary publications in the opening pages). Retired Member of the Trinity Divinity Faculty, University of Toronto, and Visiting Professor, University of Havana, Cuba, he is Founder of Nalanda College of Buddhist Studies, Toronto, and Founder / Editor Emeritus, *Canadian Journal of Buddhist Studies.* Pioneer in introducing the label *Buddhianscience* replacing the misleading term 'Buddhism', he is featured in *Canadian Who's Who* and *Canada at the Millennium*, and is a 'National Treasure' on Vision TV. He lives in Toronto, Canada, totally cut off from the world since his ordination at the age 82. For his leadership role in Canadian Buddhism, please read Hori & McLelland in Harding, Hori & Soucy, *Wild Geese: Buddhism in Canada*, McGill-Queen's University Press (2010).